The Poetry of
W. B. Yeats

EDITED BY MICHAEL FAHERTY

Consultant Editor: Nicolas Tredell

First published 2005 by
PALGRAVE MACMILLAN™
Houndmills, Basingstoke, Hampshire RG21 6XS and
175 Fifth Avenue, New York, N.Y. 10010
Companies and representatives throughout the world.

PALGRAVE MACMILLAN is the global academic imprint of the Palgrave
Macmillan division of St. Martin's Press, LLC and of Palgrave Macmillan Ltd.
Macmillan® is a registered trademark in the United States, United Kingdom
and other countries. Palgrave is a registered trademark in the European
Union and other countries.

ISBN 1–4039–4630–2 hardback
ISBN 1–4039–1137–1 paperback

This book is printed on paper suitable for recycling and made from fully
managed and sustained forest sources.

A catalogue record for this book is available from the British Library.

A catalog record for this book is available from the Library of Congress.

10 9 8 7 6 5 4 3 2 1
14 13 12 11 10 09 08 07 06 05

Printed and bound in China.

CONTENTS

Introduces the debate surrounding the editions of Yeats' collected poems, including the placement of the narrative and dramatic poems and which poem Yeats wanted to be his last, and explains why this Readers' Guide takes the form that it does.

Lives of the Poet

Surveys the numerous stories of Yeats' life, beginning with his own somewhat mythical autobiographies. Looks at early biographies by Joseph Hone, Richard Ellmann and A. Norman Jeffares, as well as recent publications by Terence Brown, Brenda Maddox, Ann Saddlemyer and R.F. Foster.

Yeats and Revivalism

Examines the part Yeats played in the Irish literary revival, as well as the consequences of that revival for the culture, for other Irish writers and for Yeats himself. Includes extracts from early histories of the movement by W.P. Ryan and Ernest A. Boyd; from essays by the poets Patrick Kavanagh and Thomas Kinsella rejecting both Yeats and revivalism; from Mary Helen Thuente's book on his radical use of Irish folklore; from studies by T.R. Henn, Donald T. Torchiana, W.J. McCormack and Seamus Deane on Yeats' later identification with the Anglo-Irish tradition; and from Declan Kiberd's recent survey of Irish literature that sees Yeats as a modern version of the Gaelic poet Aogán Ó Rathaille.

ACKNOWLEDGEMENTS

The editor and the publishers wish to thank the following for use of copyright material:

Jonathan Williams Literary Agency for Patrick Kavanagh, 'William Butler Yeats', in *Collected Prose*, MacGibbon and Kee (1967), pp. 254–6.

Routledge for T. R. Henn, *The Lonely Tower: Studies in the Poetry of W. B. Yeats* (1965), pp. 3–7; and Frank Kermode, *Romantic Image* (1957), pp. 28–33.

The Catholic University of America Press for Donald Torchiana, *W. B. Yeats and Georgian Ireland* (1966), pp. 85–90.

Thomas Kinsella, for 'The Irish Writer', in Roger McHugh (ed.), *Davis, Mangan, Ferguson?: Tradition and the Irish Writer*, Dolmen Press, Dublin (1970). Reproduced by permission of the author.

Gill and Macmillan, for Mary Helen Thuente, *W. B. Yeats and Irish Folklore* (1980), pp. 20–4; and Grattan Freyer, *W. B. Yeats and the Anti-Democratic Tradition* (1981), pp. 125–8, 132–3.

Faber & Faber for Seamus Deane, *Celtic Revivals: Essays in Modern Irish Literature 1880–1980* (1985); Ezra Pound, 'The Later Yeats', in T. S. Eliot (ed.), *Literary Essays of Ezra Pound* (1954), pp. 378–81; and W. H. Auden, 'The Public v the Late Mr William Butler Yeats', in Edward Mendelson (ed.), *The English Auden: Poems, Essays and Dramatic Writings, 1927–1939* (1977), pp. 389–93.

Cork University Press for W. J. McCormack, *From Burke to Beckett: Ascendancy, Tradition and Betrayal in Literary History* (1994). © W. J. McCormack by permission of Cork University Press Ltd, Crawford Business Park, Crosses Green, Cork, Ireland.

Harvard University Press and Granta Books for 'W. B. Yeats – Building Amid Ruins', reprinted by permission of the publisher from *Irish Classics* by Declan Kiberd, Harvard University Press and Granta Books. © 2000 by Declan Kiberd.

Farrar, Strauss & Giroux for excerpts from *Axel's Castle* by Edmund Wilson. © 1931 by Charles Scribner's Sons. Copyright renewed 1958 by the Estate of Edmund Wilson. Reprinted by permission of Farrar, Straus and Giroux, LLC.

Robin Leavis for F. R. Leavis, *New Bearing in English Poetry: A Study of the Contemporary Situation* (1932), reproduced by permission of the Leavis Estate.

C. K. Stead for *The New Poetic: From Yeats to Eliot*, Penguin (1969), pp. 19–21, 30–5. Reproduced by permission of the author.

Oxford University Press, Inc. for *Yeats* by Harold Bloom, © 1972 by Oxford University Press, Inc.; and *Stone Cottage: Pound, Yeats & Modernism* by James Longenbach, © 1988 by Oxford University Press, Inc. Used by permission of Oxford University Press, Inc.

Stephen Ellmann for Richard Ellmann, *Eminent Domain: Yeats Among Wilde, Joyce, Pound, Eliot and Auden*, Oxford University Press (1967), pp. 3, 61–7. Reprinted by kind permission of Stephen Ellmann.

David Higham Associates for Louis MacNeice, *The Poetry of W. B. Yeats* (1967), Faber, pp. 223–5, 231–2.

A. M. Heath and Harcourt, Inc. for 'W. B. Yeats', from the *Collected Essays, Journalism and Letters of George Orwell, Volume II: My Country Right or Left, 1940–1943*, by George Orwell (© George Orwell, 1945; © 1968 by Sonia Brownell Orwell and renewed 1996 by Mark Hamilton), by permission of Bill Hamilton as the Literary Executor of the Estate of the late Sonia Brownell Orwell, Secker & Warburg Ltd and Harcourt, Inc.

Palgrave Macmillan for Conor Cruise O'Brien, 'Passion and Cunning: An Essay on the Politics of W. B. Yeats', in A. Norman Jeffares and K. G. W. Cross (eds), *In Excited Reverie: A Centenary Tribute to William Butler Yeats, 1865–1939*, pp. 256–63; Elizabeth Cullingford, *Yeats, Ireland and Fascism* (1981), pp. 200–5; and Paul Scott Stanfield, *Yeats and Politics in the 1930s* (1988), pp. 67–71.

The London Magazine for Patrick Cosgrave, 'Yeats, Fascism and Conor O'Brien', *London Magazine*, 7 (1967), 22–41.

University of Minnesota Press for Edward W. Said, 'Yeats and Decolonization', in Seamus Deane (ed.), *Nationalism, Colonialism and Literature*, pp. 87–91 © 1998 by Edward W. Said.

Every effort has been made to trace the copyright holders but if any have been inadvertently overlooked the publishers will be pleased to make the necessary arrangement at the first opportunity.

INTRODUCTION

I n the famous elegy that W.H. Auden (1907–73) wrote shortly after W.B. Yeats died, he noted that Saturday, 28 January 1939, was a particularly cold and dark day:

■ But for him it was his last afternoon as himself,
An afternoon of nurses and rumours;
The provinces of his body revolted,
The squares of his mind were empty,
Silence invaded the suburbs,
The current of his feeling failed; he became his admirers. □
('In Memory of W.B. Yeats')

Not even Auden could have imagined just how prophetic that last line would become. This is true, of course, for all poets, but it has proved particularly true for Yeats. The battle over both his life and his poetry began almost at once, with some tribes proudly claiming him as one of their very own, while others insisted he had never really been one of them. To what tradition does Yeats belong? To what culture? Was he Irish or Anglo-Irish, or even English? Was he a romantic poet, a symbolist poet or a modernist poet? Was he a nationalist, a fascist or even something sometimes called a postnationalist? For anyone unfamiliar with these debates in the ever expanding field of Yeats studies, it is always a bit of a surprise to see just how much of the criticism revolves around the nagging question of where to *place* him. Even more surprisingly, these arguments do not seem any more settled now than they were decades ago.

Readers unfamiliar with Yeats should be warned that even to walk into a bookshop and buy a copy of his collected poems could be construed as supporting one side of a debate or the other. Some collections of his poetry begin with one poem and some begin with another. Some end with one poem and some end with another. And some seem chronological, while others do not. So which edition of the poems should you buy or, perhaps, which edition have you already purchased? Unfortunately, there is no such thing as a neutral edition of Yeats' collected poetry, much less a definitive one. The debate is essentially about whether new editions of his collected poems should follow the order of the 1933 edition or the 1949 edition. The 1933 edition divides the poems into two parts, a lyrical section at the front, containing all his shorter poems, and a narrative and dramatic section at the back, containing a half dozen of his longer poems, including 'The Wanderings of Oisin' (1889). The 1949 edition, on the other hand, begins with 'The Wanderings of Oisin' and follows a roughly chronological order, making no distinction between the lyrical and the narrative poems.

The debate over which of these two editions is closest to the definitive edition really began in 1983, when Richard J. Finneran published *The Poems of W.B. Yeats: A New Edition*, now the first volume of *The Collected Works of W.B. Yeats*. Warwick Gould sparked that debate in a review of Finneran's edition in the *Times Literary Supplement* in June 1984, followed by replies later that summer from Denis Donoghue, Mary Fitzgerald, A. Norman Jeffares and Finneran himself. The debate then spread to the pages of the *Irish University Review* and the *Yeats Annual*, where it continued for the next few years, with Gould and Finneran clearly the loudest voices for the opposing sides of this argument. Essentially, Gould argued that Finneran was wrong to follow the order of the 1933 edition, dividing the poems into two parts, since Yeats had only agreed to that for financial reasons. Beginning about 1930, Yeats and his publisher, Macmillan, had been preparing a so-called edition de luxe of his collected works, a multi-volume edition that the ageing poet seemed to understand might contain the last collected poems published in his lifetime. This project had been put on hold, however, due to the war and the global economic crisis, in the hope of finding a market for such an exclusive collection once these situations improved. But Yeats was having his own financial crisis and he suggested that, in the meantime, Macmillan publish the collected poems on their own, using the proofs he had corrected in 1932 for the proposed edition de luxe. However, he wondered whether it might be best to leave out the long dramatic poem 'The Shadowy Waters' (1906). His editor at Macmillan wrote back:

> ■ As regards the contents of the volume, I share our reader's view that it would be a pity to omit 'The Shadowy Waters'. There is, however, one departure from the arrangement of the Edition de Luxe volume which I should like to put before you, as it has been suggested by more than one person. We think it possible that the book would be more attractive to the potential purchaser who glances through it in a bookshop if what first caught his eye were the shorter lyrical poems contained in 'Crossways', 'The Rose', 'The Wind Among the Reeds', etc., rather than a lengthy work like 'The Wanderings of Oisin'. Our impression is that we might move the longer narrative and dramatic pieces to the end of the volume, where they would make a group more or less related in style, subject, and length, and I wonder if you would agree to our taking this course with the following longer works:-
>
> 'The Wanderings of Oisin'
> 'The Old Age of Queen Maeve'
> 'Baile and Aillinn'

'The Shadowy Waters'
and 'The Two Kings'.

If this arrangement commends itself to you, and if you could think of some general title we could use to cover this particular group, I will instruct the printers to proceed with the work on those lines. Needless to say, however, the suggestion is quite tentative, and we should not wish to do anything of the kind without your full approval. □

Yeats did not hesitate to reply:

■ I am delighted with your suggestion to put long poems in a section at the end. I wish I had thought of it before.
   You could call this group 'longer poems', & the rest of the book 'shorter poems', or you could call this group 'Narrative and dramatic poetry', and the rest of the book 'lyrical poetry'.[1] □

These poems were then shifted to the back of the book, along with 'The Gift of Harun Al-Rashid' (1923), Yeats' tribute to his wife and her talent for automatic writing. The sticking point in this debate is whether Yeats agreed to this order for both the 1933 edition and the edition de luxe or not, with Finneran suggesting that he did and Gould insisting that he did not. Gould argues that Yeats' subsequent letters to Harold Macmillan prove that there were two separate plans for two separate editions, with the 1933 edition aimed specifically at the general reader, not the sort of reader who would have been the target market for the expensive edition de luxe.

In the end, the edition de luxe was doomed, the project shelved because of the long war and the staggering economy. However, some volumes of that edition were salvaged, with Mrs Yeats (1892–1968) and her late husband's editor at Macmillan, Thomas Mark, publishing a collected poems in two volumes in 1949. This edition was not divided into two parts, but was roughly chronological, beginning with his long poem 'The Wanderings of Oisin'. The 1949 edition was all but canonised when Peter Allt and Russell K. Alspach chose it as the basic text for their variorum edition of Yeats' poems, published in 1957, and it has often been cited as the definitive edition of Yeats' collected poems. Gould believes, of course, that this was the order that Yeats had wanted for the edition de luxe, beginning with 'The Wanderings of Oisin' since that is when his poetry became recognisably Irish, despite the fact that some of the lyrics in the collection were actually composed before it. Even Gould and his supporters admit that a chronological ordering of Yeats' poems can never be better than roughly chronological, since he famously revised many of his early poems later in life and it was those revisions that Yeats approved for the edition de luxe. He seems to have inherited this inability to leave things alone from his father, the painter, who had a reputation as a bit of a Penelope figure – or, as a man once remarked to the young Yeats when he told him who his father was, 'O, that is the painter who scrapes out every day what he painted the day before.' Yeats recalls that his father would begin painting a landscape in the spring and that the painting would change as the seasons changed, eventually abandoned and left unfinished when it was covered in snow.[2] As Yeats said of his own tendency to revise his poems:

■ The friends that have it I do wrong
When ever I remake a song,
Should know what issue is at stake:
It is myself that I remake. □

(Epigraph to *Collected Works* (1908), vol. 2)

When A. Norman Jeffares published his edition of the collected poems in 1989, mostly following the order of the 1949 edition, he included an appendix by Gould defending that decision, arguing that this collection might only be quasi-chronological but it was the order that Mrs Yeats and Mark wanted, who surely would have known the poet's own intentions best. They had also respected Yeats' desire to preserve only the latest versions of his poems, with the exception of 'Three Marching Songs' and 'Three Songs to the Same Tune', which Mrs Yeats and Mark thought different enough to include both. As Gould points out, Yeats often delegated responsibility for the corrected versions of his poems to his wife and his editor and gladly accepted their corrections, partly because he was a notoriously poor speller his entire life and partly because he was no better with capitalisation or punctuation. Given the fact that Mrs Yeats and Mark played such crucial roles in the proofreading of Yeats' texts, even such an exacting editor as Finneran is forced to concede that 'no matter what new material becomes available, the editing of Yeats's poems will remain as much an art as a science, as much a subjective process as an objective one.'[3]

However, there is one problem with the 1949 edition about which Finneran, Gould and Jeffares all agree. When editing that edition, it appears that Mark suggested to Mrs Yeats that they end the collection with 'Under Ben Bulben' – the poem written for those Irish poets who would come after Yeats and in which he imagines himself in a grave in Sligo, his epitaph etched on the tombstone above him – and that is what they did. In 1961, Curtis Bradford published a short report in *Modern Language Notes* that revealed that, just weeks before his death, Yeats had made a list of what are now known as his last poems in the order that he would like to see them published, including some that he was still working on at the time.[4] The list was most likely made for his sister, Lolly, who was planning to publish his *Last Poems and Two Plays* (1939) under the imprint of the Cuala Press. That list, written in black ink and with Yeats' usual misspellings and mistakes of capitalisation and punctuation, included these poems and these plays in this precise order:

- 1 Under Ben Bulben
- 2 Three Songs to one Burden
- 3 The Black Tower
- 4 Cuchulain Comforted
- 5 Three Marching Songs
- 6 In Tara s Songs
- 7 The Statues
- 8 News for the Delphic Oracle
- 9 The Long Legged Fly
- 10 A Bronze Head
- 11 A Stick of Incense
- 12 Hound Voice
- 13 John Kinsella s Lament etc
- 14 High Talk
- 15 The Apparitions
- 16 A Nativity
- 17 Man & Echo
- 18 The Circus Animal s Desertion
- 19 Poletics
- 20 Cuchulain s Death
- 21 Purgatory[5] □

It has often been noted that Yeats did not see himself as a poet who published a volume of poems whenever he had produced enough to fill one up, but as a writer of books, and, if that is indeed the case, then the order of the poems means a lot. Bradford suggested that beginning these last poems with 'Under Ben Bulben' rather than ending with it makes those that follow read as if they were spoken from beyond the grave.[6] Seamus Heaney (born 1939) has also noted that ending not only this section but the entire collection with the poem 'Politics' and its last lines – 'But O that I were young again / And held her in my arms' – makes the reader imagine an entirely different Yeats in his final scene from the one who was slowly stiffening in Drumcliff churchyard:

■ A far cry from 'Cast a cold eye / On life, on death'; equally histrionic, but implying a radically different stance in the face of death. It is as if we were to learn that Sir Walter Raleigh's last words had not been his famous shout to the reluctant executioner – 'What dost thou fear? Strike, man!' – but that instead he had repeated the name of the maid of honor he was rumored to have seduced in the grounds of Hampton Court Palace years before.[7] □

Although almost everyone seems to agree with Heaney that this is a much more romantic and exciting exit than a cold grave in an Irish cemetery, there is still some disagreement about whether poems such as 'Why should not Old Men be Mad?', 'Crazy Jane on the Mountain' and 'Avalon' should be published as part of *Last Poems* or separately as poems from his controversial broadside *On the Boiler* (1939), as well as whether or not Finneran should have included almost 130 additional texts at the back of his collected poems. These are either poems that Yeats had decided not to reprint at some point in his career or verses excerpted from his prose and plays.

Given the controversies surrounding the various editions of Yeats' collected poems, it is probably no surprise that the meaning of those poems is the subject of even greater debate. This Guide takes the form that it does in order to reflect four key aspects of that debate. Despite the fact that much of the criticism of Yeats' poetry was written in a period when readers were told that everything they needed to make sense of a poetic text could be found in the text itself, his critics repeatedly proved that some understanding of Yeats' life and times was all but essential to an understanding of the poetry that that life and those times had produced. The first chapter, then, will begin by sampling some of these early studies of the poet's life, starting with the first authorised biography by Joseph Hone in 1943 and the subsequent ground-breaking biographies of the late 1940s, written by Richard Ellmann (1918–87) and A. Norman Jeffares (born 1920), and ending with the second and final volume of R.F. Foster's *W.B. Yeats: A Life*, only published in 2003 but already pronounced definitive by some reviewers.

The subject of the second chapter is Yeats and revivalism. When the Irish literary revival began to attract the attention of the critics in the late nineteenth century, the young poet was placed at the margins of the movement, but it was not long before those same critics were placing him – or some said Yeats had placed himself – at its very centre. But the next generation of poets and critics began to wonder whether Yeats really belonged to the Irish tradition or not. Even Yeats had begun to wonder, doing his best in his final years to cobble together an eighteenth-century Anglo-Irish tradition and make himself the last of its line. The second chapter considers the debate as to which tradition Yeats rightly belongs, particularly the arguments of the poets Patrick Kavanagh (1904–67) and Thomas Kinsella (born 1928) and the critics T.R. Henn (1901–74), Donald T. Torchiana (1923–2002), W.J. McCormack (born 1947) and Seamus Deane (born 1940), which claim that Yeats may have been at the centre of the Irish literary revival but he did not really belong there, feeling much more at home in the Big House culture of the west of Ireland with its roots in the Anglo-Irish tradition of the eighteenth century.

The third chapter of this Guide surveys criticism on the relationship between Yeats and the modernists, as well as the somewhat bigger question of the relationships between romanticism, symbolism and modernism. When the modernist poets gathered in London in the early twentieth century to sit at the feet of the somewhat older Yeats, readers wanted to know if this meant that the Irish poet had now become a member of the new internationalist tribe. The young modernist Ezra Pound (1885–1972) soon told them that it most certainly did not, that Yeats had always been (and probably always would be) a symbolist poet. Some critics thought that this was the perfect pigeonhole for Yeats, while others began to argue that he was really best read in the company of the romantic poets. Yet for many critics his association with the modernists stuck, with some suggesting that Pound had clearly modernised the older Yeats while others insisted that it was Yeats who had influenced the younger Pound. We will examine this debate in some detail in the third chapter of this Guide, which includes excerpts from major works by Edmund Wilson (1895–1972), F.R. Leavis (1895–1978), Frank Kermode (born 1919), Harold Bloom (born 1930) and C.K. Stead (born 1932).

The fourth chapter will sample the often heated debate on Yeats and politics, looking at those critics who claim he was essentially an Irish nationalist his entire life, as well as those who argue that his brief flirtation with fascism in the 1930s really reveals the most about his true political feelings. This chapter includes early concerns about the poet's anti-democratic tendencies expressed by writers such as W.H. Auden, Louis MacNeice (1907–63) and George Orwell (1903–50), but looks largely at the responses to the highly polemical essay by Conor Cruise O'Brien (born 1917), first published in 1965, in which he portrayed Yeats as a political opportunist who probably would have stuck with fascism had it succeeded in Ireland. The Guide concludes with a Selected Bibliography that, among other things, lists helpful introductions and commentaries, as well as highly recommended background reading on the Irish contexts of Yeats' poetry.

CHAPTER ONE

Lives of the Poet

U nlike some poets, who do their best shortly before their lives end to erase all traces of themselves in order to frustrate any future biographers and tell their friends and family not to have anything to do with such people, Yeats wanted biographies. As he said in the draft of a lecture that he gave in March 1910 on Lionel Johnson (1876–1902), a former member of the Rhymers Club (1891–94) to which Yeats himself had belonged,

■ I am speaking of him very candidly; probably he would not [wish] to be spoken of in this way, but I would wish to be spoken of with just such candour when I am dead. I have no sympathy with the mid-Victorian thought to which Tennyson [1809–92] gave his support, that a poet's life concerns nobody but himself. A poet is by the very nature of things a man who lives with entire sincerity, or rather, the better his poetry the more sincere his life. His life is an experiment in living and those that come after have a right to know it. Above all it is necessary that the lyric poet's life should be known, that we should understand that his poetry is no rootless flower but the speech of a man, [that it is no little thing] to achieve anything in any art, to stand alone perhaps for many years, to go a path no other man has gone, to accept one's own thought when the thought of others has the authority of the world behind it ... to give one's life as well as one's words which are so much nearer to one's soul to the criticism of the world.[1] □

In fact, Yeats began this business of giving his life to the criticism of the world himself, publishing the first contribution to what would eventually be known as *Autobiographies* in March 1916. Later contributions would be published separately in the 1920s and 1930s, particularly the five books of *The Trembling of the Veil*. Yeats had suggested the title of the collection as early as 1926 and the original plan was that *Autobiographies* would be the sixth volume of the doomed edition de luxe. In the end, the collection was not published by Macmillan until 1955, edited by Mrs Yeats and Thomas Mark.

However, biographers could, of course, read the separate published contributions before then and, to some extent, Yeats' own versions of his life became the template for many of those that would follow. As Yeats once said in a general introduction to his work that invokes Dante Alighieri (1265–1321), John Milton (1608–74), William Shakespeare (1564–1616), Sir Walter Raleigh (1554–1618), Percy Bysshe Shelley (1792–1822) and Lord Byron (1788–1824):

■ A poet writes always of his personal life, in his finest work out of its tragedy, whatever it be, remorse, lost love, or mere loneliness; he never speaks directly as to someone at the breakfast table, there is always a phantasmagoria. Dante and Milton had mythologies, Shakespeare the characters of English history or of traditional romance; even when the poet seems most himself, when he is Raleigh and gives potentates the lie, or Shelley 'a nerve o'er which do creep the else unfelt oppressions of this earth', or Byron when 'the soul wears out the breast' as 'the sword outwears its sheath', he is never the bundle of accident and incoherence that sits down to breakfast; he has been reborn as an idea, something intended, complete. A novelist might describe his accidence, his incoherence, he must not; he is more type than man, more passion than type. He is Lear, Romeo, Oedipus, Tiresias; he has stepped out of a play, and even the woman he loves is Rosalind, Cleopatra, never The Dark Lady. He is part of his own phantasmagoria and we adore him because nature has grown intelligible, and by so doing a part of our creative power.[2] □

For Yeats, a novelist might describe his accidence and incoherence, but a poet writing his autobiographies probably should not. It is from these autobiographies that many of the myths surrounding Yeats have come and most biographers have had great difficulties seeing beyond them to the more mundane facts of Yeats' life. Although they are full of factual errors, the autobiographies are, nevertheless, essential reading for anyone seriously interested in Yeats' poetry. The poet who speaks in the poems is often the same poet who tells the story of his life in the autobiographies, however much subsequent biographies have shown that this poet is one of Yeats' best inventions. It is in the autobiographies, for example, that Yeats explains how his first meetings with the old Fenian John O'Leary (1830–1907) turned him into an Irish poet with a purpose, absorbing all the books O'Leary lent him by the poet and patriot Thomas Davis (1814–45) and the Young Irelanders and engaging in the occasionally violent debates at the Young Ireland Society, where O'Leary was president:

■ From these debates, from O'Leary's conversation, and from the Irish books he lent or gave me has come all I have set my hand to since. I had begun to know a great deal about the Irish poets who had written in English. I read with excitement books I should find unreadable to-day, and found romance in lives that had neither wit nor adventure. I did not deceive myself; I knew how often they wrote a cold and abstract language, and yet I who had never wanted to see the houses where Keats [1795–1821] and Shelley lived would ask everybody what sort of place Inchedony was, because [Jeremiah J.] Callanan [1795–1829] had named after it a bad poem in the manner of [Byron's] *Childe Harold* [1812–18]. Walking home from a debate, I remember saying to some college student, 'Ireland cannot put from her the habits learned from her old military civilization and from a Church that prays in Latin. Those popular poets have not touched her heart, her poetry when it comes will be distinguished and lonely.' O'Leary had once said to me, 'Neither Ireland nor England knows the good from the bad in any art, but Ireland unlike England does not hate the good when it is pointed out to her.' I began to plot and scheme how one might seal with the right image the soft wax before it began to harden. I had noticed that Irish Catholics among whom had been born so many political martyrs had not the good taste, the household courtesy and decency of the Protestant Ireland I had known, yet Protestant Ireland seemed to think of nothing but getting on in the world. I thought we might bring the halves together if we had a national literature that made Ireland beautiful in the memory, and yet had been freed from provincialism by an exacting criticism, a European pose.[3] □

This is only one of many transformations described in the autobiographies, although a fellow Irish poet and one of Yeats' closest friends around the time of this transformation, George Russell (also known as AE) (1867–1935), said he hardly recognised Yeats from this early account of his life. According to Russell, the boy of this contribution, published separately as *Reveries over Childhood and Youth* (1916), could just as easily have turned out to be a grocer in adult life as a poet.

No doubt aware of her husband's desires, Mrs Yeats authorised the first biography of the poet only weeks after his death in the south of France in January 1939. The authorised biographer, Joseph Hone (1882–1959), not only knew Yeats well but came from the same Anglo-Irish caste as the poet and shared many of his late political concerns, including his fascination with Mussolini's experiments in pre-war Italy. Hone had published a number of other Irish biographies before tackling Yeats; these included a life of Bishop Berkeley (1685–1753) in 1932, of Thomas Davis in 1934, of Jonathan Swift (1667–1745) in 1935 and of George Moore (1852–1933) in 1938. Mrs Yeats not only put her private memories of her late husband at Hone's disposal, but also granted him access to her personal collection of the poet's letters and other papers. Yeats' sisters, Lily and Lolly, also helped Hone with his research, as did his brother, Jack, and his old friend, Madame Maud Gonne MacBride

(1866–1953). The resultant biography, published in 1943, is a massive book of almost 500 pages, which some Yeats scholars considered the most factual of all the studies of the poet's life until the recent publication of R.F. Foster's two exhaustive volumes, even though Hone did get some of those facts wrong. He was also considerably constrained by the fact that most of the people who knew Yeats best and who had played the most important roles in his life were still very much alive when the book was first published, particularly Mrs Yeats. It is understandable that he could say very little, or sometimes nothing at all, about the poet's intimate relationships with such crucial figures as Maud Gonne and Olivia Shakespear (1864–1938), as well as the significant role that Mrs Yeats had played in the composition of *A Vision* (1926; revised edn, 1937). Due to paper shortages at the height of the Second World War, Macmillan could only afford to publish a limited number of copies and the biography was out of print within five months of publication. This first attempt at a biography was almost necessarily a product of its time, with little or no interest in the psychology of the poet or even the poems he produced, with even Mrs Yeats apparently a little disappointed that it made no real attempt to see the poet in the poems.

She must have been better pleased, then, with the next scholarly attempt at a biography of her husband, Richard Ellmann's *Yeats: The Man and the Masks*, first published by Macmillan only five years later. It is a considerably shorter book but, since Hone had gathered most of the facts together, Ellmann could attempt the more complicated task of reconciling the man Hone portrays in his biography with the poet and, even more importantly, the poet with the poetry. Almost all the studies of Yeats before this, says Ellmann, have been interested in either his poetry or his past but no one has tried to combine the two. Even the previous biographical studies proved difficult to reconcile, according to Ellmann, with each new study only muddying the waters, not helping them to clear:

■ Writings about [Yeats] have tended to be either critical or factually biographical, with no bridge between. The more that is written, the more elusive he has become, as critics, friends, and biographers build up a variety of unconnected pictures. We are given the nervous romantic sighing through the reeds of the 'eighties and 'nineties and the worldly realist plain-speaking in the 'twenties; we have the business man founding and directing the Abbey Theatre in broad day, the wan young Celt haunting the twilight, and the occultist performing nocturnal incantations; we can choose between the dignified Nobel Prize winner and Senator of the Irish Free State and their successors, the libidinous old man and the translator of the Upanishads. These portraits are not easily reconcilable, and the tendency has been, instead of reconciling, to prove certain of them inessential or to split up the poet's life into dozens of unrelated episodes.

Yeats is partly to blame. He wrote a great deal about himself, but the autobiographical muse enticed him only to betray him, abandoning him to ultimate perplexity as to the meaning of his experiences. He spent much of his life attempting to understand the deep contradictions within his mind, and was perhaps most alive to that which separated the man of action lost in reverie from the man of reverie who could not quite find himself in action. Unsure which qualities were purely Yeatsian, he posed and attitudinized, then wondered whether pose and attitude were not more real than what they covered over. Afraid of insincerity, he struggled unsuccessfully to fuse or to separate the several characters by whom he felt himself to be peopled. And sometimes he yielded to the temptation of adopting convenient simplifications and pretending that they left nothing out. □

(Richard Ellmann, *Yeats: The Man and the Masks*, 1948/1961)[4]

Ellmann's solution to this problem was to accept the deep contradictions in Yeats' character that he had had so much difficulty accepting himself, that he was both a man of action and a man of reverie. Sometimes he was the one in the process of becoming the other and sometimes he was the other in the process of becoming, once again, its opposite. For Ellmann, this dialectic was not only the pattern of Yeats' own personality, but also the pattern of his paternal heritage and the pattern for his later personal cosmology. Since Yeats' grandfather had been a devout rector of the Church of Ireland, it was only natural that his father had been a rebellious sceptic and that the grandson would become someone who could accept neither his grandfather's Protestantism nor his father's positivism, forced to invent his own occult practices. While these practices seemed a bit of an embarrassment to Hone, Ellmann is one of the first Yeats scholars to take them seriously. Mrs Yeats also gave Ellmann access to her private collection of more than 50,000 pages of unpublished materials and, while Yeats may often have hidden these occult practices from the public, they are well documented there:

■ A final cause of the mistiness of the standard picture of Yeats is that he was even more obsessed with magic, occultism, psychical research, and mysticism, the whole *tradition à rebours* [decadent tradition], than he allowed to appear, partly because of solemn vows of secrecy, partly because he was sensitive to mockery and convinced that he must use in his public writings only the most traditional aspects of his own thought. For many years he deliberately suppressed or only half disclosed many of his principal preoccupations, so that the reader who wishes to understand fully what any single work means must pass through a kind of initiation in those of his ideas that never went beyond the manuscript stage.

For if he was reticent in public, Yeats was indiscreet in private. He confided almost everything to his manuscript books, diaries, and letters, and from them another picture can be elicited, which joins together the disparate fragments and episodes of his life, and reveals him in quite a different light, the embroidered coat removed. □

(Richard Ellmann, *Yeats: The Man and the Masks*, 1948)[5]

The purpose of Ellmann's biography was to read the literature alongside the life – just as he would do much more extensively in his biographical study (1959; revised edn, 1982) of James Joyce (1882–1941) and his biographical study (1988) of Oscar Wilde (1854–1900) – but the emphasis is still more on Yeats' life than on the literature. As a consequence, Ellmann wrote a companion volume called *The Identity of Yeats*, published by Macmillan in 1954, which attempts to find patterns of symbolism in the poetry in much the same way that his biography had attempted to find patterns of synthesis in the poet's life.

A. Norman Jeffares published his first study of Yeats' life only a year after Ellmann's study had appeared and the two books were often reviewed together as pioneering works in the fields of Yeats studies and literary biography. Born in Dublin, Jeffares had met Mrs Yeats as a schoolboy and, as she had done with Hone and Ellmann, she spoke with him at length about her late husband and made her private papers available to him, as did others who had been close to the poet. Jeffares' biography resembles Hone's more than it does Ellmann's in that it is more concerned with the man than with the poet, but Jeffares clearly believes that it is important to know something about the life of the man who wrote the poems in order to understand them fully and his biography includes some significant firsthand facts about that life that Hone's and Ellmann's do not. In 1988, Jeffares published his second biography of Yeats, aptly titled *W.B. Yeats, A New Biography*. Even though the approach in the second book was essentially the same as in the first, it was an obvious advance on the earlier biographies in that Jeffares could now repeat things that he had been told that he could not possibly have repeated, out of simple respect, when Mrs Yeats and others were still alive. Ellmann had even ended his biography somewhat roughly at the time when Mrs Yeats entered the poet's life. Although the children and grandchildren of those lives spoken about in these biographies were still very much alive, Jeffares now had permission from them to clarify things that had been very unclear before. Whereas Ellmann, for example, had politely spoken of Yeats' unsuccessful marriage proposal to Maud Gonne's 'beautiful adopted niece, Iseult', Jeffares could now explain that she was not actually Gonne's niece, but her daughter, conceived beside the tomb of her dead son in an attempt to reincarnate his soul. Jeffares still sometimes seems curiously incurious about Yeats' inner life and rather reticent to voice any opinions about his outer life, but it was certainly the most complete biography around until the first volume of Foster's two-volume work appeared.

Although Foster's comprehensive biography of Yeats has also been criticised for being somewhat unreflective, its recent publication has made all other biographies of the Irish poet seem almost invisible. It is the first fully authorised study of the poet's life since Hone, and Yeats' daughter and son, Anne and Michael, opened the family files to him and gave him permission to describe whatever he might find there. This project was originally begun by the historian F.S.L. Lyons, who had tutored Foster at Trinity College, Dublin, but Lyons had died unexpectedly in September 1983, just at the point where he was about to write up his notes. Foster inherited the project and the notes from Lyons and, having previously published biographies of Charles Stewart Parnell (1846–91) in 1976 and of Lord Randolph Churchill (1849–95) in 1982, he decided to take the same approach as Lyons and look at Yeats more from an historical perspective than from a literary perspective, even describing himself as an 'interloping historian' in the field of Yeats studies. For Foster, Yeats is not so much a poet as he is an actor in the drama of modern Irish history, a member of the increasingly marginalised Protestant Ascendancy who suddenly took centre stage in the nationalist struggle for Home Rule and the Irish Free State. Foster argues that what is needed is not another biography that tries to understand the influence his life had on his poetry but one that tries to understand the influence his life had on the biography of Ireland:

■ Here lies the justification for this long book; and for the fact that it is a historian who has written it. [Yeats'] life has been approached over and over again, for the purposes of relating it to his art .... Shortly after he died, Joseph Hone produced his official life; a literary biography followed from A. Norman Jeffares, and then the luminous works by Richard Ellmann, which still hold the critical field. Many other one-volume biographical studies were still to come, and more are being written at this moment; but they all tend to follow Ellmann's dazzling structure. Faced with the multifarious activities, the feints and turns, the wildly differing worlds which [Yeats] embraced, Ellmann followed his subject's example in dealing with his life thematically. [Yeats'] own *Autobiographies* dictate an arrangement for his life, and it is a thematic one; this is hard not to follow, even if it looks like the way of the chameleon. The natural reaction is to shadow him from young Celtic Revivalist to theatrical manager to witness of revolution to smiling public man; to accept his *Autobiographies* as straightforward records rather than to see them in terms of the time they were composed; and to deal with periods of frantic and diverse involvements, as in the early 1900s, by separating out the strands of occultism, drama and love, and addressing them individually. The result, in Ellmann's work, was a masterpiece of intellectual analysis and psychological penetration, to which all Yeatsians are for ever indebted. However, we do not, alas, live our lives in themes, but day by day; and [Yeats], giant though he was, is no exception. □

(R.F. Foster, *W.B. Yeats: A Life*, 1997)[6]

Foster says that, while the temptation is still there to separate out those various strands of his life and look at them one by one, that is not how Yeats actually lived his life. He often did all of these things simultaneously, not each of them separately. In fact, Foster basically agrees with George Russell's criticism of Yeats' first attempt at autobiography, that the boy in those early memoirs could just as easily have become a grocer as a poet. Foster argues that, at some moments, being a poet was not what Yeats' life was all about and that he was often a lot of other things besides just a poet. In order to avoid the misrepresentations of the thematic approach, Foster insists on 'a rigorous reliance on chronology and the reconstruction of the everyday' throughout both volumes,[7] trying to get back to that 'bundle of accident and incoherence that sits down to breakfast' that Yeats did his best to disguise. Yeats might have thought that a poet writing his poems, as well as his autobiographies, probably should not describe his accidence and incoherence but, Foster suggests, at least one of his biographers probably should.

Although the word 'definitive' has occasionally been mentioned in reviews of Foster's biography of Yeats, it is not a word Foster has used himself, arguing that his is just one of many possible treatments of the poet's life, some of which have already been written and some of which, no doubt, remain to be written still. One of those recent treatments that Foster admires is Terence Brown's *The Life of W.B. Yeats: A Critical Biography*. It is also the sort of biography that Mrs Yeats would have admired, since it was published in 1999 as part of a Blackwell series that promises to offer 'substantial critical discussion' of the poetry alongside the life and to 're-establish the notion that books are written by people who lived in particular times and places'.[8] One of Brown's own purposes in writing this biography was to draw attention to Yeats' obsession with the occult in a way that some of his early biographers would not or could not. For many critics, this particular obsession has prevented him from being accepted as a great modern poet and, rather than push it aside once again, Brown wants to take it as seriously as the poet himself did and show the extent to which it affected all other aspects of his life:

■ That undoubtedly remains a key critical issue in Yeats's reception – despite the voluminous scholarship (much of it conducted in the United States) his work has attracted on issues as diverse as his relationship to Romanticism, Modernism, politics, post-colonialism, feminism – made all the more pressing as detailed information has been made available on the centrality to Yeats's imagination of esotericism and spiritualist experiment. The present volume has sought to contribute to discussion of this critical issue by allowing that centrality to appear in its pages, to suggest that it is no longer possible simply to say that Yeats's beliefs offered him the metaphoric and symbolic means of expression for essentially humanist feelings he would have had without such 'exotic' preoccupations. This has been a study of a writer for whom magic, ritual and 'communication' with the dead and with spirits were profoundly experiential things which affected how he felt and thought about human life, about its passions and its meanings. And the artistic consequences were not always congenial to liberal humanist moral feeling. □

(Terence Brown, *The Life of W.B. Yeats*, 1999)[9]

Brown was not the first biographer, of course, to take Yeats' obsession with the occult so seriously. As early as 1954, Virginia Moore published her biographical study of the poet, *The Unicorn: William Butler Yeats' Search for Reality*, in which she offered some new information about his occult rituals and spiritualist sources, much of which came from discussions she had had with Mrs Yeats, Madame Maud Gonne MacBride and Ezra Pound. Although the book has been some help to some Yeats scholars, it sometimes seems more like literary gossip than serious academic analysis. Another study to take this subject seriously was published the same year as Brown's biography, curiously under the title of *Yeats's Ghosts: The Secret Life of W.B. Yeats* in America and as *George's Ghosts: A New Life of W.B. Yeats* in England. In her book, Brenda Maddox begins the story of Yeats' life where the Ellmann biography and the first volume of the Foster biography end, with his marriage to Georgie Hyde Lees. The two titles are appropriately descriptive, since this is more a biography of the marriage than of the poet himself, with Maddox having previously written biographies of Nora Joyce (1988) and Frieda and D.H. Lawrence (1994). Maddox's main source for this study is the 3600 pages of automatic writing that the Yeatses produced in the first few months of their marriage, which have now been transcribed by George Mills Harper and his team of scholars at Florida State University and published in three volumes as *Yeats's Vision Papers* (1992). This subject may be serious for Maddox, but the ghosts themselves, whether they belong to the 52-year-old Yeats or his 25-year-old wife, are not:

■ I see the Automatic Script as an oblique form of communication between a young wife and an ageing husband who did not know each other very well and who needed it for things they could say to one another in no other way.

My firm conviction is that at all times during the Automatic Script – even when four or five 'Controls' are recorded as gathered at the same time – there were only two people in the room. □

(Brenda Maddox, *George's Ghosts*, 1999)[10]

If two of the things the early biographies could not or would not talk about were Yeats' obsession with the occult and the role his wife played in the composition of *A Vision*, both subjects have now become central to the discussion of the poet's life, particularly with the recent publication of Ann Saddlemyer's long-awaited biography of Mrs Yeats. *Becoming George: The Life of Mrs W.B. Yeats* was published by Oxford University Press in 2002, just after Foster had submitted the manuscript of the second volume of his biography to the same publisher. Both Foster and Saddlemyer had been working from roughly the same sources, the idea for a biography of the poet's wife apparently coming from Anne and Michael Yeats, despite the fact that, as Saddlemyer herself points out, Mrs Yeats would not have approved of this project. While she assisted countless biographers, scholars and young poets in their studies of her late husband's life and work, and edited numerous volumes of his work herself, Mrs Yeats was extremely self-effacing and she did her best to make Saddlemyer's effort to tell her side of the story as difficult as possible. The 800 pages of biography that are the result of this effort are, therefore, all the more impressive and almost as essential to an understanding of Yeats' life and work as the Foster biography of Yeats himself. In fact, what the Saddlemyer biography shows is that, if some thought that Foster had put the final full stop to the story of this poet's life, they were wrong. In a review of one of these many biographies, Helen Vendler once said that every study of Yeats' life seems to suggest the need for yet another. We could use an intellectual biography of Yeats, she suggested, as well as a stylistic biography of the writer; political biographies of Yeats, that include his British, Anglo-Irish, Irish and European sympathies; and a theatrical biography, as well as occultist and erotic biographies.[11] Yeats definitely wanted biographies, but even he might be surprised now at just how many lives he actually led.

CHAPTER TWO

Yeats and Revivalism

In his *Autobiographies*, Yeats recalls that his earliest enjoyment of poetry came from a book of Orange rhymes, reading them with the stableboy in the hayloft of his grandparents' home in Sligo, and that he often dreamed in those days of dying fighting the Fenians.[1] This is quite an admission for a poet who, not all that many years later, was essentially writing rhymes for the other side. The old Fenian John O'Leary had told a young and impressionable Yeats that what Ireland needed was a revival of its all but dead culture, that Ireland had lost its claim to political independence by voluntarily surrendering its language and its literature to England. No culture exists without some sense of nationality, O'Leary told Yeats, and no nation exists without its own distinct culture. In November 1892, the scholar and cultural activist Douglas Hyde (1860–1949) said much the same thing in a highly influential lecture to the newly formed Irish Literary Society in Dublin, telling his audience it was time for Ireland to stop trying to be English and to become Irish once again. Calling his lecture 'The Necessity for Deanglicizing Ireland', Hyde argued that the imitation of English manners and tastes had become an Irish disease whose only cure was a return to the original language and the original culture of Ireland. In order to stop the rot and revive the culture, other organisations quickly formed alongside the Irish Literary Society, including the Gaelic League in 1893 and the Gaelic Athletic Association in 1894. Yeats was, of course, one of the founders of the literary society and – with the publication of *Fairy and Folk Tales of the Irish Peasantry* in 1888, *The Wanderings of Oisin and Other Poems* in 1889, *Irish Fairy Tales* and *The Countess Kathleen and Various Legends and Lyrics* in 1892 and *The Celtic Twilight* in 1893 – he was almost immediately identified as an important figure within the revivalist movement.

Another founding member of the society and the movement's first historian, W.P. Ryan (1867–1942), documented Yeats' evolving role in this literary revival, whose initial aim was simply to get more Irish readers reading Irish books and more Irish writers writing them. Although Yeats is little more than a face in the crowd of revivalists in this early account – bunched together with such formidable figures as

Jane Barlow (1857–1917), Douglas Hyde, William Larminie (1849–1900), Edmund Leamy (1848–1904), Standish James O'Grady (1846–1928), John O'Leary, George Sigerson (1836–1925) and numerous others – Ryan does put him among 'the ranks of the zealous':

■ Mr. W.B. Yeats is one of our youngest writers. He was born in Dublin in 1866. He is, however, of Sligo family, and bids fair to immortalise that Connaught county. He spent therein several years of his youth, gathering from peasant lips its faery lore and traditions, of which he was destined to make remarkable use in after years. His school education was begun in London, and completed in Dublin, but the study that moulded him most of all was that of Celtic lore and legend. When he was about twenty years old his name began to grow familiar to readers of the *Irish Fireside*[2] and one or two other Dublin publications. Critical essays of a novel nature, and dreamy and fanciful poems were his contributions. He had a triumph in 1888 [actually 1889], when his 'Wanderings of Oisin' was published. Not only did the work reveal a new poetical personality, but it opened the gates of a new world of poetical materials. Mr. Yeats ranked henceforth as the most imaginative of Irish poets; but his imagination had often the simple air of reality. Occasional extravagance there was, but it was in keeping with that faery domain of vision and phantasy where the young poet was most at home. He was soon a welcome guest to the columns of various exclusive publications. After four years came his second book of poetry, 'The Countess Kathleen.' Though meant to be as expressive of Christian Ireland as the earlier work was of Pagan Ireland, the measure of success was not as full as before. Presumably modern, the best part of the drama was that wherein the author lapsed back to the mystical and the elfin. On a stage of famine, plagues, and the schemes of demons, with one beautiful, womanly nature set against the general horror, there was scope for the grimmest tragedy. But Mr. Yeats could never awe us: his Mephistopheles would dream dreams, and speak the fairy tongue. Lyrics in the book proved his old power of effective charming. In 1893 he returned to his own ground, and gave us 'Celtic Twilight,' prose studies of dhouls [demons], fairies, and visions, which it were as possible to describe in a few words as it were to put the magic of the 'Midsummer's Night Dream' into a sonnet. Mr. Yeats has edited several books, but we forget them once we glance at his poems and Irish mysteries. Like the answered Fairy Call of Irish legends, there is no ignoring, no forgetting these latter. Of his song we may say, as he himself has sung of the bell-branch: 'All who heard it dreamed a little while' [from an early version of 'The Dedication to a Book of Stories selected from the Irish Novelists']. One of his characters, evidently after his own heart, says: –

'I would go down and dwell among the *Sidhe*[3]
In their old, ever-busy, honeyed land.'

The *Sidhe*, I think, have come to dwell with him. They are as real to him as the green grass to the more common sight, though people, he says, doubt this belief in the fairy kingdom, thinking, he adds, that he is merely trying to weave a forlorn piece of gilt thread into the dull grey worsted of this century. Critics have been concerned of late to know if he has not really done his best work, or if there is, or will be much in his poetry of the enduring kind. He will dream away and answer the questions eventually, with new books and visions. That he will be a great poet depends to a large extent on the possibility of his developing other characteristics to the same degree as that already attained by his imaginative faculty and power of vision. He must shake himself free from the passing craze of occultism and symbolism, and realise also that the universe is not tenanted solely by *soulths* [ghosts] and *sheogues* [fairies]. Even now he has done much the finest poetical work of any of those in the present movement. If it is true as John Boyle O'Reilly [1844–90] sings that 'the dreamer lives for ever,' no one is more certain than he of immortality. Round the two chief regions in which he has travelled – the land of western legends, and the fairy sphere – it is not improbable that coming cycles of Irish song will be centred. The Irish Elysium will probably inspire the greater of the two. In those beautiful legends of Hy-Brazil and the West-Irish mythology as they are in effect – there are far finer possibilities for literature than other writers have found in the story of King Arthur and his Round Table. It is to be hoped that Mr. Yeats has not made his last excursion into this immortal region – that much of the good work which we may expect from him in the future will be inspired by the Islands of Youth where the Irish Immortals

> 'Shall not grow sad
> Or tired on any dawning morrow,
> Nor ever change, or feel the clutches
> Of grievous Time on his old crutches,
> Or fear the wild, grey osprey, Sorrow.'
> ['The Wanderings of Oisin'] □
> (W.P. Ryan, *The Irish Literary Revival*, 1894)[4]

Although the passing craze of the occult eventually became a lifelong obsession for Yeats, he agreed with Ryan that what the movement needed in the 1890s was perhaps a little less work on Irish folklore and a little more on Irish mythology. As Ryan said in his early report,

■ Fine work has been done of late years for Irish folk-lore, but higher matters of Irish mythology are, strangely enough, neglected. We have taken our notions of the old gods from peasant stories; we have, as it were, surveyed the Irish Olympus through cabin-smoke. □
(W.P. Ryan, *The Irish Literary Revival*, 1894)[5]

In fact, this was only one of many mountains that Ryan believed Irish writers would have to climb before anyone would speak seriously of something called modern Irish literature. The movement lacked cohesion and a definite sense of direction, with literary societies both in Ireland and abroad all busy with their own individual projects rather than banding together on a common project. At the end of the nineteenth century, it was still not possible for Ryan to speak of a single revivalist movement, but instead of a spattering of scattered and often antagonistic movements. Like Yeats, Ryan believed that the various movements might be brought together through the formation of an Irish literary theatre in Dublin, signalling its birth as the cultural capital of the Irish nation – an ambition that was eventually realised with the purchase of the Abbey Theatre in 1904.

By the time of the next major report on the movement in 1916, Ernest A. Boyd (1887–1946) could proudly state that it was no longer a revival but a renaissance. It was also clear that Yeats was no longer just another face in the revivalist crowd but the leader of that renaissance. Not only is Yeats the only writer who gets a chapter to himself in Boyd's book, but he gets three chapters – one each on his poems, his plays and his prose. Although Boyd says this is no more than anyone would expect, given Yeats' reputation in the year of the Easter Rising, he also says that reputation may be ripe for a little deflation. Boyd sees Yeats as only one of many Irish writers who are the products of the literary revival begun by Standish James O'Grady, scholar and author of a number of popular versions of the tales of mythological figures such as Finn and Cuchulain, the earliest volume published in the late 1870s. Yeats may well be the best known writer of the renaissance, says Boyd, but his influence on other Irish writers has been less than most readers had been led to believe at the time:

■ For many years W.B. Yeats was the most widely-known name in contemporary Irish literature, and it was not until the success of [the dramatist] J.M. Synge [1871–1909] that his predominance was challenged. Even then, however, the great difference in the work and manner of the two writers resulted in there being but a slight modification in the popular estimate of Yeats's importance. To many people he was, and is, synonymous with the Irish Literary Revival, of which they believe him to be the beginning and the end. As we have seen, not Yeats, but O'Grady, was the beginning of the Revival, and, as will be shown, very little of the work done by Irish writers during the past decade, or more, is traceable to the former. In attempting to delimit the influence of Yeats there is no intention to belittle what he has done, nor to deny that such an influence exists. He has certainly affected the course of the Revival, more especially in the first years of its existence, and is mainly responsible for the ultimate development of the Irish Theatre, but in neither instance has his rôle been that popularly attributed to him. At first his influence upon his contemporaries was undeniable. He induced them to abandon their politico-literary idols, and his own example served at once to enforce his arguments. His work not only exposed the weakness of the popular models, but at the same time attracted serious attention to the poetic awakening in Ireland. But this direct impulse was not sufficiently enduring to substantiate the claim that all our modern poetry comes from Yeats. In the theatre he has not at all moulded the form of Irish drama, for his plays have found no imitators, and remain separate and utterly distinct from the work of the other playwrights. Nevertheless, his presence has been a factor of some weight in the evolution of the Revival. Poet, dramatist, storyteller and essayist, he commands attention in almost every department of literature, and the mere bulk and diversity of his writings, apart from their intrinsic excellencies, are sufficient to ensure him a position of the first importance in any survey of Ireland's literary activities during the past quarter of a century. □

(Ernest A. Boyd, *Ireland's Literary Renaissance*, 1916)[6]

Yeats never denied O'Grady's importance, stating himself that the literary revival started with the publication of O'Grady's *History of Ireland: The Heroic Period* in 1878. Boyd does, however, give Yeats credit for his vocal part in the debate as to what sort of literature the renaissance should produce. Although his own work may be as much a product of the movement begun by O'Grady as was the work of less popular writers such as William Larminie and John Todhunter (1839–1916), Yeats had been doing his best to take politics out of Irish poetry. By picking Samuel Ferguson (1810–86) and William Allingham (1824–89) as two of the older poets he admired most and praising them for generally leaving politics out of their poems, Yeats had begun to define the Irish tradition in which he hoped to place himself:

■ When, after four years of poetical activity, Yeats offered his first collection of verse to the public, in 1889, he was evidently progressing towards the realisation of his powers. Both in choice of subject and in style *The Wanderings of Oisin and other Poems* marks an advance sufficient to warrant its being described as a representative volume. In essence most of his later work is here, and, as the book contained all his poetry up to that date, it is usually regarded as the beginning of W.B. Yeats. It has, indeed, been made by many the point of departure of the Revival, but there is evidence that this is not the case. Granted that Standish O'Grady is the source, it will easily be seen that *The Wanderings of Oisin* was not the first stream of poetry to issue from him. Larminie's *Glanlua* [1899], and Todhunter's *Banshee* [1888] were the contemporaneous products of the same impulse as gave birth to Yeats's volume. Since O'Grady had sent the young generation to the roots of national culture a number of new writers were at work, and the year 1889 saw their emergence from obscurity. Hyde's *Leabhar Sgeuluigheachta* [*Beside the Fire*], which heralded the Gaelic Movement, appeared in the same year as *The Wanderings of Oisin*, and 1889 is, therefore, a date of some interest to students of contemporary Irish literature. The time had come for the realisation of various ideas and ideals which were stirring in Ireland, hence the almost simultaneous appearance of a number of writers representing or emphasising new tendencies. But neither Yeats nor Larminie nor Todhunter can be regarded as originating any movement, inasmuch as they themselves were the outcome of a movement already initiated.

Without admitting the wider claims made on behalf of *The Wanderings of Oisin*, we may justly consider it as the beginning of Yeats' career. The title poem itself sufficiently indicates a definite orientation towards national poetry, instead of the vague romances of Arcady and Spain with which the poet was at first engaged. The latter, it is true, find here their first and only republication, but the volume, in the main, is distinctly Irish. Yeats was an early champion of Ferguson against the rhetorical school and, during the first years of the Literary Societies, he had constantly to assail the theory that *The Nation* poets were unimpeachable models for all who desired to write Irish poetry. As far back as 1886 he wrote in the *Dublin University Review*, urging the merits of Ferguson, whom he recognised as the true precursor of the new spirit. This discipleship explains in some measure *The Wanderings of Oisin*. Although there is no trace of Ferguson in Yeats's style, he played, nevertheless, an important part in the literary education of the young poet. It was doubtless his study of Ferguson that prompted him to essay an epic poem upon an Irish subject, and to give, in *The Wanderings of Oisin*, the measure of his genius. From Ferguson and Allingham Yeats learned what Irish poetry could be made, once the political note was softened or entirely silenced. 'If somebody could make a style,' he wrote, 'which would not be an English style, and yet would be musical and full of colour many others would catch fire from him.' This was the thought which turned Yeats from Spain and Arcady to Ireland, and in his volume of 1889, we find him in the act of realising his ideal of national poetry. An artist in words, he had an advantage over Ferguson, whose conception and aims were lofty, but whose craftsmanship was unequal. Having been roused by O'Grady's prose, Yeats was able to bring to the old legends an admiration equal to Ferguson's, but a sense of artistry and a temperament unknown to the older writer. He constantly exhorted his contemporaries to chasten their enthusiasm for the crude outbursts of aggressive patriotism, for, as he pointed out, 'if more of them would write about the beliefs of the people like Allingham, or about old legends like Ferguson, they would find it easier to get a style.' □

(Ernest A. Boyd, *Ireland's Literary Renaissance*, 1916)[7]

Yeats' attitude towards the poets of the Young Ireland movement who had been associated with *The Nation* newspaper was almost always ambivalent, praising them for making their poetry national – making use of Irish myth and legend – but blaming them for often making it blatantly nationalist as well. In an attempt to link his sort of revivalism with the earlier work of Young Ireland poets such as Thomas Davis, James Clarence Mangan (1803–49) and (once again) Samuel Ferguson, Yeats had said in a poem originally entitled 'Apologia addressed to Ireland in the Coming Days': 'Know, that I would accounted be / True brother of a company / That sang, to sweeten Ireland's wrong, / Ballad and story, rann and song.'[8] Although Boyd could understand why the young Yeats was so keen towards the end of the nineteenth century to join ranks with the likes of those three established Irish poets, the link was still a slightly awkward one:

■ *The Countess Kathleen and Various Legends and Lyrics*, in 1892, revealed a more exclusive preoccupation with Ireland than the preceding volume. There is not a line in the book that is not instinct with the spirit of nationality, yet anything more different from what had hitherto been accepted as the typical collection of Irish national poetry it would be difficult to conceive. Perceiving this, yet conscious that his verses were none the less the expression of his country, Yeats voices his conviction in the fine *Apologia* which is now so familiar:

Nor may I less be counted one
With Davis, Mangan, Ferguson,
Because to him who ponders well
My rhymes more than their rhyming tell ...
['To Ireland in the Coming Times']

These poems belong to the period when Yeats was a member of the Young Ireland Society, and when, though fighting against the undue regard in which Davis and his school were held, he desired, like them, to write 'popular poetry.' Although convinced of the superiority of Mangan, and of Ferguson especially, he nevertheless tried to convince himself that the popular patriotic poets wrote well, and to improve upon the tradition they had created. The most successful of these attempts are the ballads, *Father Gilligan*, *Father O'Hart* and *The Lamentation of the Old Pensioner*. These, like the songs, *Down by the Salley Garden* and *The Meditation of an Old Fisherman*, from the previous volume, are the result of direct contact with the country people, and may fairly claim to be as 'popular' as is possible for Yeats. The author has suggested in later years that these poems are trivial and sentimental, weaknesses he ascribes to the fact of their being 'imitations.' But to many they will possess a charm and spontaneity preferable to the laboured obscurities of his maturity.

Distinct from the verses inspired by country lore are those which have their roots in the heroic age. Here it is possible to see the influence of Ferguson driving the poet to the libraries, where he could satisfy the appetite awakened by O'Grady for the ancient sagas. *Fergus and the Druid* and *The Death of Cuchullin* are fragments in the Fergusonian manner – for Ferguson invariably confines his treatment to some slight incident rather than to a sequence of episodes from the heroic cycles. Yeats, however, is able to supply the element of beauty whose absence made Ferguson's work so frequently colourless. The latter held his reader to the interest of the subject in itself, whereas the former compels attention by the art of his verse. One forgets the fragmentary theme in order to enjoy the expression of the poet's thought. Ferguson could not have written:

> A wild and foolish labourer is a king,
> To do and do and do, and never dream.

The lines are a formula of Yeats's attitude towards life. Even less likely is the author of *Congal* [1872] to make us lose sight of his subject in order to admire the thought.

> I see my life go dripping like a stream
> From change to change; I have been many things –
> A green drop in the surge, a gleam of light
> Upon a sword, a fir-tree on a hill,
> An old slave grinding at a heavy guern,
> A king sitting upon a chair of gold ...

Fergus and the Druid is as great an advance upon, say, Ferguson's *Abdication of Fergus MacRoy*, as the ballads mentioned were upon those of Davis and his followers. Less successful is *The Death of Cuchullin*, which deals with that intensely tragic situation of Irish legend, the slaying of Cuchullin by his father, who is ignorant of his son's identity. The tragedy is lost in the poem, nor are there any touches of personality to compensate for the author's failure to catch the proper note. Conscious, no doubt, of this ineffectiveness, Yeats later returned to the subject in the one-act play, *On Baile's Strand* [1904]. Here, at all events, the conception is more adequate. □

(Ernest A. Boyd, *Ireland's Literary Renaissance*, 1916)[9]

However much the younger Yeats had wanted to be seen as part of an Irish poetic tradition that included Davis, Mangan and Ferguson, Boyd could see that this was no longer so. That company had parted, according to Boyd, with the publication of *Poems* in 1895. In the two decades that had passed since Ryan wrote his early history of the movement, Yeats had put together a tradition, appointed himself its leader and then abandoned it for his current fascinations with the theatre and the occult. Although Boyd is still reluctant to state in 1916 that future readers will find Yeats the most important poet of the revival, he seems certain that they will find his revivalist work the best he ever wrote. Irish poets who followed Yeats disagreed, as happy as Yeats apparently was to dissociate himself from the Young Ireland poets, no matter how much he had wanted to be considered a member of that particular club in the early years of his career.

Patrick Kavanagh was one of the first of the following generation of Irish poets to question not only Yeats' membership of that club but also whether he was even Irish at all. Writing in what was supposed to be the wake of the huge success of the literary revival, Kavanagh dismissed this alleged cultural renaissance in Ireland as nothing other than 'a thoroughgoing English-bred lie'.[10] As the self-appointed leader of this renaissance, Yeats no doubt thought he was speaking for the real Irish people and expressing their humble lives, but Kavanagh argues that the revivalists were little more than tourists in rural Ireland, like Synge listening through the floorboards of his Aran Island cottage to the Gaelic conversations of the locals below:

■ The best portrait of Yeats ever produced is George Moore's in *Hail and Farewell* [1911–14]. Yeats disliked it at the time, yet it is very affectionate, and even at that time when Yeats was under forty, with his best work to come, Moore recognized his genius.

But there is one facet of the poet's life that few people have discussed – his desperate desire to be thought Irish and one of the People. Nobody will deny that he was Irish of a certain kind – a noble kind, his father was a wonderful man – yet he himself was always conscious of being something of an outsider.

And I would be accounted one
With Mangan, Davis, Ferguson.   ['To Ireland in the Coming Times']

As Plato tells us in the person of Socrates, a man cannot desire that which he has got. Joyce had it. Joyce, as he himself says, was 'Irish, all too Irish'.

Yeats took up Ireland and made it his myth and his theme. And you can see him today standing in the centre of that myth, uneasy that he doesn't belong fully. Now we can see that he does belong fully to that exciting affair with the Nation, with Pearse and Connolly and the others [Patrick Pearse (1879–1916) and James Connolly (1868–1916) were both leaders of the Easter Rising and subsequently executed]. But the fact remains that he never was at ease.

It was a weakness in his character in a way, the sort of weakness that you get in [Ernest] Hemingway [1898–1961] with his delusions of violent grandeur, bullfights and boxing. Still, as with Yeats, it gave Hemingway the basis of a theme. My own view is that men of supreme genius have no delusions of any kind about themselves. The truth is that Yeats did not belong to Sligo and Sligo is not the 'Yeats country' as our tourist people claim. A truer Yeats country would be London, the Rhymers' Club, the Pre-Raphaelites, Arthur Symons [1865–1945], that world about which he tells us so fascinatingly in the Introduction to *The Oxford Book of Modern Verse* [1936].

A great deal of his poetry of this period has Sligonian themes – Innisfree, The Fiddler of Dooney, but the central emotion in them is that of *fin de siècle* decadence.

I am not one of those who think that a brilliant poet should be accessible to the ordinary people. No, in the words of Ezra Pound, Yeats's great friend (he was best man at Yeats's wedding), 'the lordliest of the arts and the solace of lonely men' was not created for the amusement of the ignorant man in the street. The traditional idea of the poet in Ireland is that he sings for the people. True poetry could not be created if it had to depend on the common man. The ability to recognize and enjoy the poetic content of a poem as distinct from its emotional wrapping is quite rare. Much of Yeats comes over on its Irishness. Incidentally, I think his poem on Nineteen Sixteen shows him at his worst. 'The grey eighteenth-century houses' are phoney and Pre-Raphaelite. In my opinion, Yeats's finest work was written when he was over fifty, up to but not including the *Last Poems*. The bawdy of the *Last Poems* is not true to the full Yeatsian life.

Having written this, something smote my conscience and I looked up the *Last Poems* and some of them are really splendid and so poetically exciting.

> *I sing what was lost and dread what was won*
> *I walk in a battle fought over again.*   ['What Was Lost']

There are two things in particular that are the marks of the poet – his gay youthfulness and his authority. Yeats always had both. He speaks from a height.

The condition of being young is, as [the French novelist François] Mauriac [1885–1970] recently said, a 'state of mind'. To be old is to be dead. But can a poet die? More and more I am finding it difficult to imagine the discontinuity of that which once was. I have started a new form of literary criticism. Is he young or is he old?

I do not think that those poems in *Last Poems*, which are bawdy and noisy about wild women, show Yeats's youngness but rather those in which he is his own serene authoritative self. In one of his *Last Poems* he writes of the world he has known.

> *Beautiful lofty things: O'Leary's noble head;*
> *My father upon the Abbey stage ...*
> *Maud Gonne at Howth station waiting for a train.*

> Pallas Athene in that straight back and arrogant head:
> All the Olympians; a thing never known again.
>
> ['Beautiful Lofty Things']

But was it not he who made them Olympians? Yeats was the god, the authority, the Mother Mind to whom all things could be referred. Any person possessing this myth-making quality can transform a commonplace society into an Olympian one. There were others to be sure who had authority, not the least being George Moore. In many ways it was through his *Hail and Farewell* that the Irish Literary Revival, Abbey Theatre, etc., became a reality. He gave it a history, a form. Movements are born of The Word. No expression, no existence. I am sure that Yeats writing –

> And did some words of mine send out
> Certain men the English shot?
>
> ['Man and the Echo']

was not so far off the mark. He was a poet. One knew he was there. □
(Patrick Kavanagh, Collected Pruse, 1967)[11]

While Boyd could at least understand why the young Yeats wanted to be considered in the company of Davis, Mangan and Ferguson, Kavanagh believes his true brothers were the old decadents of the Rhymers' Club back in Victorian London, such as Ernest Dowson (1867–1900), Lionel Johnson and Victor Plarr (1863–1929). Yeats may have written an awful lot of revivalist poems about the sort of peasant life that Kavanagh had been born into but, like Synge in his Aran Island cottage, he would always be the outsider. Although Kavanagh argues that Yeats was much more a product of urban English culture than of rural Irish culture, critics in the 1960s began to wonder whether Yeats did not belong to Sligo after all – or at least County Sligo as it was in the late nineteenth and early twentieth centuries.

T.R. Henn was one of the first to look closely at the Sligo Yeats knew as a boy during the summers he spent at his grandparents' house there, pointing out that it was an Ireland quite different to the one Kavanagh knew as a boy in County Monaghan. It was an aristocratic Big House culture, whose proudest period had been the eighteenth century prior to the Act of Union that abolished the Irish Parliament in 1800. Henn suggests this Sligo, where he spent his own childhood, was a somewhat idyllic world unto itself, rather unique even within Ireland at the time. Yeats may have identified himself with one group of writers and one version of Ireland in his early revivalist years but, following such events as the Easter Rising in 1916 and the ratification of the Irish Free State by the Dáil in 1922, he began to identify himself with another group of writers and another version of Ireland, one which had only recently all but ceased to exist:

■ The society and life of the early part of the century was in many ways peculiar. It is a very different world from that of Synge or of [the dramatist Sean] O'Casey [1880–1964]. Everywhere the Big House, with its estates surrounding it, was a centre of hospitality, of country life and society, apt to breed a passionate attachment, so that the attempt to save it from burning or bankruptcy became an obsession (in the nineteen-twenties and onwards) when that civilization was passing. The gradual sale of the outlying properties, as death duties and taxation rose higher, is recorded in Lady Gregory's struggle to save Coole Park, and was the fate of many estates.[12] [Lady Augusta Gregory (1852–1932), a close friend of Yeats, was a dramatist, folklorist and translator who was active in the running of the Abbey Theatre.] The great families were familiar with each other and with each other's history; often, perhaps commonly, connected by blood or marriage. They had definite and narrow traditions of life and service. The sons went to English Public Schools, and thence to Cambridge, or Oxford, or Trinity College, Dublin: the eldest would return to the estate and its management, the younger went to the Services, the Bar, the Church. There were

... Great rooms where travelled men and children found
Content or joy; a last inheritor
Where none has reigned that lacked a name and fame
Or out of folly into folly came.   ['Coole and Ballylee, 1931']

The great age of that society had, I suppose, been the eighteenth and early nineteenth centuries; from the eighteen-fifties onwards it seems to have turned its eyes too much towards England, too conscious of its lost influence in its hereditary role of The Ascendancy. By 1912 it was growing a little tired, a little purposeless, but the world still seemed secure:

We too had many pretty toys when young:
A law indifferent to blame or praise,
To bribe or threat; habits that made old wrong
Melt down, as it were wax in the sun's rays;
Public opinion ripening for so long
We thought it would outlive all future days.
                                        ['Nineteen Hundred and Nineteen']

The image of the house and its fall lingered with Yeats to the end, as in the play *Purgatory* [1939]:

Great people lived and died in this house;
Magistrates, colonels, members of Parliament,
Captains and Governors, and long ago
Men that had fought at Aughrim and the Boyne ...
                    ... to kill a house

Where great men grew up, married, died,
I here declare a capital offence.

In the furnishings of a great house, or in its library, one became aware that most of the work had been done between, say, 1750 and 1850, over the bones of a rebellion and two famines. The original building might date from Cromwell's time [1599–1658], or before; modernized, perhaps, by adding a frontage from a Loire chateau, or a portico from Italy. Some of these were of great beauty:

Many ingenious lovely things are gone
That seemed sheer miracle to the multitude,
Protected from the circle of the moon
That pitches common things about.

['Nineteen Hundred and Nineteen']

But the whole Anglo-Irish myth, the search for beauty and stability in the midst of poverty and defeat, the dreams that oscillated between fantasy and realism, has yet to be described.

It is against this background, I believe, we must see the Recognition and Reversal in Yeats' poetry that came out of the Rebellion and its aftermath. Before the First World War that aristocratic culture seemed to have given so much: pride of race, independence of thought, and a certain integrity of political values. It could be perceived (even then) in relation to the great eighteenth-century tradition, which, foreshortened and perhaps not wholly understood, held so much fascination for Yeats. It could be seen as representing the Anti-Self or Mask to which he was striving: whether in the image of the hero, or soldier, or horseman, or that symbolic Fisherman who occurs repeatedly:

… I choose upstanding men
That climb the streams until
The fountain leap, and at dawn
Drop their cast at the side
Of dripping stone; I declare
They shall inherit my pride,
The pride of people that were
Bound neither to Cause nor to State,
Neither to slaves that were spat on,
Nor to the tyrants that spat,
The people of Burke and of Grattan
That gave, though free to refuse –
Pride, like that of the morn …

['The Tower']

Lady Gregory and the Gore-Booths had shown him the security that came from the wealth of the great estates, and the life, leisured and cultured, that it seemed to make possible:

Surely among a rich man's flowering lawns,
Amid the rustle of his planted hills,

Life overflows without ambitious pains;
And rains down life until the basin spills,
And mounts more dizzy high the more it rains
As though to choose whatever shape it wills
And never stoop to a mechanical
Or servile shape, at others' beck and call.

['Meditations in Time of Civil War']

To this society, in the main Protestant, Unionist, and of the 'Ascendancy' in character, the peasantry was linked. The great demesnes had their tenantry, proud, idle, careless, kindly, with a richness of speech and folk-lore that Lady Gregory had been the first to record.[13] The days of *Castle Rackrent* [1801, a novel by Maria Edgeworth (1767–1849)] and the absentee landlord were, in the main, over; the relationship between land-lord and tenant varied, but was on the whole a kindly one, and carried a good deal of respect on either side. The bitterness of the Famine, the evictions and burnings described by Maud Gonne in *A Servant of the Queen* [1938], belonged to an earlier period. The members of the family would be known either by the titles of their professions: the Counsellor, the Bishop, the Commander, and so on: or by the Christian names of their boyhood. They mixed with the peasantry more freely and with a greater intimacy (especially in childhood) than would have been possible in England.[14] Yeats' memories of conversations with servants, and particu-larly with Mary Battle, gave him much material. Sport of every kind was a constant bond: the ability to shoot, or fish, or ride a horse was of cen-tral importance. At its best there was something not unlike a survival of the Renaissance qualities:

... Soldier, scholar, horseman, he,
And all he did done perfectly
As though he had but that one trade alone.

['In Memory of Major Robert Gregory']

But even at its best the tradition had outlived its usefulness, as Yeats knew:

O what if gardens where the peacock strays
With delicate feet upon old terraces,
Or else all Juno from an urn displays
Before the indifferent garden deities;
O what if levelled lawns and gravelled ways
Where slippered Contemplation finds his ease
And Childhood a delight for every sense,
But take our greatness with our violence?

['Meditations in Time of Civil War']

There were other aspects of that life. Land or local troubles flared out from time to time. There were times, even in my own boyhood, when one did not sit in the evening between a lamp and the open; though Lady Gregory, in reply to threats on her life during the Civil War, replied proudly that she was to be found each evening, between six and seven, writing before an unshuttered window. ☐

(T.R. Henn, *The Lonely Tower*, 1965)[15]

Not only did the peasants and the aristocrats generally get on quite well, but so did the Catholic and the Protestant communities, both of whom comfortably accommodated pagan beliefs – as well as the other community's beliefs and practices – in their everyday lives. Another curious feature of the small society of Sligo around the turn of the century, reports Henn, was its apparent lack of a middle class, something he suggests Yeats only encountered in urban Ireland:

■ In this society there was (outside the big cities) no middle class, and this was in itself a fundamental weakness. A barrister was honoured for his profession: a solicitor was in a very different category. The doctor and the clergyman had positions in the social scale not wholly unlike those in the world of Swift. The relations between Protestants and Catholics might be bitter, and memories of the Penal Laws were long; but in the years before the First World War I remember little trouble in the West. Indeed, my grandfather had given land for the local chapel, so that the front pew was reserved for members of the family in case they should one day be converted. And for many years, in accordance with some old tradition, a light was kept burning on our behalf in the ruined abbey on one of the islands in the Shannon – a ritual that hardly belonged to Protestantism, but was accepted as natural and proper. In every district there were many superstitions, with a curiously ambivalent attitude to them on the part of country-folk and gentry alike. The early Christian missionaries had taken over many of the features of the Elder Faiths of the locality. Holy wells are numerous and display the offerings of the pious. In my own youth pieces of gorse were placed on the lintels of the cottages on May Day to discourage the Good People from alighting there. A relic of the Baal Fire ritual was rehearsed in the lane below our house on St John's Eve when young men leaped through the flames of bonfires.[16] The sacred pilgrimage to Croagh Patrick fired Yeats' mind with a vision of a new synthesis of paganism and Christianity. The 'cleft that's christened Alt' ['Man and the Echo'] is near Sligo, and has magical associations; it was no violence of Yeats to think of it in terms of the chasm at Delphi, just as the Sphinx might be transplanted to the Rock of Cashel ['The Double Vision of Michael Robartes']. A good Catholic might well half-believe in the older magic and yet go to Mass with a clear conscience; a Protestant, while in theory superior to all superstitious practices, might yet catch something of a fearful half-belief from speech with servants, grooms and fishermen, and innate romanticism could readily build upon their stories.

I believe that it is important to realize something of this background of Yeats' work. It has many bearings. The world of the great houses offered security, a sense of peace, beautiful things to look on and handle:

> Great works constructed there in nature's spite
> For scholars and for poets after us,
> Thoughts long knitted into a single thought,
> A dance-like glory that those walls begot.   ['Coole Park, 1929']

The truth about the great houses of the South and West lies, perhaps, somewhere between Yeats' pictures of Coole Park, the romantic descriptions of some recent novelists, and MacNeice's 'snob idyllicism'. [This is a reference to the account in *The Poetry of W.B. Yeats* (1941) by the poet Louis MacNeice. See Chapter Four of this Guide.] For every family that produced 'travelled men and children' there was another that produced little but 'hard-riding country gentlemen', who had scarcely opened a book. An eighteenth-century house might be half-filled with Sheraton and Adam work, and half with Victorian rubbish. Families nursed the thought of past greatness, fed their vanity with old achievement or lineage or imagined descent from the ancient kings; and in the warm damp air, with its perpetual sense of melancholy, of unhappy things either far off or present, many of them decayed. Standish O'Grady could write bitterly of *The Great Enchantment*, that web of apathy in a country with an alien government and an alien religion, subject at every turn to patronage and the servility it brings, into which Ireland had fallen. That, too, is a narrow view of the whole. The aristocracy had, at its best, possessed many of the qualities that Yeats ascribed to it: the world of Somerville and Ross [Somerville and Ross was the joint pseudonym of the cousins Edith Somerville (1858–1949) and Violet Martin (1862–1915), who wrote short stories and novels of life in Big House Ireland that at one time were very popular], the Dublin of Joyce or of Sean O'Casey differ merely in accordance with the position of the onlooker. □   (T.R. Henn, *The Lonely Tower*, 1965)[17]

Henn notes that Yeats' ancestors were much more likely to have been hard riding than well travelled, even if he sometimes pretended otherwise. Yeats would occasionally trace his family tree back to the Ormondes, the Butlers and the High Kings, but he took considerably more pride in whatever he may have inherited from those forefathers who really knew how to sail a boat or how to ride a horse. At this point in his life, says Henn, Yeats was also emotionally attracted to the general decay and dilapidation of this dying Big House culture, as well as its remains of hillforts, Norman castles and round towers. His attempt to restore his own round tower, Thoor Ballylee, not far from Coole Park, became as much a personal as it was a poetic symbol for the now middle-aged poet.

After reading this brief description of Sligo in Henn's book, Donald T. Torchiana decided to dedicate an entire study to Yeats and his post-revivalist obsession with Georgian Ireland, first published in 1966. Having tried somewhat unsuccessfully to join the tribe of Davis, Mangan and Ferguson, Yeats invented a whole new tribe of Anglo-Irish writers, philosophers and politicians – whose glory days, like the Big Houses of Sligo, were in the eighteenth century – that included Bishop Berkeley, Edmund Burke (1729–97), Thomas Davis, Robert Emmet (1778–1803), Oliver Goldsmith (1728–74), Henry Grattan (1746–1820), Jonathan Swift and Wolfe Tone (1763–98). Yeats had been born into this culture, had temporarily rebelled against it and then, following his decades with the literary revival, returned to it and embraced it. Torchiana argues that, as Yeats became more and more disenchanted with nineteenth-century Ireland, he became increasingly fascinated with eighteenth-century Ireland, the one culture gradually yielding to the other. Although Yeats was well aware that this change of enthusiasms would not prove popular amongst many of his readers in Ireland and America, the weeks and months he was spending at Coole Park with Lord and Lady Gregory, Robert Gregory (1881–1918) and Sir Hugh Lane (1875–1915) made him wonder whether the real Irish were not, perhaps, the Anglo-Irish. In the Big Houses of Sligo and Galway, it seemed to Yeats that landlords like Gregory still had an almost feudal attachment to and concern for their tenants, while nobles like Lane showed an almost renaissance sense of artistic patronage and civic obligation. This culture had begun to die, of course, with the Act of Union in 1800 and the dissolution of the Irish Parliament but, with the formation of the Dáil Éireann and the Irish Free State, Yeats had hopes it might assume its old role once again:

■ With the establishment of the Free State, Yeats recognized that at long last the artist in Ireland had been freed from his insistent preoccupation with being Irish. At long last he could devote himself entirely to his work.[18] Looking back some ten years, Yeats reviewed how he had then also turned wholeheartedly to the eighteenth century to seek traditions of intellect and government for the new state and, just as importantly, to remind the hesitant twentieth-century Anglo-Irish of the essential Irish patriotism of Protestant leaders like Swift and Grattan. This turn, its source in his friendship with the Gregorys and Synge, and the new array of authors and ideas he pursued – all these are recorded in the exuberant pages of his essay, 'Ireland, 1921–1931.' Its central portion is crucial to this argument:

Freedom from obsession brought me a transformation akin to religious conversion. I had thought much of my fellow-workers – Synge, Lady Gregory, Lane – but had seen nothing in Protestant Ireland as a whole but its faults, had carried through my projects in face of its opposition or its indifference, had fed my imagination upon the legends of the Catholic villages or upon medieval Irish poetry; but now my affection turned to my own people, to my ancestors, to the books they had read. It seemed we had a part to play at last that might find us allies everywhere, for we alone had not to assume in public discussion of all great issues that we could find in St. Mark or St. Matthew a shorthand report of the words of Christ attested before a magistrate ... . Now that Ireland was substituting traditions of government for the rhetoric of agitation our eighteenth century had regained its importance. An Irish Free State soldier, engaged in dangerous service for his Government, said to me that all the philosophy a man needed was in Berkeley. Stirred by those words I began to read *The Dialogues of Hylas and Philonous* [1713]. From Berkeley I went to Swift, whose hold on Irish imagination is comparable to that of [the Catholic political leader Daniel] O'Connell [1775–1847]. The Protestant representatives in Dail and Senate were worthy of this past; two or three went in danger of their lives; some had their houses burnt; country gentlemen came from the blackened ruins of their houses to continue without melodrama or complaint some perhaps highly technical debate in the Senate. Month by month their prestige rose. When the censorship of books was proposed certain Protestant Bishops disassociated themselves from it, and had the Government persisted with the Bill in its first form and penalized opinion we might have had a declaration, perhaps from the Episcopacy as a whole, that private judgement implied access to the materials of judgement. Then, just when we seemed a public necessity, our Episcopacy lost its head. Without consulting its representatives in Dail or Senate, without a mandate from anybody, in the teeth of a refusal of support from Trinity College, terrified where none threatened, it appealed, not to the Irish people, but to the Colonial Conference, to keep the Irish Courts in subordination to the Privy Council, thereby seeming to declare that our ancestors made the independence of the legislature and the Courts the foundation of their politics, and of Ireland's from that day, because those Courts and that legislature protected not a nation but a class. When these blind old men turned their backs upon Swift and Grattan, at a moment too when the past actions of the Colonial Conference itself had already decided the issue, they had forgotten, one hopes, or had never learnt, that their predecessors sat in the Irish House of Lords of 1719, when it sent the Irish Court of Exchequer to prison for accepting a decision of that Privy Council.[19]

A question at once arises. Who were the Anglo-Irish, historically speaking, from the Battle of the Boyne [1690] down to the founding of the Free State? Until now, a general understanding of the term has been good enough. But now that we are following Yeats's growing concept or myth or fixed idea of the Anglo-Irish – something of all three are involved – it is time to get a glimpse of what he could include or work with. For this purpose, an excellent definition was formulated by Hugh A. Law in 1929:

... whom do we mean by the Anglo-Irish? Note that the name was not chosen by those of whom I speak. *They* have been content, and commonly proud, to call themselves simply 'Irish.' But that word has of late been so much used as a synonym for 'Gaelic' that, for the sake of clearness and convenience, some distinction had to be made in speaking of one particular body of Irish citizens. Very roughly then the term is taken to denote a well-known, though never accurately defined, section of our people, differing from the rest very little in blood (since for centuries past we have been, all of us, of mixed race) – but differing more or less widely in religious belief, or in social habits or in political associations, and not infrequently in all three. Endless exceptions must be made; but for our present purpose it may be assumed that the typical Anglo-Irishman is Protestant in faith, has some connection with the land-owning class as it existed here from the end of the 17th to the end of the 19th century, and cherishes family traditions of service to the Crown of these islands.[20]

The first point, then, is that the Anglo-Irish include those who designated themselves the 'Irish interest' in Swift's time and who, well into Yeats's own boyhood, identified themselves – even though part of the nineteenth-century Garrison – with Ireland. Swift was being characteristic of his class when he dryly observed the 'English colonies' in Ireland to be 'much more civilized than many counties in England, and speak better English, and are much better bred.'[21] It was no less characteristic that Synge's famous ancestor, the Archbishop of Tuam, should have defended the Catholics in a sermon before the Irish House of Commons in 1725.[22] Nor is Yeats any less himself in remarking of his youth: 'Everyone I knew well in Sligo despised the Nationalists and Catholics, but all disliked England with a prejudice that had come down perhaps from the days of the Irish Parliament.'[23] And all would have probably agreed that no small part of this disdain for England rested in her supposed vulgarity.[24]

It was in the 1880's, with the rise of the Land League, that the term Anglo-Irish came into generally opprobrious use; so much so that the Irishman of English ancestry frequently fell a sacrificial victim – by virtue of his name or ancestry alone – to the rigors of the new nationalism.[25] Captain John Shawe-Taylor [1866–1911] ... may be counted one severe example. Many a professional peasant or Dubliner, of course, has seen the distinction as but a silly myth of social snobbery.[26] Yet it seems, despite the disclaimers of Denis Ireland,[27] that [the dramatist George Bernard] Shaw [1856–1950] put his finger once and for all on the dangers of this nationalistic denial of Protestant Irish worth when he had Larry Boyle rebuke Matthew in the third act of *John Bull's Other*

Island [1904] thus:

> Do you think, because youre poor and ignorant and half-crazy with toiling and moiling morning noon and night, that youll be any less greedy and oppressive to them that have no land at all than old Nick Lestrange, who was an educated travelled gentleman that could not have been tempted as hard by a hundred pounds as youd be by five shillings? Nick was too high above Patsy Farrell to be jealous of him; but you, that are only one step above him, would die sooner than let him come up that step; and well you know it.

Part of Yeats's insistent iteration that Protestant Ireland's eighteenth century was once again important lay in the fact that the Lestranges had been altogether too acquiescent to the shrill demands of the Gael since the Union, had in fact become too preoccupied with England; yet, for all their separation from public life, still possessed a genius, mournful as that separation made it.[28]

But what attracted Yeats most in eighteenth-century Protestant Ireland was more an attitude or quality of intellect than any necessary class distinction. Whatever the provenance, the mind Yeats celebrated was like that of the Irish airman ['An Irish Airman foresees his Death'] – capable of selfless, independent choice. Yeats himself, on the evidence of a genealogical-minded cousin, acknowledged his family to have been never more than small gentry at best.[29] Land was not the measure of intellect. Joseph Hone, among his friends, tirelessly reminded the modern Gaelic detractors of the Anglo-Irish that

> The term Anglo-Irish has ... some value of convenience, but is misleading in many ways, especially as used by political and religious propagandists, who wish to discredit the great figures of Protestant (episcopalian) Ireland by identifying them with the Plantations and so with records of confiscation and oppression. In fact, landlordry, whether Norman, Cromwellian or mixed Irish, can claim credit for comparatively few of Ireland's famous sons. Neither Swift nor Berkeley was born in a great house; Goldsmith came from a country rectory; Burke was the son of a lawyer, Wolfe Tone of a coachmaker; Grattan's father was a Recorder, Thomas Davis's an Army surgeon; Bernard Shaw's ancestor was a lawyer in Kilkenny; and these men were not only born in Ireland but educated there, not at Eton, Oxford and Cambridge, where since the seventeenth century Irish rank and riches have chiefly sent their young.[30]

However boastful Yeats's later reminder to his countrymen that the Anglo-Irish had 'created nearly all the literature of modern Ireland and most of its political intelligence' may have sounded, it also tellingly underlined what he chose to single out in 'the people of Burke and of Swift ... of Grattan, of Emmet, of Parnell'[31] for modern contemplation. □

(Donald T. Torchiana, *W.B. Yeats & Georgian Ireland*, 1966)[32]

Yeats' eyes began to open to all of the accomplishments of Georgian Ireland, not only the Big Houses of Sligo and Galway but, more conspicuously, the great buildings, townhouses and squares of Dublin that were built when Grattan sat in the Irish Parliament. In Yeats' understanding of history at this time, the Battle of the Boyne may have meant the final defeat of medieval Ireland, but it at last brought to the island renaissance thinking and other modern ideas. With those ideas, of course, also came the eventual impact of the French Revolution, rebellious peasants and the resultant Garrison mentality of the nineteenth century, yet it produced a culture to which Yeats could cling. As much as he detested eighteenth-century English literature, notes Torchiana, Yeats relished eighteenth-century Irish literature and even suggested a syllabus for Irish students that would begin with the old stories of Conchubar and Cuchulain and end with books by Berkeley and Burke.

In a paper presented to the Modern Languages Association in New York the same year Torchiana published his study, the Irish poet Thomas Kinsella said he could fully appreciate Yeats' desire to find a tradition to call his own and the necessity of inventing one when he could not readily find one to identify with. Kinsella points out that, when he looks back as an Irish poet and tries to trace his own tribal ancestry, he finds Yeats and then nothing but silence for more than a century:

■ A writer who cares who he is and where he comes from looks about him and begins by examining his colleagues. In that very act a writer in Ireland must make a basic choice: do I include writers in Irish among my colleagues? Or am I to write them off as a minor and embattled group, keeping loyal – for the best of reasons – to a dead or dying language? Some of the best writers in Irish already believe that their language is doomed, rejected by its people. They are pessimistic, but my instinct tells me they are right. So I turn only toward those who are writing in English. And, to speak only of the poets, the word 'colleague' fades on the lips before the reality: a scattering of incoherent lives. It will seem on a bad day that they are a few madmen and hermits, and nothing more. I can learn nothing from them except that I am isolated.

So I begin again, and look for the past in myself. An English poet would have an easier time of it. His course is clear. No matter what his preoccupations may be, he will find his forebears in English poetry; as inheritor of the parent language he is free to 'repatriate' a great American poet or a great Irish poet. As he looks backward, the line might begin with Yeats and T.S. Eliot [1888–1965] and continue with Matthew Arnold [1822–88] and Wordsworth [1770–1850] and Keats and Pope [1688–1744] – and so on through the mainstream of a tradition. An Irish poet will have only the first point in common with this. Or so I find in my own case, when I try to identify my forebears. Who are those whose lives in some sense belong to me, and whose force is there for me to use if I can, if I am good enough, as I try to write my own poetry?

The line begins, again, with Yeats. Then, for more than a hundred years, there is almost total silence. I believe that silence, on the whole, is the real condition of Irish literature in the nineteenth century – certainly of poetry. There are enough hideous anthologies to bear me out: collections in which one falls with relief on anything that shows mere competence – say, John Todhunter's lyrics or Robert Dwyer Joyce's [1830–83] political ballads – not to speak only of Ferguson and Mangan and Allingham and [Thomas] Moore [1779–1852]. But there is nothing that approaches the full literary achievement of an age. It is all tentative, or displaced.

If I look deeper still, further back, in the need to identify myself, what I meet beyond the nineteenth century is a great cultural blur. I must exchange one language for another, my native English for eighteenth century Irish. After the dullness of the nineteenth century, eighteenth century Irish poetry seems to me suddenly full of life: expertise in the service of real feeling – hatred for the foreign land-owner; fantasies and longings rising from the loss of an Irish civilisation (the poets putting their trust in the Stuarts or the Spanish fleet or even the Pope of Rome); satires, love-songs, lamentations: outcries of religious fervour or repentance. And all of this in full voices, the voices of poets who expect to be heard and understood, and memorised – Eoghan Ruadh O Súilleabháin [1748–84], Donnchadh Ruadh Mac Connmara [1715–1810], Seán Clárach Mac Domhnaill [1691–1754], Tadhg Gealach O Súilleabháin [?1715–95]; they are the tragic, almost-doggerel end of Gaelic literature – but they have no more need to question the medium they write in than, say, John Clare [1793–1864] writing in English.

Beyond them is the poet Aogán O Rathaille [?1670–1729] writing at the end of the seventeenth century and the beginning of the eighteenth. I am sure he is a major poet: the last great poet in Irish, and the last Irish poet, until Yeats, whose life can be seen as a true poetic career. It is a career that begins in the full light of Gaelic culture and ends in darkness, with the Gaelic aristocracy ruined and the death-blow already delivered to the Irish language.

Then beyond O Rathaille, the course of Irish poetry stretching back for more than a thousand years, full of riches and variety: poetry as mystery and magic, in the earliest fragments and interpolated in the early sagas; poetry as instant, crystalline response to the world, in a unique body of nature lyrics; poetry as a useful profession – the repository of historical information and topography and custom; love poems and devotional poems of high dignity and technique; conventional bardic poetry stiff with tradition and craft. Here, in all this, I recognise simultaneously a great inheritance and a great loss. The inheritance is mine, but only at two enormous removes – across a century's silence, and through an exchange of worlds. The greatness of the loss is measured not only by the substance of Irish literature itself, but also by the intensity with which we know it was shared; it has an air of continuity and shared history which is precisely what is missing from Irish literature, in English or Irish, in the nineteenth century and today.

Why can I not make living contact with that inheritance, my own past? Others have. It is because I believe I would have to make a commitment to the Irish language; to write in Irish instead of English. And that would mean loss of contact with my own present – abandonment of the language I was bred in for one which I believe to be dying. It would also mean forfeiting a certain possible scope of language: English has a greater scope, if I can make use of it, than an Irish which is not able to handle all the affairs of my life. So that even with a commitment to the Irish language, a full contact with the old tradition – a contact between two whole entities – is, I believe, impossible. But in the end it is really not a matter of choice; for my own part I simply recognise that I stand on one side of a great rift, and can feel the discontinuity in myself. It is a matter of people and place as well as writing – of coming, so to speak, from a broken and uprooted family, of being drawn to those who share my origins and finding that we cannot share our lives. □

(Thomas Kinsella, 'The Irish Writer', 1970)[33]

Following a suggestion by the Irish poet John Montague (born 1929), Roger McHugh published this paper in 1970 alongside Yeats' early essays on Davis, Mangan and Ferguson – possibly to show the sheer awkwardness of those early arguments and just how desperate Yeats was in those days to make himself a 'true brother' of that company. Clearly, Kinsella is not convinced by any of them and, despite his own attempt to bridge the gap in the tradition by spending years on the translation of such Irish epics as the *Táin Bó Cuailnge* [*Cattle Raid of Cooley*, sixth to eighth century AD], he can understand why Yeats had to come up with yet another culture and place himself at the fag end of it:

■ The only semblance of an escape – consonant with integrity – is into a greater isolation still, as Yeats's career shows. Yeats looks back over the course of literature in Ireland and sees it very differently. He values what he can in Gaelic literature, and uses it, as we know; but his living tradition is solely in English. And it has its high point, not its almost-doggerel last gasp, in the eighteenth century. Its literature and its human beings are specialised and cut off, an Anglo-Irish annex to the history of Ireland. He yokes together Swift and Burke and Berkeley and Goldsmith for his writers, and for his chosen people finds a race of 'swashbucklers, horsemen, swift indifferent men'. It is English literature, not Irish, that lies behind them, and their line – as he sees it – is ending in his own time. You might feel that Yeats created this brief Anglo-Irish tradition for himself, by special selection, and then projected his own values into it. But it is still a coherent entity, at a graceful elegiac height above the filthy modern tide. Yeats is isolated to begin with, like Aogán O Rathaille, at a turning point in history – there is a notable similarity in the way these poets regard their times: turning away from a miserable present and a terrible future to lament and celebrate an old nobility at the end of the line. But I believe that Yeats's isolation is at least partly a matter of choice. He refuses to come to terms with the real shaping vitality of Ireland where he sees it exists; to take the tradition in any other way would have been to write for Daniel O'Connell's children, for De Valera and Paudeen at his greasy till; to recognise these as the heirs of Anglo-Ireland's glory, and of the fruits of the 1916 Rising (which – for its 'gallantry' – Yeats is almost tempted to include in his Anglo-Irish system). [Eamon de Valera (1882–1975) was Taoiseach of Ireland 1932–48, 1951–4, 1957–9, and President 1959–73.]

Yeats is of course *in* the tradition of Irish literature; he gives it body and – in many ways – meaning. But he is isolated in the tradition. That isolation is the substance of his life. Early in his career, in an essay in 'Ideas of Good and Evil' [1903], he remembers standing on the side of Sliabh Echtge, looking out over the Galway plains. He thinks of the continuing generations of poetry and poetical life:

> There is still in truth upon those great level plains a people, a community bound together by imaginative possessions, by stories and poems which have grown out of its own life, and by a past of great passions which can still waken the heart to imaginative action. One could still, if one had the genius, and had been born to Irish, write for these people plays and poems like those of Greece. Does not the greatest poetry always require a people to listen to it?

There is the isolation: from a people whose language is not his own and whose lives, therefore, he cannot touch. At the end of his life, in 'A General Introduction for my Work', written in 1937, he returns to the same fact. He recalls that he had found in the poetry of Thomas Davis and others on the *Nation* newspaper (though it was not good poetry) 'one quality I admired and admire: they were not separated individual men: they spoke or tried to speak out of a people to a people'. Then he dramatises his isolation remembering the past persecutions of the Irish people:

> No people hate as we do in whom that past is always alive, there are moments when hatred poisons my life and I accuse myself of effeminacy because I have not given it adequate expression. It is not enough to have put it into the mouth of a rambling peasant poet. Then I remind myself that though mine is the first English marriage I know of in the direct line, all my family names are English, and that I owe my soul to Shakespeare, to Spenser [1552–99] and to Blake [1757–1827], perhaps to William Morris [1834–96], and to the English language in which

I think, speak and write, that everything I love has come to me through English; my hatred tortures me with love, my love with hate.

But Yeats is a great artist, and it is clear that this passionate frustration, though deep, did not take over his soul. Sanity is embodied in his career, in his final rejection of politics and its shrieking women, and his rejection of the people as an audience for his work. He writes: 'I am no Nationalist, except in Ireland for passing reasons; State and Nation are the work of the intellect, and when you consider what comes before and after them they are, as Victor Hugo [1802–85] said of something or other, not worth the blade of grass God gives for the nest of the linnet.'

As poet he is preoccupied with the leading work of the imagination which renders demagoguery – and all the doings of history that are not embodied in his own imagining self – of no account. The continuity or the mutilation of traditions becomes, in itself, irrelevant as the artist steps back from his entire world, mutilations and all, and absorbs it.

Yeats bestrides the categories. He had a greatness capable, perhaps, of integrating a modern Anglo-Irish culture, and which chose to make this impossible by separating out a special Anglo-Irish culture from the main unwashed body. ☐   (Thomas Kinsella, 'The Irish Writer', 1970)[34]

Kinsella's notion of the Irish poetic tradition as a gapped, broken, discontinuous, even mutilated tradition has been essential to the Yeats debate ever since he first presented his paper in the mid-1960s, but that does not mean that either critics or readers were as willing to dismiss the poems Yeats produced during his revivalist period as Yeats himself apparently was.

In fact, Mary Helen Thuente argues in her book *W.B. Yeats and Irish Folklore*, published in 1980, that Yeats' attempt to place himself within an Irish tradition in the late nineteenth century was considerably more radical than it has sometimes seemed. Irish folklore was not taken seriously at that time – even by those who had collected it themselves, often presenting it as the nonsense and foolishness of poorly educated peasants. Thuente notes that even Yeats did not take it seriously until John O'Leary told him to. Mythological materials were not much better, since what was available to Yeats then was either too pedantic to interest anyone other than Gaelic scholars and philologists or too popular to interest a serious poet like Yeats, including Ferguson's and O'Grady's versions of these old stories:

■ While Yeats praised Ferguson's use of ancient Irish myth, in actuality such materials were of little interest and of little use to him in the 1880s and 1890s. Ancient Irish myths available to Yeats in scholarly translations and in popularisations were equally unsatisfactory. The impetus for the translation of some of the numerous old manuscripts of Irish heroic sagas had come from Johann Caspar Zeuss's [1806–56] *Grammatica Celtica* (1853), which had shown that the Irish and Welsh languages were part of the same great Indo-European group of languages from which Latin and Greek had come. Ancient Irish manuscripts had thus been given a new prestige that made them seem worth translating, although only a small portion had actually been translated by the 1880s. The translation and studies which Zeuss had inspired had not lost their dry, philological form by the time Yeats began looking for an Irish subject matter. Articles by Celticists in journals such as the *Revue Celtique* treated the ancient Irish myths more as problems of semantics than as imaginative literature. Most articles in the *Revue Celtique* were written in French, a language which Yeats barely knew in the late 1880s. Other treatments of ancient Irish myth available to Yeats provided materials for Irish historians rather than for Irish literature. In *Lectures on the Manuscript Materials of Ancient Irish History* (1861), Eugene O'Curry [1794–1862] had listed and briefly described the manuscripts available to the Irish historian and archaeologist; he had not told the stories contained in the manuscripts. Years later Yeats recalled his response to O'Curry's work: 'His unarranged and uninterpreted history defeated my boyish indolence.'[35]

On the other hand, nineteenth-century popularisers of ancient Ireland had arranged and interpreted their materials until comic caricature, sentimentality, moralisation, and a false sublimity almost overwhelmed the myths. Yeats's enthusiastic early articles on Samuel Ferguson's poems about ancient Irish heroes convey what Yeats hoped to find in such popularisations of ancient Ireland rather than their real nature. Significant discrepancies are apparent when Ferguson's poems are compared with Yeats's comments. Yeats chose to ignore the scholarly and antiquarian aspects of Ferguson's work, and Ferguson's many slighting references to the vulgarity and exaggerations of the old legends. The poems convey a vague, shadowy grandeur much more than the heroic passions which Yeats claimed to have found in them. Yeats's emphasis on the 'strange' and 'fantastic' and 'passionate' elements in Ferguson's poetry is a more accurate reflection of Yeats's own attitudes concerning what such poetry about ancient Ireland should be than of Ferguson's work. Ferguson had described his epic poem *Congal* as an account of 'the expiring effort of the Pagan and Bardic party in Ireland', but Yeats, in his earliest articles about Ferguson, emphasised the vitality and energy of the poem.[36] Yeats praised the 'continual' introduction of the supernatural into the poem; however, the encounter between Congal and the prophesying hag which Yeats described is the only such incident in the poem and is quite brief. In a similar vein, Yeats considered Ferguson's 'Conary' and 'Deirdre' as his best poems about ancient Ireland. However, 'Conary' had more Irish folk and fairy lore in it than any of Ferguson's other heroic poems. Although Ferguson had based his 'Deirdre' on a manuscript source, the ancient tale of Deirdre had remained a living oral tradition among the peasantry. The qualities which Yeats admired the most in Ferguson's heroic poems – the supernatural, the grotesque, the weird – abounded in Irish folklore, which was much more readily available to Yeats than the stories of the heroes in the old manuscripts were.

Ancient Irish gods had often become human heroes, and occasionally mock-heroic giants, in peasant tradition. For example, William Carleton's [1794–1869] tale, 'A Legend of Knockmany', which Yeats included in his first anthology of Irish folklore, *Fairy and Folk Tales of the Irish Peasantry* (1888), could never have satisfied Yeats's need for a serious Irish subject matter. In Carleton's tale Finn and Cuchulain are mock-heroically portrayed as giants – Finn uses the trunk of a huge fir tree as a walking stick and when a neighbour wanted to borrow some butter, Finn's wife handily threw a piece 'about the weight of a couple dozen mill-stones' across a valley four miles wide. The plot turns on broad comedy and trickery. When Cuchulain arrives at Finn's pleasant Irish cottage, Finn pretends to be a baby in order to unnerve Cuchulain. In Carleton's story, Cuchulain's stature depends on the strength of his magic finger; by 1903 when Yeats began writing his series of plays about Cuchulain, he would portray Cuchulain as the embodiment of tragic passion and heroic energy.

Other literary popularisations of Irish myth available to Yeats in the 1880s represented an approach completely different from Carleton's comic treatment, but one that attempted a false sublimity which even Yeats, no matter how much he wanted to convey the seriousness of Irish literary materials, could not accept. In *Old Celtic Romances* (1879), Patrick Weston Joyce [1827–1914] had bowdlerised unacceptable passages and embellished his materials with English literary conventions. His brother, Robert Dwyer Joyce, wrote poems which frequently altered the ancient Irish tales almost beyond recognition – calling Cuchulain and the other heroes 'knights', and inventing episodes imitative of medieval romance. Although in later years Yeats praised Standish James O'Grady's *History of Ireland Vol. I: The Heroic Period* (1878) and *Vol. II: Cuchulain and His Contemporaries* (1880), O'Grady's style, which reminded Yeats of Carlyle's [1795–1881], and O'Grady's treatment of the ancient heroes, which was often reminiscent of the Victorian domestic novel, had actually not appealed to Yeats in the 1880s. Standish J. O'Grady ... might have remained a typical member of the Protestant and Unionist Irish upper class and believed that Irish history and tradition were beneath his notice had he not happened upon Sylvester O'Halloran's [1728–1807] history of Ireland [*General History of Ireland* (1774)], the first history of his country he had ever read although he had been educated at Trinity College Dublin. O'Grady was impressed with O'Halloran's rational, scholarly and impassioned approach to his materials. Soon deep in his own research on the subject, O'Grady was amazed at Ireland's rich store of heroic literature and in 1878 began to write his own 'history' of Ireland which he published at his own expense because there was no contemporary market for such subjects. In O'Grady's view, ancient literature was filled with 'a noble moral tone', 'breathes sublimity', and contained numerous incidents of 'chivalry' and others which 'inculcated chastity'.[37] O'Grady deleted or transformed passages which did otherwise. The proud, aggressive Maeve became a delicate fainting heroine out of a nineteenth-century novel. O'Grady preceded his chapters with excerpts from Milton, Keats, and classical writers. He argued for the 'general historical credibility' of the tales and deplored the presence of marvellous and extravagant episodes – illustrating two attitudes about ancient Ireland which Yeats vehemently opposed. Yeats's description in 1937 of his dissatisfaction with the translations of Standish J. O'Grady's cousin, Standish Hayes O'Grady [1832–1915], in *Silva Gaedelica* (1892) sums up his literary evaluation of both men: 'He worked at the British Museum compiling their Gaelic catalogue and translating our heroic tales in an eighteenth-century frenzy; his heroine "fractured her heart", his hero "ascended to the apex of the eminence" and there "vibrated his javelin", and afterwards took ship upon "colossal ocean's superficies".'[38]

Such translations and popularisations obviously did not encourage Yeats's early enthusiasm for the literary possibilities of Irish myth. Even if Yeats had found the Ferguson translations entirely suitable, his achievement was, like that of Callanan and [Edward] Walsh [1805–50], based on a knowledge of Irish which Yeats lacked. So, like O'Grady who did not know Irish, Yeats would have had to rely for materials upon dry, scholarly translations which have been described recently by O'Grady's biographer as 'wretched' and in 'virtual chaos'.[39] Ferguson's and O'Grady's literary purposes were also somewhat different from Yeats's at the time Yeats began using an Irish subject matter. Their ambition had been to raise ancient Irish history to a dignified level, to recast Irish heroic subjects in the lofty dignity of the Homeric epics. Yeats agreed that the status of Irish literature and the Irish character needed to be elevated; however, he felt that his own verse needed simplicity rather than lofty dignity. In 1888, after completing 'The Wanderings of Oisin', a long poem set in Irish heroic times, Yeats felt that his own poetry had been 'sluggish, incoherent, and inarticulate' and that in order to 'simplify' it, he needed 'the landscape of familiar nature substituted for the landscapes of art'.[40] The Irish poems which Yeats valued the least were 'literary', having 'more of the study, less of the earth' in them.[41] Irish folklore was close to the earth and had nothing of the study about it. Yeats's conclusion ... that Shelley's poetry had had a 'mythology' but lacked 'folklore' and suffered for that deficiency because 'a mythology which had been passing for long through literary mind without any new inflow from living tradition loses all the incalculable instructive and convincing quality of popular traditions' is especially significant in this regard. Irish folklore was a living tradition to be found among the peasants in the Irish countryside, and not, like the ancient Irish sagas, a dry, confused body of materials found only in philological and historical studies if one did not read Irish. Moreover, Irish folklore was considered by Yeats and many others at the time to be a living continuation of the same Irish folk mind which had produced the Irish heroic sagas of the past. Sophie Bryant [1850–1922] argued in *Celtic Ireland* (1889), a book which Yeats reviewed favourably in 1890, that there was more ancient belief in peasant lore than in ancient bardic tales. According to Yeats, the Irish peasant lived in a world where little had changed since Adam and Eve, especially in the West of Ireland where 'the second century is nearer than the nineteenth, and a pagan memory is more of a power than any modern feeling'.[42] Thus, when Yeats began to use an Irish subject matter in his own poetry of the 1880s, the oral traditions of the peasantry had a more immediate influence on his work than the manuscript tradition of ancient Irish myth did. □

(Mary Helen Thuente, *W.B. Yeats and Irish Folklore*, 1980)[43]

It soon became clear to Yeats that the poetic tradition as it was being passed on to him through Ferguson and O'Grady was more of a middle-class English literary tradition than an Irish folk tradition and that his source would have to be the folk themselves rather than the collections currently available to him. The other problem Yeats had with these collections, according to Thuente, was that they were internationalist rather than nationalist in their attitudes towards these tales. Most collectors of folklore in the nineteenth century were motivated by comparative mythology, wanting to see how much Irish myths were like the myths that had been collected from other cultures around Europe and elsewhere. Yeats' motivation, on the other hand, was essentially nationalist, to show how much Irish culture was unlike other European ones, particularly English culture. As he began to question the contribution of the work of Ferguson and O'Grady to the literary revival, Yeats praised the work of Lady Wilde (1826–96) and Douglas Hyde as examples of folklorists who did not put themselves above the peasants whose stories they were essentially retelling, who retold those stories much the same way the peasants had told them themselves and who saw the distinct singularity of their practices and beliefs.

About the time Thuente published her book on Yeats and folklore, a group of writers, actors, directors and scholars loosely formed around the Field Day Theatre Company in Derry – which included Seamus Deane, Brian Friel (born 1929), David Hammond (born 1928), Seamus Heaney, Tom Paulin (born 1949) and Stephen Rea (born 1949) – began a debate to rethink Irish cultural identity. Deane had been active in this debate since the 1970s as editor of the journal *Atlantis*, often arguing that the whole literary revival was little more than a myth, particularly Yeats' attempt to revive Big House culture in the Irish Free State. In order to do this, says Deane, Yeats had to misread those writers he wished to include in his new version of the Anglo-Irish tradition and, more importantly, he had to persuade his readers to misread them, too:

■ Briefly, Yeats claims that the eighteenth-century Irish writers have in common a specifically anti-modernist outlook. Berkeley's refutation of Locke [1632–1704], Swift's attacks on the Royal Society and on the mercantile system, Goldsmith's lament for the old way of life destroyed by 'luxury' and the agrarian revolution and, above all, Burke's great tirade against the French Revolution, were all, in his view, attempts to stem the 'filthy modern tide' ['The Statues'] for which empiricism, science and parliamentary democracy were responsible. It had been a standard charge since the first generation of Romantic writers, that Locke and/or Newton [1642–1727] were to blame for the afflictions of modernism. This was as much a stock response for literary men as was the attribution of Europe's political problems to Voltaire [1694–1778] and Rousseau [1671–1741] by political commentators. 'C'est la faute à Voltaire, c'est la faute à Rousseau' ['It's Voltaire's fault, it's Rousseau's fault'] was a refrain adaptable to almost any persuasion. Yeats's selectivity is revealed in his omission from the Anglo-Irish pantheon of John Wilson Croker [1780–1857] – the outstanding Government spokesman against the revolution, France and the new 'Jacobinical' world.[44] Croker's hostility to the new literature (especially towards Shelley) probably disqualified him in Yeats's eyes. But this one example reveals what an oddly constructed Anglo-Irish tradition we are offered. It is more comprehensible as a version of the Romantic polemic against the Enlightenment than as an account of Irish intellectual history in the eighteenth century.

Yeats, however, was unique in attributing the shared anti-modernism of his eighteenth-century heroes to their Irishness. The Irishness is, for him, partly genetic, partly environmental:

Born in such a community, Berkeley with his belief in perception, that abstract ideas are mere words, Swift with his love of perfect nature, of the Houyhnhnms, his disbelief in Newton's system, and every sort of machine, Goldsmith and his delight in the particulars of common life that shocked his contemporaries, Burke with his conviction that all States not grown slowly like a forest tree are tyrannies, found in England the opposite that stung their own thought into expression and made it lucid.[45]

This particular version of eighteenth-century literary and intellectual history is manifestly absurd. In that short paragraph, Yeats misreads Berkeley and Swift, makes Goldsmith appear far more eccentric and controversial than he actually was, attributes to England a role in Burke's thought which really belongs to France – and yet he manages to escape derision. □

(Seamus Deane, *Celtic Revivals*, 1985)[46]

Or at least escape derision until Deane and his fellow Field Day critics came along. What Yeats had managed to do, in both his revivalist and postrevivalist years, was to persuade his readers that Irishness had something to do with a hatred of the modern world, especially as it had expressed itself in England during the Enlightenment and the subsequent Industrial Revolution. He also had to persuade them that the Protestant Ascendancy to which his chosen thinkers and writers belonged was essentially aristocratic, even though historical documents seem to suggest that the Anglo-Irish of the eighteenth century were basically bourgeois, usually considered no better (and sometimes worse) than their Irish-speaking neighbours. As Burke himself said, Ireland may have had an oligarchy in the days of the original Irish Parliament, but it did not have an aristocracy, with its Protestants as plebeian as its Catholics:

> ■ Nevertheless, it is this group which Yeats refers to as an aristocracy and it is to Burke and others he looks for an intellectual justification for this description. It may be argued that he had more grounds for his view of the Ascendency by the twentieth century. Yet Yeats's defence of this 'aristocracy' is developed in the twenties and thirties, after its defeat and, as O'Grady had pointed out, its rather ignoble demise. Since the death of Parnell, modern Irish writing has been fond of providing us with the image of the hero as artist surrounded by the philistine or clerically-dominated mob. This is a transposition of the political theory of aristocracy into the realm of literature and it has had, since Yeats, a very long run in Irish writing. The Big House surrounded by the unruly tenantry, Culture beseiged by barbarity, a refined aristocracy beset by a vulgar middle class – all of these are recurrent images in twentieth-century Irish fiction which draws heavily on Yeats's poetry for them. □
>
> (Seamus Deane, *Celtic Revivals*, 1985)[47]

Yeats first thought he had found an aristocratic Irish ember still burning in the tumbledown cottages of the Celtic peasantry and then thought he had found another in the Big Houses of the Protestant Ascendancy, seeing both as potential antidotes to all the damage done to Irish culture by the growing middle class. For Yeats, aristocracy had something to do with Irishness, says Deane, and Irishness had something to do with anti-modernism. The irony is that Yeats could not see that he looked down on the Catholic middle class in the early twentieth century in much the same way the Catholic community had looked down on the Anglo-Irish in the eighteenth century, with many Protestants doing the same jobs as themselves. This is not Irish history as historians now know it, but Irish history as Yeats wanted it to be known:

> ■ O'Connell and Parnell had mobilized Irish political energies into national movements. Yeats mobilized Irish cultural energies in a similar way,

enhancing the distinction between Irish and English culture and providing the leadership to make this institutionally effective. The élite company which he envisaged would govern a community rather than represent a public. Therefore his aristocratic views needed reinforcement from the belief in the possibility of such a community in Ireland and, of course, the peasantry were there to supply it. The astonishingly swift decline of the Irish language in the years after the Famine and the increasing prominence of shopkeepers, publicans and innkeepers in the Land League and Home Rule movements were clear indications that Yeats's view of the peasantry was outmoded by the 1870s.[48] Their language was dying, their social formation had been drastically altered, their nationalism was fed on the Young Ireland diet of Thomas Moore, James Clarence Mangan and the pervasive emblems of harp, wolfhound and round tower. In addition, the literature of the Gaelic civilization was making its way into Yeats's and indeed into the national consciousness in the form of translation, most of it inept. Yeats came at the end of a long line of amateur antiquarians, most of whom regarded the translation of Gaelic poetry into English as a contribution to the enlightenment of an English (or English-speaking) audience on the nature of the Irish Question. Charlotte Brooke's [?1740–93] *Reliques of Irish Poetry* (1789), James Hardiman's [1782–1855] *Irish Minstrelsy* (1831), Samuel Ferguson's *Lays of the Western Gael* (1867) and even Douglas Hyde's *Love Songs of Connacht* (1894) helped to consign Gaelic poetry to the bookshelf, transforming it into one of the curiosities of English literature.[49] They were little more than obituary notices in which the poetry of a ruined civilization was accorded a sympathy which had been notably absent when it was alive. The same can be said for Standish O'Grady's *History of Ireland: Heroic Period* (1878–80), the work which so coloured Yeats's mind that he believed all modern Irish writing owed part of its distinctive tincture to that source. Much of what Yeats believed about the Irish peasantry, its past and its native literature, was formed by the literature produced by the more cultivated sections of the nineteenth-century landlord class. The paradox does not seem to have troubled him unduly.

Nevertheless, it might trouble his readers. The flimsy basis upon which Yeats built his conception of the Ascendancy and of the peasantry ultimately affects his poetry and drama. All his ideas and images of tradition and communion are predicated on the idea of spiritual loneliness. Even when he sees himself as being in some sense the inheritor of Young Ireland, he envisages the crisis of his own times as one in which the individual is liberated from conformity, in which the lonely aristocratic spirit can survive only because it lives within an organic community:

> Ireland is passing through a crisis in the life of the mind greater than any she has known since the rise of the Young Ireland party, and based upon a principle which sets many in opposition to the habits of thought and feeling come down from that party, for the seasons change, and need and occupation with them. Many are beginning to recognise the right of

the individual mind to see the world in its own way, to cherish the thoughts which separate men from one another, and that are the creators of distinguished life, instead of those thoughts that had made one man like another if they could, and have but succeeded in setting hysteria and insincerity in place of confidence and self-possession.[50]

His heroes – Parnell, John O'Leary, Synge and Hugh Lane – were all men whose aloofness and loneliness were a product of their immersion in some aspect of the national consciousness. They were embodiments of individuality, enemies of individualism; aristocrats, not democrats. Three of them, Parnell, Synge and Lane were at the centre of three great controversies – the O'Shea divorce case, the *Playboy* riots and the Lane bequest. In each instance, Yeats viewed them as heroic and aristocratic figures attacked by the plebeian mob. Events like these, and the carnage of the First World War and of the revolutionary period in Ireland 1916–22, deprived him of that sanguine spirit which had informed his early writings, especially those essays in which he declared his faith in the sense of a beginning which the revived Ireland of his youth provided. Thereafter, from about 1913 onwards, he is, like so many of his Edwardian contemporaries, preoccupied with gloomy predictions and fears of the end of civilization.[51] Perhaps Yeats had a more pronounced sense of disappointment than [H.G. Wells (1866–1946), Joseph Conrad (1857–1924), E.M. Forster (1879–1970), Bernard Shaw or John Galsworthy (1867–1933)] precisely because he had so recently entertained such high hopes for his country. The frailty of his conception of the Irish tradition and community made its collapse inevitable. Yet, in Auden's famous phrase, Ireland did 'hurt' him 'into poetry' ['In Memory of W.B. Yeats'], not by being mad but simply by being other than he had imagined. After the death of Swinburne [born 1837] in 1909 Yeats, with the Bullen edition of his *Collected Works* published in 1908, was the senior poet of the English-speaking world. At the age of 43 he already appeared to be 'one of that generation of massive late Victorians who were to dominate our literature'.[52] At the age of 50 he had become one of the great modernists. It is in 1915 that his poem 'Scholars' opens Pound's *Catholic Anthology*, followed by [T.S. Eliot's] 'The Love Song of J. Alfred Prufrock'; it is in 1922, the *annus mirabilis* [year of wonders] of the modern movement, that his *Later Poems* appeared. With an almost inexhaustible resourcefulness, he maintains the privileged role for Ireland in his thought, contrasting the self-sacrifice of Easter Week with the mindless slaughter of the trenches, using the bitterness of the Civil War as the ground for a great threnody [lament] on the disappearance of the civilization of the Big House, the Anglo-Irish spirit and, by extension, of Western Christendom itself. But in the thirties Yeats's fidelity to his governing ideas of aristocracy and community was to betray him into absurdity through his association with the fascist Blueshirt movement. Romantic Ireland was dead and gone but Yeats seemed to be less ready to believe this in 1933 than he had been in 1913.

Still, the power and influence of Yeats's versions of Irish community and tradition remain, no matter how insubstantial their basis in our contemporary understanding of history. They retain their life because they are rooted in his poems and plays although our inclination is to think of the poems and plays as rooted in them. The principle of continuity which he established in literature, stretching from Swift to the Revival, and that which Pearse established in politics, stretching from Wolfe Tone to the men of 1916, are both exemplary instances of the manner in which tradition becomes an instrument for the present. Without such a tradition, or the idea of it, history appears gapped, discontinuous, unmanageably complex. The period between 1880 and 1940 made a fetish of continuity in part because the generation before had witnessed the final rupturing of the Gaelic civilization. The glamorization of the Celt and of the Ascendency was an attempt to reconcile on the level of myth what could not be reconciled at the level of politics. It was, in effect, an Arnoldian 'healing measure' which failed. It offered the Irish the opportunity to be unique but refused them the right to be independent on the grounds that independence would lead to a loss of their uniqueness. Yeats's unhappiness with the new Irish state stemmed from this. In refusing to accept an Ascendency-led cultural nationalism of Yeats's sort, with its aristocratic claims, post-Treaty Ireland effectively put an end to the Revival, a fact for which many of its writers and artists have not forgiven it. The great myths had gone. The best of the poets after Yeats quickly learned that the local and the ordinary defined the horizon for literature as it did for politics. With the emergence of Patrick Kavanagh, the new state found its characteristic, if adversary, voice. The day of the literary peasant and of the aristocratic hero was over. □

(Seamus Deane, *Celtic Revivals*, 1985)[53]

Deane certainly understands why Yeats needed to rewrite Irish literary history and why he needed to feel as if he belonged to either the Young Ireland or the Anglo-Irish tradition but, with his eventual rejection of the first and his inevitable failure to convince many critics of the second, Yeats almost made things worse for Irish poets who came after him, not better. These rather desperate-looking attempts to bridge the gap in the tradition only made that gap all the more obvious and insuperable to them. What had seemed a problem to be solved for Yeats became an inexplicable riddle for later poets like Thomas Kinsella, John Montague and Derek Mahon (born 1941). As Kinsella said before, Yeats may have felt comfortable in the company of old Augustans like Berkeley, Burke, Goldsmith and Swift, but he definitely did not. If Yeats had succeeded in inventing an Anglo-Irish tradition, it was one that, in the twentieth century, began and ended with him.

In *From Burke to Beckett: Ascendancy, Tradition and Betrayal in Literary History*, a book published the same year as Deane's *Celtic Revivals*,

W.J. McCormack argued against all those who seemed to think that this Anglo-Irish tradition was entirely Yeats' own invention. While it is often believed that Yeats created this tradition in response to the creation of the Irish Free State and his eventual disappointment with the way in which it was being governed, McCormack suggests these aristocratic attitudes can be found in his work much earlier than that, clearly connected to his friendships with Lady Gregory and John M. Synge. However, this tradition and these attitudes took some time to form and, according to McCormack, Yeats had more than a little help with this from a rather unlikely source: the Catholic press and pamphleteers, who sometimes invoked the names of the old Irish Augustans to support the republican cause and sometimes to attack Yeats and other prominent Protestants suspected of having their own plans for the new Irish Parliament:

> ■ It may seem unlikely that any connection could be established between the sonorous and disciplined verse of W.B. Yeats and the kind of ephemeral, shapeless productions in pamphlet form which were treated in earlier pages [in McCormack's book]. It may seem – the appearance is again deceptive – that a progressive development has been traced in which literary sublimity emerges out of inchoate party feeling and disputation, just as Michelangelo's David is said to have emerged from a mass of stone. For disputation and composition lie closely together in Yeats's activities, and not simply as source and product. The extent of his political writing in prose is only now recognizable when it is collected and formally organized between two covers. Prior to such republication, it had seemed as if the poet transcended the quarrels of his day or – at worst – commented upon them from an olympian detachment.
>
> Such detachment owed not a little to the dignity implicit in his affiliation to the Protestant Ascendancy, even if there were those who questioned whether this affiliation had been a birth-right or an act of personal appropriation. The right or, at least, the power to link his name with those of Jonathan Swift, George Berkeley, Oliver Goldsmith, Edmund Burke, and Henry Grattan, underpinned his re-creation of an eighteenth century to which he provided a splendid, elegiac last flourish. But the eighteenth century served a variety of rhetorical and propagandistic purposes at the beginning of the twentieth: through Wolfe Tone links were forged between latter-day separatism and Irish Jacobinism, and even so distinctly non-Protestant a journal as The Catholic Bulletin mobilized eighteenth-century allusions to bolster its own politics. What's more, Yeats was repeatedly a victim of this strategy, to the point where his subsequent elaboration of a Protestant Ascendancy rhetoric might be suspected of being a defensive reaction rather than an initiative launched on its own terms.
>
> Through 1921, the Bulletin's editorials were naturally preoccupied with the course of the Anglo-Irish war and the negotiation of a treaty. In the

issue of January 1922, they dwelt on ambiguities emerging in the London talks, especially those relating to the status which Ireland might possess after a successful treaty. 'Dominion' was not readily definable, and the *Bulletin* was impatient with the failure to establish exactly what was conceded by the British government in the course of negotiations: 'Apparently this "mystery" status, which Ireland has received, is not the same status which Molyneux, Swift, and Lucas interpreted as being hers, and which they had not the slightest difficulty in lucidly defining in their time.'[54] [The scientist and political writer William Molyneux (1656–98) and the journalist Charles Lucas (1713–71) had both loudly attacked the right of Westminster to dictate to the Irish Parliament.] This litany of names was repeated, with the addition of others, as if the eighteenth-century contexts in which these figures had worked constituted a single, unified political occasion comparable to that in which de Valera, Michael Collins [1890–1922], and Lloyd George [1863–1945] now found themselves. The same conglomeration of discrete moments and highly different figures will characterize Yeats's Ascendancy tradition when he comes to invent it ten or more years later. □

(W.J. McCormack, *From Burke to Beckett*, 1994)[55]

While the name of Wolfe Tone, the Protestant republican and revolutionary, was often invoked with considerable reverence and respect in the *Bulletin* at this time, other Anglo-Irish heroes began to take a bit of a drubbing, seen as obvious father figures for the so-called New Ascendancy which, of course, included Yeats. His name was hardly mentioned at all in the Catholic press in the early 1920s but, by the middle of that decade, Yeats had become a popular target for *Bulletin* writers and other political propagandists. Having taken his seat as a senator in the Dáil and having recently received the Nobel Prize in Stockholm, Yeats was not only seen as a part of this new Anglo-Irish conspiracy but as its suspected ringleader:

■ The editorial for January 1924 referred to 'the newly enriched New Ascendancy' of whom (it seems) the trustees of the National Library were representative. The campaign against 'the most utterly depraved, beastly filth' [as the *Bulletin* described James Joyce's *Ulysses* (1922)] now merged with the excoriation of the (allegedly) eighteenth-century Ascendancy, and this done by targeting the neologistic New Ascendancy. The prompt to this alteration of the *Bulletin*'s approach was undoubtedly the appointment of several writers – not including Joyce of course, for government had its reservations also!–to the Senate. On 28 November 1923 the editorial noted with precision

Senator Oliver St John Gogarty [1878–1957], writer of odes in ordinary and extraordinary to Trinity College as well as to the Tailteann Games Committee, and sole author of much else that is curious and perhaps facetious, moved congratulations to Senator William Butler Pollexfen Yeats, on the award of the Nobel Prize for Literature.[56]

The writer's grasp of irony was unable to handle even so palpably ironic a poem as 'September 1913', quoting the line 'Romantic Ireland's dead and gone' as a literal statement, though adding 'which, being interpreted, means a notice to quit issued to all who adhere to Irish ideals, as affecting the education and the spirit of the country'. This foolishness might be ascribed to the writer's unfamiliarity with the techniques of poetic discourse – he had invariably quoted prose literature – but the description of Alfred Nobel [1833–96] as 'a deceased anti-Christian manufacturer of dynamite', and the characterization of the Prize as 'the Stockholm dole', reveal incipient monomania. Yeats was challenged to defend both his art and the superlatives which Gogarty had used in congratulating the poet. 'What music, what perfection, what ideal? Let Senator Yeats answer.'[57]

No answer was the firm reply. But the New Ascendancy continued to feature in the *Bulletin*, notably in a series of articles by Conor Malone.[58] The April 1924 editorial identified the Royal Irish Academy as an 'Ascendancy Institution' and this despite its long record of devotion to Gaelic scholarship. Discussion as to where the parliament of the Free State should establish its permanent seat – a topic on which Yeats spoke in the Senate – led the editor into a prolonged denunciation of 'The Old House' in College Green, where the eighteenth-century parliament had met until the Union of 1800. 'Some of the New Ascendancy, Senator Pollexfen Yeats and his satillites' were mocked for their alleged longing to re-occupy the old house. 'But none of the Pollexfen propagandists, none of the pullulating penmen of the daily press' had equalled Agnes O'Farrelly's enthusiasm in this cause – and she is mockingly quoted to prove the point. Two prominent lexical extravagances are mobilized to support this onslaught – Yeats is repeatedly named Pollexfen, and the generality of eighteenth-century grandees branded as 'Ascendancy bashaws'.[59]

Is this just the further derangement of a propagandist keen to associate ascendancy with exotic names? On the contrary, the bashaw – a corrupt version of *pasha*, used in English as a synonym for grandee or any imperious figure – had been frequently used in the late eighteenth century (cf. [*Caleb Williams* (1794), a novel by William Godwin (1756–1836)]) in conjunction with the kind of *soi-disant* [self-styled] dignity also associated with the term Protestant Ascendancy. The *Bulletin*'s line of supply was [the historian W.E.H.] Lecky [1838–1903], drawing on Burke or on contemporaries of Burke. If bashaw had a broad provenance as a term of abuse, Pollexfen in contrast was highly specific. Yeats's mother, Susan Pollexfen, was the daughter of a Sligo family notable for its freemasonic activities, and for these reasons the surname was a useful synopsis of much that ultra-Catholic propagandists loathed in 1924. In deriding the modest efforts of Agnes O'Farrelly in the same breath as dismissing the Pollexfen propagandists, the *Bulletin* reiterated what was virtually a challenge to Yeats, for it dubbed her poem a 'poetic plea for the preservation of the Ascendancy'.[60]

When Yeats served on a Senate committee charged to inquire into the state of learning in Celtic Studies, he was again presented as Senator W.B. Pollexfen Yeats in an article which quoted derisively from the report he and Alice Stopford Green [1847–1929] had written, and which damned the Academy as 'the notorious mismanaging stronghold of the Ascendancy'. Later in the same issue, a meditation on Dublin Corporation's ethical standards permitted allusion to 'ascendancy business methods': as in its references to the 1790s, the *Bulletin* retained a shrewd sense of the term's mercantile origins.[61]

Nevertheless, at the end of 1924 the New Ascendancy rhetoric was still loudly audible. Alongside this latter-day political campaign against the assimilation of non-Catholic intellectuals to the Free State went a retrospective associating not only the generation of Swift but even that of Queen Elizabeth [1533–1603] with the hated Old Ascendancy.[62] But Yeats had been tempted into retaliation, and consequently his contributions in *To-Morrow* were roundly condemned in successive editorials. That Yeats, [the dramatist] Lennox Robinson [1886–1958], [the novelist] Francis Stuart [1902–2000] and other writers in the short-lived paper loudly declared that they founded their art on the immortality of the soul mattered little. 'Leda and the Swan' served only to remind the editor of *Ulysses* – 'the recent Augustan Ascendancy and the Associated Aesthetes shows that when they exalt one and other they only expose one another. Their Swan Song has been penned, printed, and produced: the putrescence of their output has now to stink in public.'[63]

The *Kulturkampf* [cultural struggle] continued. Catholics were warned against any collaborating with a public library system sponsored by the Andrew Carnegie Trust, and a certain pride was taken in the collapse of 'a rather pretentious Catholic charitable enterprise' which had acknowledged the help of 'Catholic "rats" who frequent Trinity College'.[64] Of course, this is deplorable, but it would be a mistake to ignore how skilfully the argument is deployed, not only to a relatively unsophisticated readership but simultaneously against the most sophisticated readership in the country. Ascendancy was a central element in linking the persecution of Catholics in the past with the frustration of their self-appointed literary advisers in the Free State. Ascendancy paved the way for the incrimination of Yeats in the columns of the *Bulletin*, and Yeats's chosen medium of response (*To-Morrow* [1924]) ignominiously ceased publication after two issues.

When the government decided to introduce legislation prohibiting divorce, Yeats was a government nominee in the Senate; he was also vehemently opposed to the curtailment of civil rights in this area. His speech is well known: in practice, he prepared two speeches, one which he sent to *The Irish Statesman* from his holidays in Mussolinian Italy (where divorce was prohibited) in March 1925, and one which he con-tributed to the actual Senate debate in June of the same year. Though he deliberately referred to meetings of the Catholic Truth Society, cited the legal position in several predominantly Catholic countries, and generally displayed an awareness of variety in Catholic attitudes towards sexuality and marriage, and though he also delivered himself of a splendid rhetori-cal performance – 'we are the people of Grattan; we are the people of Swift, the people of Emmet, the people of Parnell ...' – nothing in either speech was heard of the Protestant Ascendancy.[65] That concept was evi-dently not yet required, even if Yeats's defeat in 1925 contributed to the build-up of political tensions which saw the exploitation of Ascendancy in the 1930s. By then, the European context in which Yeats was increas-ingly engrossed gave an added flavour to the vocabulary of élitist poli-tics, while the passage of time had further confirmed the associations with Ascendancy which the *Catholic Bulletin* had striven over several years to inculcate in the public mind.

Yeats's later celebration of Protestant Ascendancy in 1934 can thus be seen as a reactive development in which the initiative had been seized by a significant sector of the Catholic intelligentsia. It may be argued that the *Bulletin* was scarcely representative of public opinion in the Free State, being ardently republican as well as relentlessly clericalist. In its promotion of a comprehensive off-the-peg ideology, it reproduced some items from Yeats's bespoke philosophy, at least as the latter developed in the next decade – approval of Mussolini [1883–1945], concern for education, anxiety over the electoral success of the left in France, untrammeled hatred of England. The poet's thought was subtle where the *Bulletin* was blunt, and yet in noting the growth of antagonism between them we should also acknowledge common interests. Thus, while it is usual to reserve the term 'intelligentsia' for an alienated corps of advanced opinion, at odds with authority and generally sympathetic to the claim of the arts, the unusual circumstances of the Free State in the 1920s allowed a magazine almost craven in its several orthodoxies to become a beacon of *la petite intelligentsia*, a thoroughly philistine paper which published poems.

The skill of the *Bulletin's* campaign is nowhere better reflected than in its coinage of 'the New Ascendancy'. The phrase simultaneously identi-fied Yeats and his associates with the corruption and exploitation of eighteenth-century Ireland *and* suggested they were not that old ascen-dancy but some latter-day, presumptive simulacrum thereof. Perhaps Fr Corcoran [the editor of the *Bulletin*] was unaware that, in a profound sense, Ascendancy always was a simulacrum. ☐

(W.J. McCormack, *From Burke to Beckett*, 1994)[66]

Even though Yeats sometimes pretended that circumstances in the Free State had forced him to come up with a new tradition – or at least revive

one that would help solve what he considered to be the biggest problems Ireland faced in the 1930s – McCormack shows that it was the
Catholic middle class who first placed him within that tradition. Once
put there, he seemed quite happy to stay where he was, but Yeats did
put some effort into refining that tradition and defining exactly what it
stood for, personally excluding John Wilson Croker from his chosen
few, as Deane has pointed out, as well as the novelist Henry Brooke
(?1703–83), the Shakespeare scholar Edmond Malone (1741–1812)
and the dramatist R.B. Sheridan (1751–1816), as McCormack points
out. He may have ignored all the old Augustans in his revivalist years
but, once his opponents began to see them as their opponents and to
include him as the newest member of that Anglo-Irish club, Yeats saw
no reason to persuade them otherwise. In his versions of their lives,
Yeats also saw his own, with Swift 'evicted from court circles, Berkeley
sequestered in remote Cork, Goldsmith jeered into eccentricity, and
Burke held in continued opposition'.[67]

In a massive survey of Irish literature from its ancient bards to the
modern Gaelic verse of Seán Ó Ríordáin (1916–77), Declan Kiberd has
recently argued that Yeats may have felt himself at home amongst the
ghosts of these cantankerous Augustans but his real Irish family was
probably the filí whose culture fell as the Anglo-Irish culture rose. The
filí were the poets of medieval Ireland who were forced to flog their
poems on the open market following the collapse of the feudal system
that had provided them with both the security of patronage and incred-
ible social prestige. For more than four centuries, these poets had written exclusively for the Irish courts, in a language that only the educated
could understand, but now they had to write for whomever would lis-
ten, often lamenting the loss of those courts and that high culture as it
gave way to a clearly lower English culture. Kiberd says this was the
beginning of the myth of a dying Ireland, yet one that ironically revived
(and even thrived) while it sang of its own imminent death. And this
was essentially Yeats' song, too:

■ The greatness of Yeats lay in his constant capacity to adjust to ever-
changing conditions. He began in his teens writing poetry of octogenar-
ian senility, yet ended his days creating passionate celebrations of the
human body. 'When I was young, my muse was old,' he later explained
with a glint, 'but now I am old my muse is young.'[68] As the years passed,
he grew simpler in expression, using shorter lines dominated by monosyllables, with more nouns and fewer adjectives. He said himself that a poet
should think like a wise man, but express himself as one of the common
people.[69] That sounds rather like the plight of the filí after the collapse of
the bardic system compelled them to seek a popular audience. The fascination of reading Yeats is in witnessing a poet whose understanding of

culture was based on ancient, mandarin assumptions seeking to adjust to the violent, jagged modern world, and then having the courage to let that world flow through him.

He believed that he was, by right of inheritance, an Anglo-Irish gentleman of the lower aristocracy. The world, however, had a different fate in store for him. In 1874 at the age of nine, he prepared to leave Sligo for school in London and his aunt said to him, 'Here you are somebody. There you will be nobody at all.'[70] The great revelation of his early career was a meeting with Oscar Wilde, a talker unequalled in eloquence among the London personalities of the day. 'I never before heard a man talking with perfect sentences', he recalled, 'as if he had written them overnight with labour, and yet all spontaneous.'[71] It was only when he saw beads of sweat running off Wilde's drooping hand at a dinner table that the young Yeats realized how all the epigrams were the outcome of rigorous rehearsal. He learned three useful lessons from Wilde: on the value of wearing a mask; on the nature of art as concentrated utterance; and on the need to disguise all complications of thought in the most direct of language. Wilde had made many of the old aristocratic notions of pleasure marketable in an age of the bourgeoisie.

For Yeats, Wilde's *Intentions* [1891] was a wonderful book, since it confirmed his hunch that art, far from being representative of its age, is more often written against its prevailing spirit. Yeats, accordingly, was less interested in being read by his age than in providing his own strong, adversarial readings of it. Nor was his a version of the war of the nineteenth century against the twentieth (though, being thirty-five as the century turned, he might have been forgiven for taking that view). It was the sheer breadth of his perspectives on historical time that allowed him to look forward as well as back. Even the death of the old imagination might become the greatest challenge to forms of consciousness intrepid enough to imagine such a thing:

> Shakespearean fish swam the sea, far away from land;
> Romantic fish swam in nets coming to the hand;
> What are all those fish that lie gasping on the strand?

> ['Three Movements']

Because he took long views, Yeats was able to see the disorder of the modern world as rooted in its foolish devotion to mere mechanism. In the early poems, he sought a relief from all this in a certain formlessness, but the new century had brought in its harsh geometry a drastic return to fixed structures. The search for a freer form had been answered by the old, familiar imposition. This sickness had its source in the Enlightenment, said Yeats, which reduced everything to quantities and fractions. Swift and Burke had foretold all this with distaste, but the rude mechanicians mocked by Gulliver were already carrying the day. However, since no victory was ever final, their time of humiliation and defeat would come.

Yeats knew that not even Swift was wholly 'clean' in this matter, since he was a nominal representative of that Anglo-Irish society which, three centuries earlier, had extirpated the *filí*. In their fate Yeats saw a prophecy of his own. Like them, he wrote a poetry of praise and blame: and he saw it as his duty to speak for an entire civilization which he felt to be under threat. Yet he soon tired of the bardic role, and often sought to shrug it off. In 'At the Abbey Theatre', upset by the fickleness of public taste, he all but appoints the populist Douglas Hyde as national poet to a rather infantile people. This would leave Yeats free to pursue his own more mandarin art, in keeping with the deeper agendas of the *filí* – the production of that heroic verse now so unpopular with most Abbey playgoers. The irony of the poem is rich: Hyde, allegedly the sponsor of bardic values, will be given the leadership of the *vulgus* [the common people], while Yeats, the resigned national bard, will in fact keep a deeper faith with the underlying inheritance.

Much of that faith declared itself in a refusal to uphold low artistic standards. When bad poets began to imitate Yeats's style, far from feeling flattered, he voiced outrage and a disinclination to praise his imitators:

> You say, as I have often given tongue
> In praise of what another's said or sung,
> 'Twere politic to do the like by these;
> But was there ever dog that praised his fleas?
> ['To a Poet, who would have me Praise certain Bad Poets, Imitators of His and Mine']

This is also a refusal to found a school of Yeatsian poetry. The poet who could not recognize Davis, Mangan or Ferguson as real progenitors of his own aesthetic of the Unconscious is resolved to be the first and last of his line, a sponsor of what he would elsewhere call (in a marvellous phrase) 'the tradition of myself'.[72]

The thinking behind the refusal is clear enough: imitation is suicide for any self-respecting artist. It is a point to which he returns in 'A Coat', where again he tries to disperse with savage mockery his growing band of disciples;

> I made my song a coat
> Covered with embroideries
> Out of old mythologies
> From heel to throat;
> But the fools caught it,
> Wore it in the world's eyes
> As though they'd wrought it.
> Song, let them take it,
> For there's more enterprise
> In walking naked.

This is also a dismissal of his own earlier Nineties mode, literally of its 'embroidered cloths' ['He wishes for the Cloths of Heaven']. Now the outline is more stark and clear, in lines whose tight-lipped terseness amounts to a determination to confront reality, however distasteful. Even the broken rhythms of the close, and the half-rhyme between 'take it' and 'naked' point to the future and to a world no longer felt to be regular. Of the forty-five words in the lyric, thirty-nine are monosyllables, used with all the deliberation of a man who understands very well the force of Synge's prediction that verse would have to become brutal again before it could be fully human.

The situation of Yeats is very close to that of [the French poet Charles] Baudelaire [1821–67], when he describes the poet dropping his halo in a city street and preferring that some bad imitator should pick it up instead of its owner. The aura attaching to earlier traditions is now a bauble worn only by fifth-rate practitioners: it can be of no interest to those who walk naked. Yet the loss of the old halo forces Baudelaire into the marketplace, where he must sell his songs to whomever will buy. His way of imprinting himself on popular consciousness was to choose a drastically limited number of exemplary poses which made him instantly recognizable to the public. Yeats learned that lesson well and used his own images: hero, saint, sage, lover, fool. Yet the aim of self-renewal with which he sought to defeat the commodification by market forces of his styles was never wholly successful. Not only did Yeats repudiate earlier styles; he often rewrote entire poems, long after they had appeared in published books, prompting frustrated admirers to complain that they would never have a definitive edition of his work. His riposte was as radical as any delivered to his bad imitators:

> They do not know what is at stake;
> It is myself that I remake.[73]

> [Epigraph to *Collected Works* (1908), vol. 2]

No doubt – but the resale value of reworked poems in further volumes showed that even art for art's sake had its own cash worth as an aspect of the fashion system.

Driven to survive in market conditions, Yeats (like Wilde before him) had little choice but to sell himself as a commodity. Years of struggle in winning audiences for the high art of the Abbey Theatre reminded him of the realities of a world in which a *file* must find a purchaser for a poem, which in its lines would sell off what remained of the older values:

> When I was young
> I had not given a penny for a song
> Did not the poet sing it with such airs
> That one believed he had a sword upstairs;
> Yet would be now, could I but have my wish,
> Colder and dumber and deafer than a fish.

> ['All Things can tempt Me']

The selling of penny songs in Yeats's youth had been done mostly by mendicants and beggars rather than by ruined noblemen with swords secreted in their wardrobes: but the point is fair enough. The songs were a link back to a lost world of heroism, grace and leisure: hence the discrepancy between the poet's memories and current condition. The tramp or wanderer in Yeats's poems is one who knows 'the exorbitant dreams of beggary', the relation between imaginative sumptuousness and material destitution. If Augusta Gregory was impressed on her visits to Galway workhouses by the contrast between the poverty of the storytellers and the splendour of their tales, Yeats could see in these deracinated figures an image of Anglo-Ireland on the skids. So did Synge, who signed his love letters to [the Abbey actress] Molly Allgood [1887–1952] 'Your Old Tramp'.[74] So did Samuel Beckett [1906–89] whose tramps talk as if they possess doctorates ('How do you know they don't?' Beckett once asked an interviewer)[75] but whose clothes (dented bowler, shabby morning suit) told a story of the decline of a bardic class. 'You should have been a poet,' says Didi. 'I was once,' answers Gogo, looking down at his rags: 'Is it not obvious?' □

(Declan Kiberd, *Irish Classics*, 2000)[76]

In fact, Kiberd suggests that the situation of the filí in seventeenth-century Ireland was probably not all that unlike the situation of many unemployed PhD graduates today, or perhaps like poet laureates forced to play to music halls.[77] Yet Yeats did not despair, believing that if his generation of poets simply pointed out that the culture lay in ruins, it became the responsibility of the next generation to begin to build upon them once again:

■ To kiss a sculpture in 'The Statues' is to bring it back to life, much as Yeats reanimates the despised husks of a discarded past. Ever vigilant, he realizes that no past civilization is ever wholly lost, for it has its fifth columnists in the present dispensation: and he is surely one of them. Just as Cuchulain had the magical capacity to draw strength and guidance from his *sidhe* fathers under the ground, so Yeats can draw inspiration from the last lines of Aogán Ó Rathaille in 'The Curse of Cromwell':

And there is an old beggar wandering in his pride –
His fathers served their fathers before Christ was crucified.

Access to such sources may, of course, disable a man in the eyes of the living, but he is consoled by the virtual community:

That the swordsmen and the ladies can still keep company,
Can pay the poet for a verse and hear the fiddle sound,
That I am still their servant though all are underground.

That ground is like the buried consciousness of the community, a landscape of layered memories, any one of which might flash forth and bring

the old world back, so that the ruins of the past would be truly illumi-
nated in the present:

> I came on a great house in the middle of the night,
> Its open lighted doorway and its windows all alight,
> And all my friends were there and made me welcome too;
> But I woke in an old ruin that the winds howled through;
> And while I pay attention I must out and walk
> Among the dogs and horses that understand my talk.
>   O what of that, O what of that,
>   What is there left to say?

Like the *filí*, Yeats was a mortician of the old culture, one for whom
there would be only one radical novelty: death itself. His gift for perpetual self-liquidation had strong roots in his Protestant conception of
selves, ever dying, being ever reborn, on a strenuous path to identity: 'A
writer must die every day he lives, be reborn, as it is said in the Burial
Service, an incorruptible self, that self opposite to all that he has named
"himself" '.[78] However, it drew an equal sanction from a Gaelic tradition
which, for centuries, had revolved around near-death experiences. The
more one excavated dead bones or lost experiences, the more strength
one drew from a past forever coming back to life. The earth preserved
not just bodies but consciousness itself:

> A brief parting from those dear
> Is the worst man has to fear.
> Though grave-diggers' toil is long,
> Sharp their spades, their muscles strong,
> They but thrust their buried men
> Back in the human mind again.   ['Under Ben Bulben']

The dead spirits one embraced should always be those which filled whatever gaps were to be found in the present. The test of a civilization was
its capacity to offer (or at least dredge up) antithetical images with
which a person might unite. This was not the much-vaunted inner conflict
of Romantic poetry, but a conflict with an identity which returned from
outside the self, from the remote past.[79] A man might at first feel a deep
enmity towards this destiny, and yet come to love nothing but that destiny, another name for which might be 'tradition' ... the painted woman
who comes out of the past to haunt his dreams. The discarded potentials
of a lost past turn out to be the 'woman lost', encountered a second time
as the literary tradition:

> When a man loves a girl it should be because her face and character
> offer what he lacks; the more profound his nature the more should he
> realise his lack and the greater be the difference. It is as though he
> wanted to take his own death into his arms, and beget a stronger life
> upon that death.[80]

Necrophilia, like nostalgia, might not be what it used to be, but Yeats had no compunction about resorting to it, for the image of the despised harlot had indeed been the Gaelic poets' own description of their inherited culture. What gave him the courage to record the collapse of one civilization was his confidence that such an account would be the very basis of its successor. After all, the *filí* had shown the way. ☐

(Declan Kiberd, *Irish Classics*, 2000)[81]

Kinsella was probably the first to detect a resemblance between Yeats and Ó Rathaille, noting how they both mourned the present state of Ireland and celebrated its past, but Kiberd takes this almost off-hand remark by Kinsella a step further. He suggests not only that there is a definite and unmistakable resemblance between the two poets but also that this is the tradition to which Yeats really belongs, even though it is one of the few Irish traditions in which he never put himself. Sometimes Yeats claimed membership of clubs that said they did not want him and sometimes Yeats was given membership of clubs to which he did not want to belong, but it must come as some relief to some of his readers that, at the beginning of the twenty-first century, at least some of his critics have finally decided that he might be Irish after all.

CHAPTER THREE

Yeats and Modernism

While Yeats' early poetry is most often described as revivalist, his late poetry is probably most often described as modernist. With the publication of the first edition of *Responsibilities* by the Cuala Press in 1914, Yeats went from being seen as the self-appointed leader of one movement to an elder honorary member of another. However, just what modernism meant at that time was anyone's guess. Even today, the definition of modernism depends, to some extent, on who is doing the defining and what it is he or she is trying to describe – whether a poem, a play, a painting or any other work of so-called modernist art. This tag was not attached to poetry until Robert Graves (1895–1985) and Laura Riding (1901–91) successfully did so in 1927 in *A Survey of Modernist Poetry*, though their intention was to blast recent developments in English verse not bless them. Even if this movement lacked a coherent name during what turned out to be its most productive years, no one could deny that something drastic was happening to the arts. Pressed by readers in both Britain and America to explain what was happening to poetry, Ezra Pound invented the term 'imagism' to describe his own new work as well as the latest work of poets such as Richard Aldington (1892–1962), H.D. (Hilda Doolittle, 1886–1961), John Gould Fletcher (1886–1950), F.S. Flint (1885–1960), D.H. Lawrence (1885–1930), Marianne Moore (1887–1972) and William Carlos Williams (1883–1963). Since Pound was spending his winters with Yeats at Stone Cottage in Sussex and since their obviously close relationship seemed to be having an effect on the recently published work of both writers, readers also wanted to know whether that meant Yeats was now an imagist, too.

Pound had sailed from America to Europe in 1908 with the hope of studying under Yeats, the only writer alive who Pound thought could teach him what he needed to know. Summing up the state of things in literary London five years later for *Poetry* magazine, Pound told his American readers that he still found Yeats the only poet there 'worthy of serious study', although Pound was beginning to wonder whether he might learn more from slightly younger writers like Ford Madox Ford (1873–1939) than he could from Yeats.[1] In a review of *Responsibilities* for the same magazine the following year, however, Pound agreed with all those readers who thought they detected a 'new note' in Yeats' poetry that had not been there before he met Pound, but that still did not make him a member of the imagist movement:

■ I live, so far as possible, among that more intelligently active segment of the race which is concerned with today and tomorrow; and, in consequence of this, whenever I mention Mr Yeats I am apt to be assailed with questions: 'Will Mr Yeats do anything more?', 'Is Yeats in the movement?', 'How *can* the chap go on writing this sort of thing?'

And to these inquiries I can only say that Mr Yeats' vitality is quite unimpaired, and that I dare say he'll do a good deal; and that up to date no one has shown any disposition to supersede him as the best poet in England, or any likelihood of doing so for some time; and that after all Mr Yeats has brought a new music upon the harp, and that one man seldom leads two movements to triumph, and that it is quite enough that he should have brought in the sound of keening and the skirl of the Irish ballads, and driven out the sentimental cadence with memories of *The County of Mayo* and *The Coolun*; and that the production of good poetry is a very slow matter, and that, as touching the greatest of dead poets, many of them could easily have left that *magnam partem* [great part], which keeps them with us, upon a single quire of foolscap or at most upon two; and that there is no need for a poet to repair each morning of his life to the *Piazza dei Signori* to turn a new sort of somersault; and that Mr Yeats is so assuredly an immortal that there is no need for him to recast his style to suit our winds of doctrine; and that, all these things being so, there is nevertheless a manifestly new note in his later work that they might do worse than attend to.

'Is Mr Yeats an Imagiste?' No, Mr Yeats is a symbolist, but he has written *des Images* as have many good poets before him; so that is nothing against him, and he has nothing against them (*les Imagistes*), at least so far as I know – except what he calls 'their devil's metres'.

He has written *des Images* in such poems as *Braseal and the Fisherman*; beginning, 'Though you hide in the ebb and flow of the pale tide when the moon has set' ['The Fish']; and he has driven out the inversion and written with prose directness in such lyrics as, 'I heard the old men say everything alters' ['The Old Men admiring Themselves in the Water']; and these things are not subject to a changing of the fashions. What I mean by the new note – you could hardly call it a change of style – was apparent four years ago in his *No Second Troy*, beginning, 'Why should I blame her,' and ending –

Beauty like a tightened bow, a kind
That is not natural in any age like this,
Being high and solitary and most stern?
Why, what could she have done being what she is?
Was there another Troy for her to burn?

I am not sure that it becomes apparent in partial quotation, but with the appearance of *The Green Helmet and Other Poems* [1910] one felt that the minor note – I use the word strictly in the musical sense – had gone or was going out of his poetry; that he was at such a cross roads as we find in

> *Voi che intendendo il terzo ciel movete.*
> [You who by understanding move the third circle.
> Dante, *Convivio* (*The Banquet*) (1304–06), Second
> Treatise, Canzone 1, line 1; *La Divina Commedia:*
> *Paradiso* (*The Divine Comedy: Paradise*) (1315–21),
> Canto 8, line 37]

And since that time one has felt his work becoming gaunter, seeking greater hardness of outline. I do not say that this is demonstrable by any particular passage. *Romantic Ireland's Dead and Gone* is no better than Red Hanrahan's song about Ireland, but it is harder. Mr Yeats appears to have seen with the outer eye in *To a Child Dancing on the Shore* ... The hardness can perhaps be more easily noted in *The Magi*.

Such poems as *When Helen Lived* and *The Realists* serve at least to show that the tongue has not lost its cunning. On the other hand, it is impossible to take any interest in a poem like *The Two Kings* – one might as well read the *Idylls* of another [Tennyson's *Idylls of the King* (1842–85)]. *The Grey Rock* is, I admit, obscure, but it outweighs this by a curious nobility, a nobility which is, to me at least, the very core of Mr Yeats' production, the constant element of his writing.

In support of my prediction, or of my theories, regarding his change of manner, real or intended, we have at least two pronouncements of the poet himself, the first in *A Coat*, and the second, less formal, in the speech made at the Blunt presentation.[2] The verses, *A Coat*, should satisfy those who have complained of Mr Yeats' four and forty followers, that they would 'rather read their Yeats in the original'. Mr Yeats had indicated the feeling once before with

> Tell me, do the wolf-dogs praise their fleas?
> [Pound's version of a line from 'To a Poet, who would have me Praise
> certain Bad Poets, Imitators of His and Mine']

which is direct enough in all conscience, and free of the 'glamour'. I've not a word against the glamour as it appears in Yeats' early poems, but we have had so many other pseudo-glamours and glamourlets and mists and fogs since the nineties that one is about ready for hard light.

And this quality of hard light is precisely what one finds in the beginning of his *The Magi*:

> Now as at all times I can see in the mind's eye,
> In their stiff, painted clothes, the pale unsatisfied ones
> Appear and disappear in the blue depth of the sky
> With all their ancient faces like rain-beaten stones,
> And all their helms of silver hovering side by side.

Of course a passage like that, a passage of *imagisme*, may occur in a poem not otherwise *imagiste*, in the same way that a lyrical passage may occur in a narrative, or in some poem not otherwise lyrical. There have always been two sorts of poetry which are, for me at least, the most 'poetic'; they are firstly, the sort of poetry which seems to be music just forcing itself into articulate speech, and secondly, that sort of poetry which seems as if sculpture or painting were just forced or forcing itself into words. The gulf between evocation and description, in this latter case, is the unbridgeable difference between genius and talent. It is perhaps the highest function of art that it should fill the mind with a noble profusion of sounds and images, that it should furnish the life of the mind with such accompaniment and surrounding. At any rate Mr Yeats' work has done this in the past and still continues to do so. The present volume contains the new metrical version of *The Hour Glass*, *The Grey Rock*, *The Two Kings*, and over thirty new lyrics ... In the poems on the Irish gallery we find this author certainly at *prise* [grappling] with things as they are and no longer romantically Celtic, so that a lot of his admirers will be rather displeased with the book. That is always a gain for a poet, for his admirers nearly always want him to 'stay put', and they resent any signs of stirring, of new curiosity or of intellectual uneasiness. ☐

(Ezra Pound, 'The Later Yeats', 1914)[3]

When Macmillan published its edition of *Responsibilities and Other Poems* two years later, Pound reviewed it for *Poetry* magazine once again. This time, he seems even more reluctant to drag Yeats into the modernist camp, talking somewhat less enthusiastically about a 'new robustness' in his work rather than the celebrated 'new note' of the first review. Pound praises the older poet for not having 'gone off' – saying Yeats is the 'only poet of his decade who has not gradually faded into mediocrity, who has not resigned himself to gradually weaker echoes of an earlier outburst' – but he still tags him as 'a romanticist, symbolist, occultist, for better or worse, now and for always'.[4]

Pound was not the first poet to call Yeats a symbolist. An old occultist friend of Yeats, Arthur Symons, had dedicated his book *The Symbolist Movement in Literature* to him in 1899, dubbing Yeats 'the chief representative of that movement in our country'. With a bit of inspiration from the American poet Edgar Allan Poe (1809–49), the symbolist movement was essentially a late nineteenth-century French phenomenon, as expressed in the work of writers such as Charles Baudelaire, Stéphane Mallarmé (1842–98), Arthur Rimbaud (1854–91), Paul Valéry (1871–1945) and Paul Verlaine (1844–96). However, Edmund Wilson was the first critic to take a serious look at Yeats' relationship to these symbolist writers and to attempt to separate symbolist literature from romantic literature, which it was often seen to be a part of. In his book *Axel's Castle* (1931), Wilson argues that, although symbolism is often regarded as simply a second wave of romanticism following a period of naturalism in the mid to late nineteenth century, it is actually something quite different. But in order to understand how symbolism developed out of romanticism, one has to understand first how romanticism developed out of neo-classicism. In the following passage, Wilson selects four works to represent neo-classicism and four to represent romanticism. In the neo-classical camp are three plays – *Le Misanthrope* (1666) by Molière (1622–73), *Bérénice* (1670) by Jean Racine (1639–99) and *The Way of the World* (1700) by William Congreve (1670–1729) – and Swift's satire *Gulliver's Travels* (1726); on the romantic side are the prose fiction *René* (1802) by Chateaubriand (1768–1848) and three poems: *Rolla* (1833) by Alfred de Musset (1810–57), Byron's *Childe Harold's Pilgrimage* (1812–18) and Wordsworth's *Prelude* (1805, 1850):

■ Romanticism, as everyone has heard, was a revolt of the individual. The 'Classicism' against which it was a reaction meant, in the domain of politics and morals, a preoccupation with society as a whole; and, in art, an ideal of objectivity. In *Le Misanthrope*, in *Bérénice*, in *The Way of the World*, in *Gulliver's Travels*, the artist is out of the picture: he would consider it artistic bad taste to identify his hero with himself and to glorify himself with his hero, or to intrude between the reader and the story and give vent to his personal emotions. But in *René*, in *Rolla*, in *Childe Harold*, in *The Prelude*, the writer is either his own hero, or unmistakably identified with his hero, and the personality and emotions of the writer are presented as the principal subject of interest. Racine, Molière, Congreve and Swift ask us to be interested in what they have made; but Chateaubriand, Musset, Byron and Wordsworth ask us to be interested in themselves. And they ask us to be interested in themselves by virtue of the intrinsic value of the individual: they vindicate the rights of the individual against the claims of society as a whole – against government, morals, conventions, academy or church. The Romantic is nearly always a rebel. □
(Edmund Wilson, *Axel's Castle*, 1931)[5]

According to Wilson, naturalism was simply a temporary swing in the opposite direction, back to neo-classicism and its interest in society and its belief in scientific objectivity. That only led, of course, to another swing of the pendulum and another romantic rebellion – or the movement that is usually called symbolism. However, Wilson argues that this second rebellion was quite distinct from the first. While the romantics rebelled by going out into the world and trying to discover something other than the middle-class society they had rejected, the symbolists simply shut their doors and pretended it did not exist. For Wilson, the young Rimbaud may have been the typical symbolist poet but, when he left the France he detested for the otherness of East Africa, he became more a romantic than a symbolist rebel. The best example of the symbolist rebel, argues Wilson, was invented by the French writer Philippe-Auguste Villiers de l'Isle-Adam (1840–89) in his occultist play *Axël* (1890), a work that Symons introduced to Yeats during his first visit to Paris and one that would remain a sacred text to him throughout his life. In the play, Axel discovers that the real world can never compare with the dream world, that reality can never match what the imagination can do with it. As a result, he shuts himself up in his castle and lives in the imagination and works of the imagination alone, not unlike Yeats who eventually bought his own tower and disappeared into his books of mysticism and the occult:

■ The later movement, as I have already said, was an antidote to nineteenth-century Naturalism, as the earlier had been an antidote to the neo-classicism of the seventeenth and eighteenth centuries: Symbolism corresponds to Romanticism, and is in fact an outgrowth from it. But whereas it was characteristic of the Romantics to seek experience for its own sake – love, travel, politics – to try the possibilities of life; the Symbolists, though they also hate formulas, though they also discard conventions, carry on their experimentation in the field of literature alone; and though they, too, are essentially explorers, explore only the possibilities of imagination and thought. And whereas the Romantic, in his individualism, had usually revolted against or defied that society with which he felt himself at odds, the Symbolist has detached himself from society and schools himself in indifference to it: he will cultivate his unique personal sensibility even beyond the point to which the Romantics did, but he will not assert his individual will – he will end by shifting the field of literature altogether, as his spokesman Axel had done the arena of life, from an objective to a subjective world, from an experience shared with society to an experience savored in solitude.

The heroes of the Symbolists would rather drop out of the common life than have to struggle to make themselves a place in it – they forego their mistresses, preferring dreams. And the heroes of the contemporary writers with whom I have been dealing in this book [Yeats, Valéry, Eliot, Marcel Proust (1871–1922), Joyce and Gertrude Stein (1874–1946)] are in general as uncompromising as Axel – sometimes, indeed, the authors themselves seem almost to have patterned their lives on the mythology of the earlier generation: the Owen Aherne and Michael Robartes of Yeats, with their lonely towers and mystic chambers, their addiction to the hermetic philosophy – and Yeats himself, with his astrology and spiritualism, his own reiterated admonitions (in spite of considerable public activity) of the inferiority of the life of action to the life of solitary vision: Paul Valéry's M. Teste, sunken also in solitary brooding so far below the level where the mind is occupied in attacking particular practical problems that it is no longer interested even in thoughts which have for their objects particular fields of experience, but only in the processes of thought itself – and

Teste's inventor, the great poet who can hardly bring himself to write poetry, who can hardly even bring himself to explain why he cannot bring himself to write poetry; the ineffectual fragmentary imagination, the impotence and resignation, of the poet [T.S. Eliot] of 'Gerontion' and *The Waste Land*; the supine and helpless hero of [Proust's] *A la Recherche du Temps Perdu* [*Remembrance of Things Past / In Search of Lost Time*, 1913–27], with his application of prodigious intellectual energy to differentiating the emotions and sensations which arise from his passive contacts with life and with his preference for lying in bed by himself and worrying about Albertine's absences to getting up and taking her out – Proust himself, who put into practice the regime which Huysmans [1848–1907] had invented for his hero [in the novel *A Rebours* (*Against Nature*), 1884], keeping his shutters closed by day and exercising his sensibility by night, whose whole elaborate work might have been based on Axel's contention in regard to foreign travel that the reality never equals the dream; Joyce's Bloom, with his animated consciousness and his inveterate ineptitude; Joyce's new hero [H.C. Earwicker] who surpasses even the feats of sleeping of Proust's narrator and M. Teste by remaining asleep through an entire novel [*Finnegans Wake*, 1939]; and Gertrude Stein, who has withdrawn into herself more completely, who has spun herself a more impenetrable cocoon, than even Michael Robartes, M. Teste, Gerontion, H.C. Earwicker or Albertine's asthmatic lover.

There is a difference between Proust's cork-lined bedroom and Alfred de Vigny's ivory tower. Vigny [1797–1863] was dealing, even in his art, with that active life of the world in which he had participated, but the post-Romantic writer who sleeps by day has lost touch with that world so completely that he no longer knows precisely what it is like. We recognize in a Romantic like Coleridge [1772–1834], with his mulling, metaphysics-weaving mind and his drugs, much of the temperament and mentality of the author of *A la Recherche du Temps Perdu*; but even Coleridge has more politics than Proust. ☐

(Edmund Wilson, *Axel's Castle*, 1931)[6]

Romantic poets like Coleridge, argues Wilson, saw middle-class society as their enemy and attacked but, for symbolist poets like Yeats, that battle had been lost years ago. The poet no longer had a place in the modern industrial world so he simply withdrew from it, not fighting it or moaning about it but simply ignoring it as best he could. Or the poet could do what Rimbaud did, give up poetry and run off to East Africa in search of a more primitive, pre-industrial world:

■ There are, as I have said, in our contemporary society, for writers who are unable to interest themselves in it either by studying it scientifically, by attempting to reform it or by satirizing it, only two alternative courses to follow – Axel's or Rimbaud's. If one chooses the first of these, the way of Axel, one shuts oneself up in one's own private world, cultivating one's private fantasies, encouraging one's private manias, ultimately preferring one's absurdest chimeras to the most astonishing contemporary realities, ultimately mistaking one's chimeras for realities. If one chooses the second, the way of Rimbaud, one tries to leave the twentieth century behind – to find the good life in some country where modern manufacturing methods and modern democratic institutions do not present any problems to the artist because they haven't yet arrived. In this book, I have been occupied with writers who have, in general, taken Axel's course; but the period since the War has furnished almost as many examples of writers who have gone the way of Rimbaud – without usually, however, like him, getting to the point of giving up literature altogether. All our cult, which Wyndham Lewis [1882–1957] has denounced, of more primitive places and peoples is really the manifestation of an impulse similar to Rimbaud's – D.H. Lawrence's mornings in Mexico and his explorations of Santa Fé and Australia; Blaise Cendrars's [1887– 1961] negro anthology, the negro masks which bring such high prices in Paris, André Gide's [1869–1951] lifelong passion for Africa which has finally led him to navigate the Congo, Sherwood Anderson's [1876–1941] exhilaration at the 'dark laughter' of the American South, and the fascination for white New Yorkers of Harlem; and even that strange infatuation with the infantile – because our children are more barbarous than we – which has allowed the term Expressionism to be applied at once to drawings done by the pupils in German schools and to the dramas of German playwrights, which caused Nathalia Crane [born 1913] to be taken seriously and made Daisy Ashford [1881–1972] all the rage; that hysterical excitement over modern 'primitives' which has led the generation of Jean Cocteau [1889–1963] to talk about the douanier Rousseau [1844–1910] as their fathers did about Degas [1834–1917] – all this has followed in the wake of Rimbaud.

Yet Lawrence, for all his rovings, must come back to the collieries again; and for Anderson, though he may seek in New Orleans the leisure and ease of the old South, it is the factories of Ohio which still stick in his crop. The Congo masks in Paris are buried in galleries or in the houses of private collectors almost as completely as if they were sunk among the ruins of their vanished dynasties in the African wilderness; and when white New Yorkers, obstreperous and drunken, visit the Harlem cabarets at night, they find the negroes in American business suits, attempting modestly and drearily to conform to the requirements of Western civilization. Our shocking children soon grow up into adults as docile as their mothers and fathers. And as for those that choose Axel's course, the price paid by the man of imagination who, while remaining in the modern world, declines to participate in its activities and tries to keep his mind off its plight, is usually to succumb to some monstrosity or absurdity. We feel it in Proust's hypochondriac ailments and his fretting self-centred prolixities; in Yeats's astrology and spirit-tappings and in the seventeenth-century cadence which half puts to sleep his livest prose; in the meagreness of the poetic output of Paul Valéry and T.S. Eliot contrasted with their incessant speculations as to precisely what constitutes poetry, precisely what function it performs and whether there is any point in writing it; even in the mystifications by which Joyce, 'forging,' just behind that screen, 'the uncreated consciousness' not merely of the Irish but of the western man of our time, has made his books rather difficult of access to a public for whom a few chapter headings or a word of explanation might have enabled them to recognize more readily a mirror for the study of their own minds ...

It is true of these later writers that they have not dissociated themselves from society so completely as the original group of Symbolists: they have supplied us, as a matter of fact, with a good deal of interesting social criticism; but it is usually a criticism which does not aim at anything, it is an exercise – Proust is the great example – of the pure intelligence playing luminously all about but not driven by the motor power of any hope and not directed by any creative imagination for the possibilities of human life. If these writers ever indicate a preference for any social order different from the present one, it is invariably for some society of the past as they have read of it in its most attractive authors – as Yeats likes to imagine himself in the rôle of some great lord and patron of arts of the Renaissance, or as Eliot dedicates his credo to a seventeenth-century Anglican bishop [Lancelot Andrewes, 1555–1626]. And this tendency to look to the past, in spite of the revolutionary character of some of their methods, has sometimes given even to their most original work an odd Alexandrian aspect: the productions of Eliot, Proust and Joyce, for example, are sometimes veritable literary museums. It is not merely that these modern novelists and poets build upon their predecessors, as the greatest writers have done in all times, but that they have developed a weakness for recapitulating them in parodies. □   (Edmund Wilson, *Axel's Castle*, 1931)[7]

When this book was published in the early 1930s, it seemed to Wilson that it might be time for the pendulum to stop swinging, that perhaps these oppositions between neo-classicism and romanticism and between naturalism and symbolism were actually false oppositions. As he says above, the choice for the modern writer between the ways of Axel and Rimbaud is no longer a terribly attractive or even intellectually justifiable choice and perhaps the best option is a combination of naturalism and symbolism as he believes Joyce achieved in *Ulysses*. But when poets were still choosing between the two in the late nineteenth and early twentieth centuries, it is clear to Wilson that Yeats chose Axel, the hero of the symbolist play Symons first introduced him to in France in 1894. This identification with the symbolists, says Wilson, has been ignored by English-speaking critics simply because they are unfamiliar with this essentially French tradition, a tradition which Yeats brought back to Ireland and which perhaps connects him more with the poets of Paris than it does with the poets of either London or Dublin.

In a book published only a year later, *New Bearings in English Poetry*, F.R. Leavis also argues that Yeats was part of a poetic tradition that had concluded that poets had no place in the modern world and had, in protest, chosen to withdraw completely from that world. However, Leavis traces this tradition back to the English romantics, not the French symbolists. It was the romantics who first adopted the pose of seeing the modern world as essentially unpoetic – and it worked well for them, bringing more readers to poetry than it had had before or has had ever since. But, by the time of the Victorians, the pose had become mere gesture and readers had had enough of poets who saw themselves as cultural and social refugees and poetry as their only refuge. The exciting inventions of the romantics, argues Leavis, had become the tired conventions of the Victorians, insisting that poets express simple emotions rather than complex ideas and evoke the worlds inside their heads rather than the world outside their doors:

■ The mischievousness of the nineteenth-century conventions of 'the poetical' should by now be plain. They had behind them the prestige of the Romantic achievement and found their sanction in undoubted poetic successes. But as the situation changed and the incidence of stress for the adult sensitive mind shifted, more and more did they tend to get between such a mind and its main concerns. It clearly could not take the daydream habit seriously, though to cut free from the accompanying conventions and techniques would not be so easy as one might think. The other habits and conventions that have been indicated would be still harder to escape. But they would be equally disabling. For a sensitive adult in the nineteenth century could not fail to be preoccupied with the changed intellectual background, and to find his main interests inseparable from the modern world. Tennyson did his best. But, in spite of a great deal of allusion to scientific ideas ('If that hypothesis of theirs be sound' [*The Princess* (1847)]), and in spite of the approval of contemporary savants, his intellectual interests (of which, therefore, we need not discuss the quality) have little to do with his successful poetry, which answers to the account of 'the poetical' given above. Indeed, there could be no better illustration. To justify his ambition would have taken a much finer intelligence and a much more robust original genius than Tennyson's – much greater strength and courage. He might wrestle solemnly with the 'problems of the age', but the habits, conventions, and techniques that he found congenial are not those of a poet who could have exposed himself freely to the rigours of the contemporary climate. And in this he is representative. It was possible for the poets of the Romantic period to believe that the interests animating their poetry were the forces moving the world, or that might move it. But Victorian poetry admits implicitly that the actual world is alien, recalcitrant, and unpoetical, and that no protest is worth making except the protest of withdrawal. □
(F.R. Leavis, *New Bearings in English Poetry*, 1932)[8]

Unfortunately, the poets whom Yeats admired most, according to Leavis, were as stuck in these tired romantic ruts as Tennyson was, including Pre-Raphaelite poets like Morris and Dante Gabriel Rossetti (1828–82), members of the Rhymers' Club like Dowson and Johnson and, of course, all of those French symbolists:

■ An account of Mr Yeats's beginnings is an account of the poetical situation in the eighties and nineties. 'I had learned to think,' he tells us in *Essays*,[9] 'in the midst of the last phase of Pre-Raphaelitism.' And he describes his hostility to the later fashions in painting that his father favoured: 'I had seen the change coming bit by bit and its defence elaborated by young men fresh from the Paris art schools. "We must paint what is in front of us," or "A man must be of his own time," they would say, and if I spoke of Blake or Rossetti they would point out his bad drawing and tell me to admire Carolus Duran [1838–1917] and Bastien-Lepage [1848–84].'[10] But Mr Yeats knew differently: 'In my heart I thought that only beautiful things should be painted, and that only ancient things and the stuff of dreams were beautiful.'[11]

He had made *Prometheus Unbound* [1820] his 'sacred book', and had begun to write poetry in imitation of Shelley and Spenser, whose styles he had 'tried to mix together' in a pastoral play. His father introduced him to *The Earthly Paradise* [1868–70] and he came to know William Morris personally, and found him a congenial spirit. When he became one of the Rhymers' Club along with Johnson, Dowson, and the rest he readily adopted the current accent and idiom: 'Johnson's phrase that life is ritual expressed something that was in all our thoughts.'[12] They had their high-priest – 'If Rossetti was a subconscious influence, and perhaps the most powerful of all, we looked consciously to [Walter] Pater [1839–94] for our philosophy' – and no one exceeded Mr Yeats in devotion. His early prose is sometimes comic in its earnestness of discipleship, in its unctuously cadenced concern for 'the transmutation of art into life':

... tapestry, full of the blue and bronze of peacocks, fell over the doors, and shut out all history and activity untouched with beauty and peace; and now when I looked at my Crevelli [Carlo Crevelli, active 1457–93, Italian painter] and pondered on the rose in the hand of the Virgin, wherein the form was so delicate and precise that it seemed more like a thought than a flower, or my Francesca [Piero della Francesca, about 1410/20–92, Italian painter], so full of ghostly astonishment, I knew a Christian's ecstasy without his slavery to rule and custom ... I had gathered about me all gods because I believed in none, and experienced every pleasure because I gave myself to none, but held myself apart, individual, indissoluble, a mirror of polished steel.[13]

Yet if, dutifully, he 'noted also many poets and prose-writers of every age, but only those who were a little weary of life, as indeed the greatest have been everywhere',[14] there is a recurrent theme, a recurrent tone, as, for instance, in his reference to 'simpler days before men's minds, subtilized and complicated by the romantic movement in art and literature, began to tremble on the verge of some unimagined revelation',[15] that betrays later influences than Pater's. Pater modulates into the pronounced esotericism indicated by the title, *Rosa Alchemica* [1897]; an esotericism that was among the things brought back by Arthur Symons from Paris. The title Yeats gives to his autobiography over these years, *The Trembling of the Veil*, comes from Mallarmé, 'while', he tells us,[16] 'Villiers de L'Isle Adam had shaped whatever in my *Rosa Alchemica* Pater had not shaped.' It is difficult for us today to regard *The Symbolist Movement in Art and Literature* as a work of great importance, but it was such to Yeats and his contemporaries, and this fact, together with the Continental developments that the book offers to reflect, may serve to remind us that the Victorian poetic tradition was not merely a poetic tradition, but a response to the general characteristics of the age.

'I am very religious,' says Mr Yeats in his *Autobiographies*, 'and deprived by [T.H.] Huxley [1825–95] and [John] Tyndall [1820–93], whom I detested, of the simple-minded religion of my childhood, I had made a new religion, almost an infallible church of poetic tradition, of a fardel of stories, and of personages, and of emotions, inseparable from their first expression, passed on from generation to generation by poets and painters with some help from philosophers and theologians. I wished for a world where I could discover this tradition perpetually ... I had even created a dogma: "Because those imaginary people are created out of the deepest instinct of man, to be his measure and his norm, whatever I can imagine those mouths speaking may be the nearest I can go to truth." '[17] He hated Victorian science, he tells us,[18] with a 'monkish hate', and with it he associated the Victorian world. Of *A Doll's House* [1879, by Henrik Ibsen (1828–1906)] he says characteristically: 'I hated the play; what was it but Carolus Duran, Bastien-Lepage, Huxley, and Tyndall all over again; I resented being invited to admire dialogue so close to modern educated speech that music and style were impossible.'[19] Modern thought and the modern world, being inimical to the hopes of the heart and the delight of the senses and the imagination, are repudiated in the name of poetry – and of life.

This last clause, or the emphasis due to it, distinguishes him from the other Victorian romantics, distinguishes him too from his fellow esoterics. He may quote as epigraph to *The Secret Rose* [1897] Villiers de L'Isle Adam's 'As for living, our servants will do that for us'; but there is about his contemplated withdrawal a naïvely romantic, wholehearted practical energy that reminds us more of Shelley than of Rossetti or Pater. 'I planned a mystical Order,' he tells us in *Autobiographies*,[20] 'which should buy or hire the castle, and keep it as a place where its members could retire for a while from the world, and where we might establish mysteries like those of Eleusis and Samothrace; and for ten years to come my most impassioned thought was a vain attempt to find philosophy and create ritual for that Order. I had an unshakable conviction, arising how or whence I cannot tell, that invisible gates would open as they opened for Blake, as they opened for Swedenborg [1688–1772], as they opened for Boehme [1575–1624], and that this philosophy would find its manuals of devotion in all imaginative literature, and set before Irishmen for special manual an Irish literature which, though made by many minds, would seem the work of a single mind, and turn our places of beauty or legendary association into holy symbols.' It is not for nothing that the *Prometheus Unbound* had been his sacred book. And the latter part of this passage has another significance: Mr Yeats was an Irishman. ☐

(F.R. Leavis, *New Bearings in English Poetry*, 1932)[21]

This almost offhand remark means a lot for Leavis. While he generally condemns Victorian poets for their retreat from the real world and condemns Yeats as well for joining them, Leavis argues that Yeats' Irishness ensured that his poetry was not just private and personal. It gave the poetry a practical public purpose, lending it, according to Leavis, a sort of 'external validation' missing from most of the verse produced by Yeats' fellow poets:

■ The poetry of *The Wind Among the Reeds* [1899], then, is a very remarkable achievement: it is, though a poetry of withdrawal, both more subtle and more vital than any pure product of Victorian romanticism. We might, as bearing on the strength it was to Mr Yeats to be Irish, note further that with the Irish element in the poetry was associated a public and practical aim. Early and long service in the cause of a national renaissance, and, above all, of a national theatre, might be expected to turn even a poet of the Victorian dream-world into something else; and Mr Yeats devoted to the Irish cause rare qualities of character and intelligence. Yet his resolute attempt upon the drama serves mainly to bring out the prepotence of the tradition he started in. His plays repudiate the actual world as essentially as his incantatory lyrics and his esoteric prose repudiate it. 'As for living, our servants will do that for us' – the epigraph might cover all three. A drama thus devoted to a 'higher reality' of this kind could hardly exhibit the dramatic virtues. ☐

(F.R. Leavis, *New Bearings in English Poetry*, 1932)[22]

Like Pound and so many others, Leavis thought he could detect a definite change in Yeats' poetry from the Stone Cottage winters on. Part of this change is the 'new note' that Pound mentioned in his early review – with Leavis saying he can barely believe the same poet wrote *The Wind Among the Reeds* and *The Green Helmet*, since the later work has 'no incantation, no dreamy, hypnotic rhythm; it belongs to the actual waking world, and is in the idiom and movement of modern speech'[23] – but the bigger part of this change is Yeats' acknowledgement in his poetry that the modern world is indeed out there. He may still oppose that world with all his old notions of aristocracy and nobility, Leavis argues, but he no longer ignores it. Leavis was never convinced that Yeats was a great modern poet in comparison to someone like Eliot, being held back for so long by the bad examples of what he called the Victorian romantics, but at least he had begun to wake up from the long sleep of romanticism.

In order to place Yeats in the context of modernism, Pound made a clear distinction between symbolism and imagism, while Wilson wanted to make an even clearer distinction between romanticism and symbolism. For Leavis, all Victorian, Edwardian and Georgian poets were stuck in the romantic mode until Eliot published his modernist poems and things began to change. But for Frank Kermode, whose influential book *Romantic Image* appeared in 1957, romanticism was still the dominant mode for poets in the middle of the twentieth century, with symbolism and modernism only minor variations that had grown out of the romantic movement. From this perspective, Kermode sees Yeats as not only a romantic and a symbolist poet but also a modernist poet. The romantic poets were the product of the modern industrial age, with its attendant middle class – or the age in which we still live. Convinced that this age detested art and only rewarded those who did and made things, poets withdrew not only from society but from all physical contribution to that society whatsoever. All they made were their images or symbols, which, happily, they found came easiest and best when they did as little as possible, giving themselves over to a life of contemplation and, hopefully, the occasional vision. Visions did not come easily or best to those who led busy, engaged lives, so poets had to disengage as much as possible from life in order to earn their visions. This was the price romantic as well as modern poets paid for the images and symbols they put in their poems:

> ■ No one has written better than Yeats about that generation of poets who 'had to face their ends when young' – about Wilde, who so admired [Yeats'] 'The Crucifixion of the Outcast' [1894], about Dowson, and Johnson, who was to become crucial to Yeats's own developing idea of isolation. When the outcast counts on being crucified, indeed savours the prospect; when, bitter and gay, he abstains from morality for fear, as Yeats put it in a late letter, of losing the indispensable 'heroic ecstasy', then we know we are dealing with a tradition which has become fully, not to say histrionically, self-conscious. A movement is strong when a man like [W.E.] Henley [1849–1903] throws himself into an antithetical, activist movement to oppose it. ('To converse with him,' said Wilde after Henley had thrown him out of a café, 'is a physical no less than an intellectual recreation.')
>
> If we suspect the testimony of those who were all too deeply involved, we may turn to the detached, ironical, adverbial [Henry] James

[1843–1916], who, asked by the *Yellow Book* [1894–97] for a story, immediately began his own investigation into the relation between the quality of the work and the estrangement of its maker. As Mr. [R.P.] Blackmur [1904–65] has said, James saw the artist as an interesting theme for fiction only in his guise as a failure. If *life* is important, why be an artist? 'It's so poor – so poor! ... I mean as compared with being a person of action – as living your works.' The young artist in *The Lesson of the Master* [1888], who is in a sense James's Callicles [the young poet in Arnold's *Empedocles on Etna* (1852)], may protest against this plight; but the Empedoclean Master has his answer ready:

> 'What a false position, what a condemnation of the artist, that he's a mere disenfranchised monk and can produce his effect only by giving up personal happiness! What an arraignment of art!' Paul went on with trembling voice.
>
> 'Ah, you don't imagine by chance that I'm defending art? "Arraignment" – I should think so! Happy the societies in which it hasn't made its appearance, for from the moment it comes they have a consuming ache, they have an incurable corruption in their breast. Most assuredly the artist is in a false position! But I thought we were taking him for granted ... '

The life these artists want, and which the older of them achieves at the cost of corrupting his art, is appallingly seductive; it is represented by the girl the young man desires and the older man marries, and by 'the life she embodied, the young purity and richness of which appeared to imply that real success was to resemble *that*, to bloom, to present the perfection of a fine type, not to have hammered out headachy fancies with a bent back at an ink-stained table'. Allowing for the difference of accent, this might be Yeats speaking. A man may choose (if indeed there is a choice) perfection of the life or of the work; and, as Yeats believed, the latter choice meant sacrifice, self-sacrifice. Marchbanks in *Candida* [1897, by Bernard Shaw] is absurd and embarrassing; but, like him, the poet of the nineties was doomed, if not for the sake of the future for which Marchbanks was to legislate, then simply to guarantee his lonely access to the Image.

Lionel Johnson, the friend of Yeats, was in some ways the most distinguished of these poets. Yeats's many accounts of him dwell upon those elements in Johnson's life which he came increasingly to regard as typical. It is of Johnson he thinks first when he considers the dissipation and despair that are the inevitable lot of the modern artist, who must live in a world where what Yeats called Unity of Being is impossible – a world of division, where body and mind work separately, not moving as one, where the artist's motive and subject is his struggle with himself. When Yeats was young he used to write in autograph albums the famous words of Axel (later he substituted 'For wisdom is a butterfly and not a gloomy bird of prey'). In 1899 he admiringly credited Johnson with Axel's attitude. 'He has renounced the world and built up a twilight world instead ... [Kermode's ellipsis] He might have cried out with Axel, "As for living, our servants will do that for us." ' It was *Marius* [1885, by Pater], said Yeats, that had taught Johnson's generation 'to walk upon a rope'; for as life demanded extravagant participation, art required isolation. These men, whom he later groups in his lunar system as 'belonging by nature to the nights near the full', made, says Yeats, what Arnold called 'that morbid effort', and 'suffered in their lives because of it'. Formerly there had been ways of escape – Yeats's image for one of them is the Christian Thebaid [the upper part of the Nile Valley where Christian monasticism developed from the third century AD] – but these existed no more. Johnson might brood upon sanctity, but the Christian confessor cannot order a man not to be an artist, when 'the whole life is art and poetry'. 'Full of the Image, he could never have that empty heart which calls the Hound of Heaven.' And Johnson took pleasure in his doom, and in the torment he experienced because 'some half-conscious part of him desired the world he had renounced'; he and Dowson 'had the gravity of men who had found life out and were awakening from the dream'. Johnson 'fell' constantly; not only in the moral sense, but downstairs, off stools, brooding upon sanctity as he did so; but when Yeats calls him 'much-falling' he almost certainly has in mind that poem so much admired by Dowson, called 'Mystic and Cavalier', which is quoted in the *Autobiographies*:

Go from me: I am one of those who fall ...

And in the battle, when the horsemen sweep
Against a thousand deaths and fall on sleep:
Who ever sought that sudden calm if I
Sought not? Yet, could not die.

That such a poem exhausts action, that art exhausts life, was a notion that haunted Yeats: 'Exhausted by the cry that it can never end, my love ends,' he says magnificently in *A Vision*; and the song in *Resurrection* says the same thing. Johnson drained his life away into art, looking forward, with a kind of tragic irony, to ten years on when he would be ruined, begging from his friends; but he fell once too often before the time was up. What of the artist who continues to exist, preying gloomily upon the substance of his own life? Age merely confirms his abstraction, his exclusion from ordinary vitality, by turning him into a scarecrow. Age is as hateful as the headache and the cough, the inky laborious craft – Adam's curse – whether the artist be young or old. 'My first denunciation of old age,' said Yeats, 'I made before I was twenty.' Indeed the antithesis of living man and creator was one of the root assumptions of his life and work; he drew the artist as a tragic hero, proving life by the act of withdrawing from it. He was of the great conspiracy of contemplative men, and had made his choice of 'perfection of the work' ['The Choice']; but he retained and developed a harrowing sense of the goodness of life and action, and a conviction that 'real success was to resemble *that*'.

'Art is solitary man,' wrote J.B. Yeats [1839–1922] to his son, in the midst of their rich wartime correspondence. At that time, the poet was obviously unhappy about his abstinence from the exceptionally violent contemporary life of action; he had a taste for such violence, satisfied later when affable irregulars frequented Thoor Ballylee, and gunfights went on round the offices of Dublin, but in the English war he could not even play a poet's part. At such a time his father's emphasis on the proper detachment of the artist must have been agreeable. 'All art is *reaction from life*,' said J.B. Yeats, 'but never, when it is vital and great, *an escape* ... In Michelangelo's time it was not possible to escape for life was there every *minute* as real as the toothache and as terrible and impressive as the judgment day.' This is a very Yeatsian formula. Yet, whatever the quality of life he has to deal with, 'the poet is the antithesis of the man of action'. He does not 'meddle in ethics'; he is a magician, 'his dreams shall have a potency to defeat the actual at every point' – this is the poet *versus* the universe of death, the world of reason.

> Art exists that man cutting himself away from nature may build in his free consciousness buildings vaster and more sumptuous than these [the 'habitations of ease and comfort'] built by science; furnished too with all manner of winding passages and closets and boudoirs and encircled with gardens well shaded and with everything he can desire – and we build all out of our spiritual pain – for if the bricks be not cemented and mortised by actual suffering, they will not hold together. Those others live on another plane, where if there is less joy there is much less pain ... The artist ... out of his pain and humiliations constructs for himself habitations, and if she [Nature] sweeps them away with a blow of her hand he only builds them afresh, and as his joy is chiefly in the act of building he does not mind how often he has to do it.

Here, apart from the dubious connotations of the architectural analogy, we have something close to the essence of the younger Yeats's résumé of the tradition. What, after all, is the *Vision*, but a blueprint of a palace of art, a place in the mind where men may suffer, some less and some more, where the artist explains his joy in making at the cost of isolation and suffering? The joy of building is the same thing as Yeats's brief victory, the creation of an antithesis for fate. The father admitted his intellectual debt to his son; but nobody could have restated the Romantic case so suitably to the son's purposes.

The free, self-delighting intellect which knows that pain is the cost of its joy; the licence to look inward and paint, as Blake and [Samuel] Palmer [1805–81] painted, a symbolic world; to make a magical explanation of a divine order – all this represents the victory of Coleridge, of Blake and the French; it is the heritage, delightful and tragic, to which Yeats was born. Much in his own life made him kick against the pricks; his love of aristocratic skills, of the achievements of others in the sphere of action, of his own successes in the active life. Out of this oscillation between the two states of life came the desire, natural to a magician, to tame by explaining, to answer the question, why are men different, and why are men divided?

But long before Yeats ventured on his schematic explanations he had been concerned in a more general way with the justification of the ways of the artist and the defence of poetry. □

(Frank Kermode, *Romantic Image*, 1957)[24]

Kermode suggests that, in his antithesis of the poet and the man of action, Yeats invented a personal mythology that balanced Johnson's tragic life with the equally tragic life of Robert Gregory, Lady Gregory's only son who was killed in action on the Italian front in 1918. For Yeats, Gregory was essentially an artist who chose a life of action instead of a life of isolation, but whereas the poet purchases the image through that isolation, the combatant only purchases death. Or as Yeats puts it in 'An Irish Airman foresees his Death':

■ Nor law, nor duty bade me fight,
Nor public men, nor cheering crowds,
A lonely impulse of delight
Drove to this tumult in the clouds;
I balanced all, brought all to mind,
The years to come seemed waste of breath,
A waste of breath the years behind
In balance with this life, this death. □

While Gregory found the death that a life of such action almost necessarily demands, Yeats, well out of the war and sitting in quiet contemplation, found that he could turn that death into an image for his poetry, something that engagement in the war itself would not have allowed. In fact, Kermode argues that the poetry of Auden and the 1930s is rarely read now precisely because it was so actively engaged in war and politics, not maintaining the distance from such events that Yeats always insisted it should. While Leavis believed that poetry would only wake from its romantic slumber if it became more involved in the modern world, Kermode argues that sleep is essential if the images it supplies are to have any lasting artistic value.

In a book that began as a somewhat controversial doctoral dissertation for a Leavisite English department in the early 1960s, C.K. Stead added his critical voice to this debate on the distance between the poet, the reader and something that is sometimes called truth, sometimes reality and sometimes nature. For Stead, these three things can best be understood as the points of a triangle whose shape changes as the distances between its points change. Sometimes the poet and the reader are too close and truth is too far away from both – as happened with Rudyard Kipling (1865–1936) and the rhetorical poets in the nineteenth century – and sometimes the poet and truth are too close and the reader is too far away from both – as happened with Wilde and the aesthetic poets. According to Stead, this split between the rhetorical poets and the aesthetic poets (which includes the symbolists) developed out of romanticism, with the first group of poets close to their readers but only telling temporary truths and the second group too far from their readers, telling truths only the poets themselves could understand. Neither situation is good for poetry. Both Yeats and Eliot, argues Stead, began as aesthetic poets but wisely attempted to get closer to their readers, trying to establish an equal distance between the poet, the reader and the truth. While Kermode argued that it was important for Yeats to keep his distance from reality for the sake of his symbols, Stead says things began to change with *Responsibilities*. And from that point on, Yeats no longer saw a necessary antithesis between the private life of the poet and the life of the public man:

■ Mr Frank Kermode, in his admirable book *Romantic Image*, has placed Yeats in a 'central Romantic tradition' which runs through the poetry of nineteenth-century France and reaches Yeats, Pound, and Eliot largely through the medium of Arthur Symons. The poets of this tradition have much in common with the earlier Romantics, but differ from them in 'abstaining from any attempt to alter the social order' and in despising what Baudelaire called 'puerile Utopias'.[25] Their poems stand 'free of intention on the one hand, and affective considerations on the other'.[26] The aim of these poets, often repeated during the 1890's, was to 'wring the neck of rhetoric'; 'opinion', 'abstraction', and 'rhetoric' go together in their critical writings, invariably with disapproval. These poets, Mr Kermode says,

> are in no position to teach, and indeed have a great dread of the didactic; but they have redefined the relationship of *utile* to *dulce*, and usually believe in their moral function, so that, in short, the pleasure communicated conduces to morality. That is why George Eliot [1819–80], in some ways a typical Romantic artist, could call herself an 'aesthetic teacher' and yet protest that she had no desire to instruct or change the world.[27]

Mr Kermode is, of course, correct in placing Yeats in this tradition. The most constantly repeated idea in his prose writings is the necessity of allowing the poet freedom from single intellectualized positions, so that the imagination may be free to grasp the full complexity of life:

> We make out of our quarrel with others, rhetoric; but of our quarrel with ourselves, poetry.[28]

And the Yeatsian 'mask' is in part a means of avoiding 'passive acceptance of a code'.[29]

Mr Kermode's principal task was to trace the particular tradition, and Yeats's place in it. Beyond this, a good deal remains to be said. Many kinds of writing range themselves within such a tradition: the difference between Yeats's early and late poetry is an example of the diversity of styles within a single mode.

The point I am concerned to make is one which Mr Kermode would, I am sure, understand perfectly, though it was not his concern to make it. Symbolist attitudes are central to Yeats's work; but Yeats is more than the sum of his antecedents. His poetry enters the public world as the work of no other Symbolist poet does. The conquest is unobtrusive, but complete. By 1916 Yeats's poetry had a hold on the public world which made his English contemporaries (Kipling, [Alfred Austin (1835–1913), Sir William Watson (1858–1935), Sir Henry Newbolt (1862–1938), Alfred Noyes (1880–1958)] – poets who despised 'aesthetes' and claimed the public world as their province) seem clumsy amateurs.

Yet Yeats felt he had achieved this conquest without once offending against the Symbolist doctrine that the poet's opinions, his beliefs, his discursive ideas, had no place in poetry. This point requires explanation and illustration.

Responsibilities is the volume in which, as T.S. Eliot has said, Yeats's mature style – 'violent and terrible' – is first 'fully evinced'. 'More than half a lifetime', Eliot writes, 'to arrive at this freedom of speech. It is a triumph.'[30] The bitterness which lies behind many of the poems of *Responsibilities* was part of Yeats's long fight with those Irish patriots who had attacked his literary movement for its refusal to accept political verses as poetry. This bitterness intensified in 1907 when Synge was berated because it was thought his plays made fun of the peasantry; it reached its peak in 1913 when the Sinn Fein party opposed Hugh Lane's project for a Dublin Municipal Gallery. Lane had appointed a foreign architect, and was attacked because 'an Irish building should have an Irish architect'.[31] Yeats's poetry was now turned against 'the fumbling wits, the obscure spite' of 'old Paudeen' – his image of materialistic patriotism. Dublin is 'the blind and ignorant town'; its patriots have not 'courage equal to desire'; 'Romantic Ireland's dead and gone':

> What need you, being come to sense,
> But fumble in the greasy till,
> And add the halfpence to the pence
> And prayer to shivering prayer until
> You have dried the marrow from the bone?   ['September 1913']

The question at once arises: how did Yeats distinguish these poems from the poetry he consistently denounced? Was he making 'out of the quarrel with others rhetoric'? Certainly his Pre-Raphaelite father was alarmed by this new 'freedom of speech'. In 1913 J.B. Yeats wrote to his son:

> I know of old that from the time of your boyhood you have been liable at times, only at times, to a touch of the propaganda fiend – you get it from your father. I like the poetical rhetoric very much – yours and the French – and the Shakespearean rhetoric. But best of all I like the

music, when the bird of poesy sings to itself alone in the heart of the wood, persuading and coaxing and commanding and admonishing its own soul, and thinking nothing of others.[32]

Since we recognize a new authority in these poems of the 1914 volume, and recognize too a difference between their 'rhetoric' and the 'rhetoric' of poets whose work Yeats deplored, his answer to his father's objections is a matter of some interest. His poetry no longer looks like the work of an aesthete; but neither does it resemble in any way the public poems of Kipling, Newbolt, Watson, or their Irish counterparts. These new poems, then, represent some kind of solution of the old antagonism of artist and public man; and Yeats's justification of them offers hints towards an explanation of that solution:

Of recent years instead of 'vision' ... I have tried for more self-portraiture. I have tried to make my work convincing, with a speech so natural and dramatic that the hearer would feel the presence of man thinking and feeling ... [François] Villon [1431–63?] always and [Pierre de] Ronsard [1524–85] at times create a marvellous drama out of their own lives.[33]

This explanation was not intensely meaningful to his father,[34] but its idea of poetry as dramatic speech leads directly to Yeats's greatest poems. The terms he uses are at first misleading. 'Self-portraiture', the creation of drama out of one's own life, suggests 'self-expression'. But it must be remembered that for Yeats drama was always stylized – a non-realistic medium: to dramatize himself was not to express his own personality; it was to adopt a persona, to wear a mask. In this he is quite different from Wordsworth, whose poetic persona is inseparable from his personality.

Yeats, like Eliot later, came to believe in the necessary 'impersonality' of poetry, to believe that great poetry defines states of mind more permanent and universal than those conscious thoughts and feelings which are the expression of a single 'personality' in its passage among the accidental and the transient. This 'impersonality' – again in both poets, Yeats and Eliot – is discovered, not outside oneself, but at a level of mind deeper and more obscure than that at which conscious thought and 'opinion' are supreme: at a level where, as Yeats would put it, the mind of the individual becomes the general mind of the race. Thus the persona whose voice is heard in a poem like 'Sailing to Byzantium' is only Yeats to the degree that Prufrock is Eliot – no more. In another poem another voice may embrace the world of dying and generation – the world renounced in 'Sailing to Byzantium'; yet no question of consistency arises, for these are both universal, eternal aspirations of the human mind, different and equally meaningful gestures in the human drama. For the space of one poem the poet commits his energy to the holding of that gesture against the flux of time; the poem does not commit the poet to holding the gesture as a man.

So also, on a level slightly lower than that of his finest achievement, one poem, written in 1913, creates an image of the fervour of patriots as a mean and petty thing; another poem, written in 1916, makes of that fervour something memorable and tragic. 'September 1913' and 'Easter 1916' are choric commentaries on events; neither presents a discursive idea of patriotism; neither asks approval, as a poem on the subject by Kipling or Newbolt would ask it. It is the dramatization of speech, the infusion of life into the speech, which makes Yeats's poems at once impersonal and living, in a world of contemporary events.

With all this in mind we may understand better what Yeats wrote on hearing in 1923 that he was to receive the Nobel Prize for Literature:

> Every now and then, when something has stirred my imagination, I begin talking to myself. I speak in my own person and dramatize myself, very much as I have seen a mad old woman do on the Dublin quays, and sometimes detect myself speaking and moving as if I were still young, or walking perhaps like an old man with fumbling steps. Occasionally, I write out what I have said in verse, and generally for no better reason than because I have written no verse for a long time. I do not think of my soliloquies as having different literary qualities. They stir my interest, by their appropriateness to the men I imagine myself to be, or by their accurate description of some emotional circumstance, more than by any aesthetic value. When I begin to write I have no object but to find for them some natural speech, rhythm and syntax, and to set it out in some pattern, so seeming old that it may seem all men's speech, and though the labour is very great, I seem to have used no faculty peculiar to myself, certainly no special gift. I print the poem and never hear about it again, until I find the book years after with a page dog-eared by some young man, or marked by some young girl with a violet, and when I have seen that, I am a little ashamed, as though someone were to attribute to me a delicacy of feeling I should but do not possess. What came so easily at first, and was written so laboriously at the last, cannot be counted among my possessions.
>
> On the other hand, if I give a successful lecture, or write a vigorous, critical essay, there is immediate effect; I am confident that on some one point, which seems to me of great importance, I know more than other men, and I covet honour.[35]

This statement is interesting for more than the description it offers of Yeats assuming the 'mask'. It indicates the degree of 'impersonality' thus attained. The style achieved is always, to the reader, unmistakeably that of Yeats and no other poet, and yet to Yeats himself it seems negative, scarcely of himself at all. The point is made sharper by his contrasting attitude to his critical essays. The essays are discursive expressions of the rational will, of the personality which asserts itself and covets honour. The poems are symbols, or symbolic gestures, that come from a level of mind at which the man is every man, his mind the mind of the race. □

(C.K. Stead, *The New Poetic*, 1964)[36]

While Leavis congratulated Yeats for finally snapping out of his symbolist stupor, he attributed that change more to Yeats' Irishness than to his poetics. For Stead, this change was the 'new poetic' of modernism itself, solving the problem posed by the split between the rhetorical poets and the aesthetic poets following the early successes of romanticism. Yeats had found a way to give his poetry over to the public without giving himself over, too; he could be both a symbolist, still loyal to Symons and his French forefathers, and a politically engaged Irishman, seeming to be every bit as concerned with the state of things in the British Isles as Eliot himself was.

While Stead had gone as far as any critic up to that point to place Yeats in the modernist mainstream alongside Eliot and Pound, Harold Bloom soon put him back in the romantic tradition, though not exactly the same romantic tradition that Kermode had had in mind. According to Bloom's reading of literary history, the romantic tradition in English poetry stretched all the way back to Spenser and Milton, then taking a direct line through Blake, Wordsworth and Shelley before passing on to Robert Browning (1812–89) and Yeats. Some readers may think that Yeats is Irish and Yeats himself repeatedly claimed to belong to an Irish poetic tradition but, for Bloom, his poems are very much in the mainstream of English romanticism, not Irish revivalism or international modernism, and it is in the context of the work of those poets that his work must be considered. In order to make this argument, Bloom depends upon an idea of poetic influence that he discusses at greater length three years later in *The Anxiety of Influence: A Theory of Poetry* (1973), where he basically says that poets are always the last to know who their real poetic forefathers were. If you ask poets who their influences were, they will not tell you who they really were but who they needed them to be. Tradition, Bloom argues, necessarily causes anxiety for budding poets and in order to open up some space within that tradition and make some room for their own unique contributions to it, poets must misread and misjudge precisely those poets who influenced them most. Even though Yeats never seemed to know it, his greatest influences were the romantic poets and, from them, he borrowed the recognisable quest romance, though Bloom says Yeats 'internalized' it, most often making himself the hero of his own romantic quest:

■ A representative anthology of English poetry written by the Irish generally emphasizes twentieth-century work, as not much Anglo-Irish poetry before Yeats has received critical attention or approbation. Swift, Goldsmith, Thomas Moore, and George Darley [1795–1846] are not particularly Irish in their main achievement, and the principal Victorian Anglo-Irish poets – Allingham, [Aubrey] De Vere [1814–1902], Mangan, Ferguson, and Davis – are relatively minor figures when placed in the larger context of Victorian poetry. Yeats's true context is English Romantic tradition from Spenser through Pater and the Tragic Generation, but he saw himself as one of the Anglo-Irish line also ('Nor may I less be counted one / With Davis, Mangan, Ferguson' ['To Ireland in the Coming Times']). It seems clear that part of Yeats's exoticism, for English as for American and other English-speaking readers, is due to his deliberate Anglo-Irish coloring. The Anglo-Irish poetic tradition is not easily defined or described, but seems nevertheless an authentic one. Its inventors would appear to be Moore, in only one aspect of his work, and J.J. Callanan, like Moore a Romantic disciple of Byron. Callanan's original lyrics are most derived from Byron and Moore, but his versions from the Gaelic introduce a different kind of effect into English poetry, as in the very fine *Dirge of O'Sullivan Bear*. But the effect is not without its hazards, and an unkind critic might guess that splendid dirge to be a satire by Peacock, in some of its stanzas:

Had he died calmly,
    I would not deplore him,
Or if the wild strife
    Of the sea-war closed o'er him;
But with ropes round his white limbs,
    Through ocean to trail him,
Like a fish after slaughter! –
    'Tis therefore I wail him.

The problem is one of a certain unrestrained exuberance of rhetoric, of the kind that English Romantic poetry has been blamed for, but with small reason. Yet American and Irish Romanticism does suffer from it, as in the astonishing [Thomas Holley] Chivers [1809–58] and much of Poe, and very much in Callanan, Mangan, and Davis, the principal practitioners of the Gaelic mode in English poetry before Yeats and his contemporaries. Mangan, whom Lionel Johnson admired almost excessively, seems to me the most satisfying of Irish poets before Yeats, and is in some respects a purer poet than Yeats, and certainly a more genuine visionary. Of course, this is not to assert that Mangan is necessarily a good poet, but only that he had qualities that Yeats, even as a very great poet, contrived to lack. Mangan meant little to Yeats, as one can see by his anthology *A Book of Irish Verse* [1895], which favors the more conventional (and English) Ferguson and Allingham. To get at Yeats's true opinions on Anglo-Irish poets, we have to set aside his statements during the Nineties, when he knowingly overrated them for political as well as personal reasons, and seek instead his mature judgment at the age of forty, in a letter to John Quinn, of 15 February 1905:

Irish national literature, though it has produced many fine ballads and many novels written in the objective spirit of a ballad, has never produced an artistic personality in the modern sense of the word. Tom Moore was merely an incarnate social ambition. And Clarence Mangan differed merely from the impersonal ballad writers about him in being miserable. He was not a personality as Edgar Poe was. He had not thought out or felt out a way of looking at the world peculiar to himself. We will have a hard fight in Ireland before we get the right for every man to see the world in his own way admitted.[37]

True as this was, Mangan was perhaps a better poet than Poe, though mindless when compared to Poe, and not an artistic personality in Yeats's sense. Mangan is well worth study in his own right, but needs brief consideration here as another instance, like that of Johnson and Dowson, of a way that Yeats chose not to follow. Yeats was a very remarkable literary critic, when he wanted to be, as in his earlier essay on Shelley, but he undervalued Mangan as he did any other poet whose achievement might have helped block his own. Mangan was not so much an Irish Poe as he was a kind of Irish and lesser [Gérard de] Nerval [1808–55], a desperately haunted man with an absolute gift for vision that frequently declined into hallucination, as in poems like *Shapes and Signs*, *A Vision of Connaught*, and the self-pitying *The Nameless One*. But in at least a few poems – *Ichabod! Thy Glory has Departed*, the Clare-like *And Then No More*, and the famous *Dark Rosaleen* – Mangan frees his vision both from egregious fantasy and from pathos, and writes a kind of poetry that is distinctive and curiously national in its mixture of personal and political apocalypticism. The diffuse figure of the beloved merges perfectly here with the image of the oppressed nation:

I could scale the blue air,
    I could plough the high hills,
Oh, I could kneel all night in prayer,
    To heal your many ills!
And one ... beamy smile from you
    Would float like light between
My toils and me, my own, my true,
    My Dark Rosaleen!
    My fond Rosaleen!
Would give me life and soul anew,
A second life, a soul anew
    My Dark Rosaleen!
O! the Erne shall run red
    With redundance of blood,
The earth shall rock beneath our tread,
    And flames wrap hill and wood,
And gun-peal, and slogan cry,
    Wake many a glen serene,
Ere you shall fade, ere you shall die,
    My Dark Rosaleen!
    My own Rosaleen!

Yeats's frenzies, from the start, were to be more studied, and always highly qualified, as in the final sections of *Meditations in Time of Civil*

War and *Nineteen Hundred and Nineteen*. Though Yeats once judged his poems on Irish themes as being in the tradition of Allingham (in a letter to the poet's widow, requesting permission to edit a selected volume of Allingham), it is difficult to hear Allingham in them, as Allingham was very much a Tennysonian poet, whose work always seems rather less Irish in flavor than Tennyson's own *The Voyage of Maeldune*.[38] And Sir Samuel Ferguson, though nowhere near so dull as he is reputed to be, has only his Irish subject matter to evidence that he is a national poet. Ferguson provided Yeats with a general example; his long heroic poems prepare the way for *The Wanderings of Oisin*, but Ferguson's style and manner are less exotic and individual than Allingham's, and to Yeats he seemed at last just what he was, another minor Victorian poet.

Yeats's problem as an Anglo-Irish poet was therefore, in part, having to commence *ab ovo* [from the egg], but as though an actual achievement lay behind him, when in fact the only really good national poet before him, Mangan, made him uneasy. This uneasiness is central to Yeats; he feared rhetoric, yet Anglo-Irish poetry is rhetorical if it is to be itself. The best Anglo-Irish poets after Yeats – Kavanagh, [Austin] Clarke [1896–1974], [W.R.] Rodgers [1909–69] – are highly rhetorical, and overstatement is a prevalent (and successful) mode in Synge and O'Casey. Though the most famous lines against rhetoric since Rimbaud's are by Yeats, his vision of reality increasingly demanded a more flamboyant rhetorical procedure than his own statements could have sanctioned. This is not unique in Yeats; the most wearisome critical statements, from Wordsworth to the present day, are those against poetical diction and in favor of the rhythms of supposedly common speech. These statements, whether in Wordsworth, Pound, Eliot, or in the host of little poundlings or elioticians, invariably turn out to have no relation whatsoever to any good poet's actual performance. Whatever the rhythms of Yeats became, they never were conversational. If one wants that, one can go, I suppose, to Auden, Betjeman [1906–84] or Larkin [1922–85], but not to the High Romantic, Anglo-Irish Yeats.

The Wanderings of Oisin is Yeats's principal, overt attempt at Anglo-Irish mythological poetry. It is probably Yeats's most underrated major poem, in proportion to its high merits, and it is certainly a very rhetorical performance. But it is more than that, for the whole of Yeats is already in it, as he himself always knew. And it is a much better poem than a number of late, famous poems by Yeats that have been consistently overvalued by Yeats's critics; I would much rather reread it than rehearse again, to myself or others, the mere complication of *Among School Children* or the blatancy of *Under Ben Bulben* and *The Gyres*.

The matter of *Oisin* is Irish, based largely upon an eighteenth-century poem by Michael Comyn [1688–1760] that Yeats found translated in the *Transactions of the Ossianic Society*. At a later time, Yeats perhaps received his material a bit more directly from the folk, through Lady Gregory, if we are to believe him in this regard. But, with *Oisin*, the reader must begin by remembering how far the poet actually is from his supposed sources; he sits in the British Museum, himself knowing no Gaelic (he never bothered to learn any) and he reads a version of a version. He is so far from mythology, and indeed in every sense so far from Ireland, that we need not be surprised to discover that his poem, despite its Celtic colorings, is in the center of English Romantic tradition, and indeed in one particular current of that tradition, which I have called the internalization of quest-romance.

Spenser is the great ancestor-poet of this tradition, as Yeats shows, not so much in the surprisingly weak essay on Spenser with which he prefaced a volume of selections, as in his choice and arrangement of poems and passages in that book. Our studies of poetic influence, as a critical subject, are still so primitive in theory and pedantic in procedure that we really know very little about the relation of English Romantic poetry to its ancestors in the English Renaissance, or for that matter the relation between Romantic and modern poetry. Yet the poetic line leading to *The Wanderings of Oisin* is clear enough. It goes from Spenser through Milton and on to Blake and Wordsworth. There the tradition splits, the Blake influence coming to Yeats's *Oisin* direct (though with the aid of [the French novelist Honoré de] Balzac [1799–1850], and of some esoteric writers) but the Wordsworthian internalization of the quest reaching Yeats rather through Shelley and Keats and their followers than through Yeats's direct reading of Wordsworth, whom he always tended to dislike and ignore. Nevertheless, it is a genuine peculiarity of literary history that Yeats's *Oisin*, his true starting point as a poet, owes a great deal to a poem Yeats probably never read in full and was repelled by when he looked at, the frigid but all-important Wordsworthian anti-climax, *The Excursion* [1814]. It is from the figure of the Solitary in *The Excursion* that the heroes of [Shelley's] *Alastor* [1816], [Keats'] *Endymion* [1818], and [Byron's] *Childe Harold III* [1816] derive, and from these questers and their followers in Browning's *Pauline* [1833], *Paracelsus* [1835], and *Sordello* [1840], and throughout early Tennyson, that Yeats takes his *Oisin*. After Yeats, the tradition appears to end, though it has its satyr-epilogue in the ferocious parody of [*The Comedian as the Letter C* by Wallace Stevens (1879–1955)], where the Paterian quester subsides into a domesticated scholar of the quotidian, his centuries-old journey after the Ideal having led him past so many charmers only at last to leave him in the refuge of 'daughters with curls.' □

(Harold Bloom, *Yeats*, 1970)[39]

It is not difficult to see why Yeats did not place himself within the English romantic tradition, particularly within such a broad definition of that tradition. Such an admission, according to Bloom, would require him to place his poems beside those of Spenser, Milton, Keats, Shelley, Browning and even the tellingly disagreeable Wordsworth rather than beside those of fellow Anglo-Irish poets or even those of Eliot and Pound. From that perspective, Bloom thinks that Yeats looks like a fairly talented, but

clearly confused, romantic poet, though he does consider him to be one
of the major poets of the twentieth century, together with Thomas Hardy
(1840–1928) and Wallace Stevens – unlike Pound and Eliot, whom
Bloom believes will soon be forgotten in the same way that John
Cleveland (1613–58) and Abraham Cowley (1618–67) so quickly were.

Bloom's book certainly touched a raw nerve or two amongst
Yeatsians in the early 1970s, especially because of his insistence on seeing Yeats almost exclusively within an English poetic tradition.
However, the debate on Yeats and modernism only became more
heated about this time rather than less. Richard Ellmann had, of course,
published hugely influential and semi-biographical studies of Yeats in
the late 1940s and early 1950s but, in 1967, he brought out yet another
important book called *Eminent Domain* that looked at Yeats' relationship
to other contemporary writers, including Wilde, Joyce, Pound, Eliot and
Auden. Like Bloom, Ellmann is basically concerned with poetic influence and, like Bloom, he sees influence as a rather brutal, occasionally
violent business:

> ■ 'Influence' is a term which conceals and mitigates the guilty acquisi-
> tiveness of talent. That writers flow into each other like waves, gently
> rather than tidally, is one of those decorous myths we impose upon a
> high-handed, even brutal procedure. The behavior, while not invariably
> marked by bad temper, is less polite. Writers move upon other writers not
> as genial successors but as violent expropriators, knocking down estab-
> lished boundaries to seize by the force of youth, or of age, what they
> require. They do not borrow, they override. □
>
> (Richard Ellmann, *Eminent Domain*, 1967)[40]

But, unlike Bloom, Ellmann sees the influence of contemporary poets
upon one another as a game of constant give and take, with Yeats and
Pound providing a particularly good example of just that. When Pound
first came to London, he wanted to be Yeats' student, but it was not too
long before Pound began to think that it was Yeats who needed teaching,
not him. Having come to a similar conclusion on his own, Yeats first
rejected and then requested Pound's advice about modernising his verse –
though he later rejected that same advice once again. In the end, says
Ellmann, both poets took just about as much as they gave in this elaborate game of influence:

> ■ Pound, as he began to flabbergast London with his passionate selec-
> tions and rejections, found that his allegiance to Yeats was not shared by
> other writers whom he respected. The movement away from nineteenth-
> century poetry had begun. As John Butler Yeats wrote to his son, 'The
> poets loved by Ezra Pound are tired of Beauty, since they have met it so
> often … . I am tired of Beauty my wife, says the poet, but here is that

enchanting mistress Ugliness. With her I will live, and what a riot we shall have. Not a day shall pass without a fresh horror. Prometheus leaves his rock to cohabit with the Furies.'[41] The vogue of ugliness was sometimes companioned by an insistence on man's limited and finite condition. T.E. Hulme [1883–1917] was already in 1908, when he and Pound met, denouncing the romantic bog and leading the way to the classical uplands; by his rule, Yeats was wet and dim when he should have been dry and clear.[42] On still other grounds T.S. Eliot, who battled Yeats for Pound's soul a few years later, declared Yeats an irrelevance in the modern world.[43] By 1912 D.H. Lawrence, originally an admirer of Yeats, could say, 'He seems awfully queer stuff to me now – as if he wouldn't bear touching,'[44] and he objected to Yeats's method of dealing with old symbols as 'sickly'.[45] Another friend of Pound's, Ford Madox Ford, though not unreceptive to other monstrosities, informed Pound that Yeats was a 'gargoyle, a great poet but a gargoyle.'[46]

Pound's determination to make it new combined with this voluble pressure to stint a little his admiration for Yeats as a model. Writing in *Poetry*, the then new Chicago review, in January 1913, he explained that Ford and Yeats were diametrically opposed because one was objective, the other subjective. While he grandly pronounced Yeats to be 'the only poet worthy of serious study,' he felt compelled to warn that the method of Yeats 'is, to my way of thinking, very dangerous.' The magistrate was severe: 'His art has not broadened much during the past decade. His gifts to English art are mostly negative; i.e., he has stripped English poetry of many of its faults.'[47] Yeats continued to fall short. In 1913 Pound wrote Harriet Monroe [1860–1936] that Ford and Yeats were the two men in London, 'And Yeats is already a sort of great dim figure with its associations set in the past.'[48] In the *Pisan Cantos* (LXXXII), the two men are weighed again,

> and for all that old Ford's conversation was better,
> consisting in *res* non *verba*,
>> despite William's anecdotes, in that Fordie
>> never dented an idea for a phrase's sake
> and had more humanitas

Such reservations did not prevent Pound from regarding Yeats as a splendid bridge from Mallarmé and the symbolists,[49] which he could afford to cross on his way to founding imagism and then vorticism. These movements, full of don'ts, extolled light, clarity, and in general a Polaroid view of the verse line.[50] Pound knew, however, as Hulme, Lawrence, and Ford did not know, that Yeats was still adaptable, and as eager to leave the '90s behind as they were. The books of verse he published in 1904 and 1910 reacted against his early manner, but he was still dissatisfied, and kept looking about for incitements for further change. Pound was a perpetual incitement, mixing admiration with remonstrance.

Another spur, now improbable, was Rabindranath Tagore [1861–1941], whom Yeats met in June 1912. Tagore's poetry brought together, Yeats felt, the metaphors and emotions of unlearned people with those of the learned, coupling the fastidious with the popular[51] in the way that he had commended to Joyce ten years before. Yeats remarked to Pound, unhinged by the same enthusiasm, that Tagore was 'someone greater than any of us – I read these things and wonder why one should go on trying to write.'[52] Pointing to a description in Tagore's poem, 'The Banyan Tree,' 'Two ducks swam by the weedy margin above their shadows, and the child ... longed ... to float like those ducks among the weeds and shadows,' Yeats proclaimed, 'Those ducks are the ducks of real life and not out of literature.'[53] His friend Sturge Moore [1870–1944] was helping Tagore with the translation, and Yeats joined in the task, arguing with Moore about words.[54] (He allowed Tagore to use the word 'maiden,' though in a later stage of dictional disinfection, when he was translating the *Upanishads* with another Indian, he insisted upon the word 'girl.'[55]) Soon he recognized that Tagore was 'unequal' and sometimes dull, but he saw mainly 'great beauty,'[56] and wrote a fulsome introduction to *Gitanjali* [*Handful of Songs*, 1909].

Pound's own role in the modernization of Yeats began at first, like that of most mentors, uninvited. In October 1912 he persuaded Yeats to give *Poetry* a start with some new poems. Yeats sent them to Pound for transmittal, appending a note to ask that the punctuation be checked. The note was bound, as Pound said ruefully later, to 'create a certain atmosphere of drama.'[57] He could not resist exceeding mere compliance by making three changes in Yeats's wording. In 'Fallen Majesty,' he impudently if reasonably deleted 'as it were' from the final line: 'Once walked a thing that seemed as it were a burning cloud.' In 'The Mountain Tomb,' he worried over the lines, 'Let there be no foot silent in the room, / Nor mouth with kissing or the wine unwet,' and altered 'or the' to 'nor with.' Then, with 'To a Child Dancing upon the Shore,'

> Being young you have not known
> The fool's triumph, nor yet
> Love lost as soon as won,
> Nor he, the best labourer, dead,
> And all the sheaves to bind,

Pound thought long and deep and then changed 'he' to 'him.'

At peace, he sent the poems to Harriet Monroe with the comment: 'I don't think this is precisely W.B.Y. at his best ... but it shows a little of the new Yeats – as in the "Child Dancing." "Fallen Majesty" is just where he was two years ago. "The Realists" is also tending toward the new phase.'[58] Pound, though he had liked the hardness of 'No Second Troy,'[59] was weary of prolonging the celebrations of Maud Gonne as she had been twenty years before. On the other hand, he welcomed the increasing directness that Yeats now usually aimed at. He conveyed something of these opinions to Yeats, and at the same time duly informed him of the small changes he had made. To his surprise, Yeats was indignant at this

American brashness, and Pound had to carry out mollification proceedings as recorded in his letters to Miss Monroe. For rhythm's sake Yeats insisted upon restoring the spiritless 'as it were' to 'Fallen Majesty,' though a year later he rewrote the line to get rid of it. But Pound's other two revisions shook him. At first he modified the second passage to read, 'Nor mouth with kissing nor *the* wine unwet,' but by the proof stage he recognized that unwet wine would not do, and Pound's version, 'nor with wine unwet,' appears in *Poetry*. In the third instance, the battle of the pronouns, he insisted upon 'he' rather than 'him,' but, made aware of the grammatical sin, put a period after the third line to replace the comma. On November 2, Pound transmitted these partial restorations to Miss Monroe with the remark, 'Oh *la la*, ce que le roi désire!' [whatever the king wants!][60] Later the same day, he reported a last change, eliminating 'Nor' before 'he':

> Final clinic in the groves of philosophy.
> Love lost as soon as won. (full stop)
> And he, the best labourer, dead

peace reigns on parnassus.[61]

Still enthralled by Tagore's verse, and still stung by Pound's criticism, Yeats felt the challenge to his powers. It was probably now that he confided to Pound, 'I have spent the whole of my life trying to get rid of rhetoric. I have got rid of one kind of rhetoric and have merely set up another.'[62] For the first time in years he asked for help, as his letters to Lady Gregory of 1 and 3 January 1913 make clear. In the former he writes: 'I have had a fortnight of gloom over my work – I felt something wrong with it. However on Monday night I got Sturge Moore in and last night Ezra Pound and we went at it line by line and now I know what is wrong and am in good spirits again. I am starting the poem about the King of Tara and his wife ['The Two Kings'] again, to get rid of Miltonic generalizatons.'[63] (Pound had made 'Miltonic' a derogatory epithet.) He was later to redefine what he and Pound had crossed out as 'conventional metaphors,'[64] presumably those turned abstract by overuse. In his second letter to Lady Gregory he indicates that the whole experience has given him diarrhea:

> My digestion has got rather queer again – a result I think of sitting up late with Ezra and Sturge Moore and some light wine while the talk ran. However the criticism I have got from them has given me new life and I have made that Tara poem a new thing and am writing with a new confidence having got Milton off my back. Ezra is the best critic of the two. He is full of the middle ages and helps me to get back to the definite and the concrete away from modern abstractions. To talk over a poem with him is like getting you to put a sentence into dialect. All becomes clear and natural. Yet in his own work he is very uncertain, often very bad though very interesting sometimes. He spoils himself by too many experiments and has more sound principles than taste.[65]

A letter which Pound sent Harriet Monroe summarizes the sound principles if not the questionable taste he must have communicated to Yeats. In terms ostentatiously graceless he called for 'Objectivity and again objectivity, and expression; no hind-side-beforeness, no straddled adjectives (as "addled mosses dank"), no Tennysonianness of speech: *nothing* that you couldn't in some circumstance, in the stress of some emotion, *actually say*. Every *literaryism*, every book word, fritters away a scrap of the reader's patience, a scrap of his sense of your sincerity.'[66] Though Yeats had been able to reconstruct much of his diction, he needed a jolt to complete the process. This Pound, by virtue of his downrightness, his good will, his unintimidatable character, his sense of himself as shocker, was peculiarly fitted to administer. For him, as for Auden later,[67] poems were contraptions, and most of them were inefficient and needed overhaul. He had trained himself, like no one else, for the very task Yeats demanded of him. That Pound was able to give advice, and Yeats, notwithstanding age and fame, to take it and to admit having taken it, made their friendship, unlike many relations of literary men, felicitous.

The experience was, like most medicine, more than a little painful for Yeats; having requested Pound's help once, he had to submit to occasional further reproofs. He showed Pound 'The Two Kings' when it was finished, and Pound informed him (and said later in a review of *Responsibilities*[68]) that it was like those *Idylls* written by a poet more monstrous even than Milton [Tennyson]. Yeats wrote his father of this harsh verdict, and his father reassured him by saying that the poem had supremely what Tennyson never achieved – namely, concentration. Yeats took heart and believed that Pound this time was wrong. But he was nonetheless gratified when Pound, on reading the untitled last poem in *Responsibilities*, and especially the last lines – 'till all my priceless things / Are but a post the passing dogs defile' – remarked that Yeats had at last become a modern poet.[69] An image of urination had finally brought Pound to his knees. □

(Richard Ellmann, *Eminent Domain*, 1967)[70]

During those three winters at Stone Cottage in Sussex, Yeats and Pound continued this game of give and take, with Yeats particularly pleased to take what he could from Pound's work with Japanese Noh drama at this time and make it part of his attack on the naturalistic plays being staged at the Abbey Theatre in Dublin. Their personal lives soon became as entwined as their poetic lives, with Pound marrying the daughter of a woman with whom Yeats had once been passionately involved and Yeats then marrying the cousin and good friend of Pound's bride. There was no longer any need for one poet to assume the role of teacher while the other played student, says Ellmann, and, following the Stone Cottage years, they took turns 'be-uncling' one another, with Yeats assuming the avuncular position at some points during this long relationship and Pound playing the wise old uncle at others.

Ellmann's argument that Pound had turned Yeats into a modern poet had such an impact that Stead felt the need to revisit his earlier discussion of Yeats and modernism and make a subtle, but significant distinction between modern and modernist poets. While he had suggested in his first book, published in 1964, that Yeats, Pound and Eliot were all good examples of what he had called the 'new poetic' of modernism, Stead suggests in his second book on this subject, published in 1986, that while Pound and Eliot were modernist poets, Yeats was only a modern poet. Back in the early 1960s, Stead had taken on the Leavisites and tried to place Yeats amongst the modernists but, more than twenty years later, he had come to the conclusion that perhaps he did not belong in their company after all. Although Stead is still convinced that Yeats went from being a symbolist poet to a modern poet and that Pound was absolutely essential to that transformation, he also argues that it did not take the genius of Pound to tell Yeats that something had gone wrong with his poetry. In the same year that Pound arrived in London, Yeats published an eight-volume edition of his *Collected Works*, a set of books that Stead says not only sold surprisingly poorly but felt like 'tombstones' to a poet who had barely written a poem for years. Yeats was ready for something, or anything, new and, if anyone was an advocate of the new at that moment, it was Pound. Yeats obviously thought Pound could help him modernise his verse and Pound probably thought so too but, Stead argues, this was mostly wishful thinking. Even though the review Pound wrote of *Responsibilities* that begins this chapter – with its mention of the 'new note' in Yeats' later work – is sometimes seen as the official announcement of Yeats' membership in the modernist club, Stead says it reads more like an obituary, mostly remembering what a great poet Yeats had once been. This old dog was just not getting the hang of these new tricks:

■ Pound's review is interesting because it shows him arguing out with himself, and with those of his younger associates who felt Yeats not to be part of the modern movement, the question of what value was to be placed on Yeats's achievement. He is careful first to insist that Yeats has already done something new and is still 'the best poet in England': 'one man seldom leads two movements to triumph ... and ... Mr Yeats is so assuredly an immortal that there is no need for him to recast his style to suit our winds of doctrine.' 'Nevertheless', he goes on, there is 'a manifestly new note in his later work' and the younger writers might do worse than attend to it. Yeats is not an Imagist, Pound goes on; he is a Symbolist. But it is clear Pound feels he is moving out of Symbolism in the direction of Imagism – not in form, since Yeats cannot hear their music and describes it as 'devil's metres', but in having 'driven out the inversion and written with prose directness', 'becoming gaunter, seeking greater hardness of outline', in getting rid of 'glamour' and replacing it with a new quality of 'hard light'. All this began to be apparent, Pound says, with the appearance of *The Green Helmet and Other Poems*, where 'one felt that the minor note – I use the word strictly in the musical sense – had gone or was going out of his poetry.' *Responsibilities* confirms that development.

   Scholars and critics are apt to read this review in the light of what Yeats later achieved, and thus to take it casually, as if it were a statement of the obvious. What needs to be remembered is that at the time Pound was writing, 'the later Yeats' as we now know it did not exist. Pound was encouraging Yeats to go against the wishes of his admirers, to disappoint them in the interests of bringing that 'later Yeats' (with whom the scholars and critics have felt so much more at home than with Pound) into being. The very least one can say is that here is another example of Pound's acumen in dealing with contemporary writing. Stylistically this was the final heave for Yeats into the manner that would remain constant until his death. His material would change, there would be increasing confidence and mastery, but in the purely technical sense, no further change. And that for Pound was to become the crucial point and to render him ultimately indifferent – not to Yeats the man, who had figured and would continue to figure so importantly in his life – but to Yeats the poet. Yeats had moved from Pre-Raphaelitism into Symbolism; Pound was able to help him move out of that Symbolism which had about it the trappings and airs of the 1890s and to become a poet of the twentieth century. But there was a further step which Yeats would not take; and to Pound that placed limits on Yeats. At first these did not seem absolute limits ('Mr Yeats is … assuredly immortal') but only historical ones. There was a time gap which Yeats could not cross, and no reason why he should. Later, the limits must have come to seem to him more fundamental. Yeats could not free himself from the well-made poem, the isolated self-enclosed unit, into something of epic scope. His sole conception of the larger scale in poetry was narrative, and in consequence he was to become (as Pound jocularly put it) 'the greatest minor poet who ever lived'. ☐

   (C.K. Stead, *Pound, Yeats, Eliot and the Modernist Movement*, 1986)[71]

This further step that Yeats would not take is what, for Stead, made Yeats only a modern poet while Pound and Eliot were modernist poets. According to Stead, modern poets like Yeats and Hardy worked with closed forms, while modernist poets like Pound and Eliot worked with open forms, the difference being that closed poems complete and conclude while open poems do not. It is like the difference, he says, between the finished works of the museum and the unfinished works of the studio, with the one leaving nothing more to be said and the other still in the act of saying something, even though we may not know exactly what that something is. This is the crucial distinction that Stead feels he failed to make in his first book and it is a distinction that he feels Kermode also failed to make in *Romantic Image*, which supports its argument by a curious misreading of Yeats' elegy for Robert Gregory:

■ The enormous value of Kermode's book is that it firmly places the whole Symbolist-Imagist-Modernist movement as it occurs in English poetry in a tradition that has its roots in Romanticism. It thus cuts right through the historical confusions brought about by Eliot and T.E. Hulme when they described themselves and the literary movements they belonged to as 'Classicist' or 'anti-Romantic'. Further, Kermode shows how a dislike of didacticism belongs squarely in the same tradition, and that didacticism is disliked, not simply for what it is, but because it depends upon and issues in a kind of discursiveness which is contrary to the pure poetic image – the Romantic Image, as he properly calls it. Thus the various movements in poetry which have sought to purify the Image have been a continuation of what begins in English Romanticism as a revolt against the norms of Augustan poetry – against poetry as the versification of ideas which exist in full though undecorated form outside of the poem.[72] This historical fact is of the utmost importance; and the reason why Kermode's book continues to merit special attention is perhaps best illustrated by the precise piece of literary history contained in his parenthesis on p. 43:

As throughout this essay I here use 'Romantic' in a restricted sense, as applicable to the literature of one epoch, beginning in the late years of the eighteenth century *and not yet finished*, and as referring to the high valuation placed during this period upon the image-making powers of the mind *at the expense of its rational powers*, and to the substitution of organicist for mechanistic modes of thinking about works of art. [Italics added C.K.S.]

But there is at the same time something curiously unresolved, or confused, or perhaps even evasive about the early chapters of *Romantic Image*. Isolation (it is argued) is necessary to the production of art, and the poet must suffer it if he is to wrest his images free of those rational modes which govern ordinary discourse. Hence for Kermode the relevance of 'In Memory of Major Robert Gregory', which he sees as a poem about the isolated artist. Kermode's book is useful in showing the common Romantic source which Symbolism and Imagism share. At the same time, in doing so, it (perhaps inevitably) confuses them and blurs the distinction between the Mallarméan musical structure and the Poundian sculpted image. Further, in so far as it recognizes a distinction between Yeats and the Modernists, it favours Yeats critically – but more than that, it favours him precisely because he does *not* follow out to the full the poetics of the Romantic Image. Thus the Yeats who, with much solemnity about the artist's 'tragic solitude' (p. 43), is offered in Chapters II and III as the chief modern exponent of the Romantic Image and is commended for the 'passionate integrity' (p. 48) he achieves in its pursuit is the same Yeats praised in Chapter VII for not being over-scrupulous about the theory:

> What it comes down to in the end is that Pound, like Hulme, like Mallarmé and many others, wanted a theory of poetry based on the non-discursive *concetto* [idea]. In varying degrees they all obscurely wish that poetry could be written with something other than words, but since it can't, that words may be made to have the same sort of physical presence 'as a piece of string'. The resistance to words in their Image is explained by the fact that words are the means of a very different sort of communication; they are so used to being discursive that it is almost impossible to stop them discoursing.
>
> This linguistic difficulty has been tackled very seriously since Hulme's day, and certainly *it is enough in itself to provoke radical criticism of the whole tradition*. Should it invariably be deplored that poems tend to 'say' something? There is that tell-tale 'binding-matter', as Pound calls it, in the *Cantos*. Yeats, *untroubled by the stricter theoretical limitations*, makes no bones about having plenty of binding-matter, and criticises the *Cantos* in terms I have already alluded to. [pp. 136–7. Italics added C.K.S.]

The first paragraph quoted is not as good as it might be but it is good enough. (It is not quite that these poets wish poetry to be written with something other than words, nor quite that they want words to have a physical presence. It is more that they wish to enforce the clearest possible recognition, the sharpest possible *sense*, that language can have another function than the discursive – one which is never analytical and which Pound described as 'presentative'.) However it is in the second paragraph that Kermode lays his cards upon the table – or is it just (to change the metaphor) that his guard slips? For at this point he finds reason to suggest a 'radical criticism' might be in order of 'the whole tradition' of which he is acting as historian – a criticism from which, however, Yeats would be exempt.

Thus Kermode does make the distinction between Yeats and the Modernists which is my present concern – but he makes it either unwittingly, or in a way which is self-contradictory. How can Yeats be the greatest modern exponent of the Romantic Image and at the same time exempt from a 'radical criticism' which 'the whole tradition' calls for – exempt because he is 'untroubled by [its] stricter theoretical limitations'? And what is Kermode's opinion of those poets who do attempt more vigorously to achieve the pure non-discursive Image which the tradition calls for? Eliot's poetry is evaded; Pound is dismissed, along with 'the radicalism of Blake ... the forlorn hopes of Mallarmé, and ... the disastrous *déréglement* [derangement] of Rimbaud' (p. 160). What emerges in the end is a somewhat grandiose design on Kermode's part to be not merely historian but herald – herald of a new literary dawn which will shed the extravagances of the Romantic Image and once again respect 'order' and 'reason' in poetry (p. 160).

With all this in mind we may now turn more cautiously to his treatment of 'In Memory of Major Robert Gregory', which he describes as 'a poem worthy of much painful reading, perhaps the first in which we hear the full range of the poet's voice'. And he continues: 'with this heroic assurance of harmony goes an authentic mastery of design. After it, for twenty years, Yeats's poems, whenever he is using the whole range, are identifiable as the work of the master of the Gregory elegy' (p. 30).

Kermode's approach to the poem is via an obituary on Gregory which Yeats wrote for the *Observer*, expressing a view of Gregory which Kermode finds repeated in the poem. This obituary treats Gregory chiefly as an artist – 'To me he will always remain a great painter in the immaturity of his youth'[73] – and not merely an artist, but one who sought escape from the 'ever-growing absorption in subjective beauty' which is the artist's lot, and found it in the life of action. The war brought Gregory 'peace of mind, an escape from that shrinking, which I sometimes saw upon his face, before the growing absorption of his dream'. Here is the Yeats mythology machine under full steam. Gregory is not individualized. He becomes the Artist, a symbol, and Kermode finds him so used in the poem.

It is not of primary importance but it needs to be said that Kermode's reading of the poem is wrong in the very simple sense that the view of Gregory put forward in the obituary is *not* the view put forward in the poem. The emphasis in the obituary is entirely upon Gregory the artist, and upon his escape from the artist's 'dream' into action and death. The emphasis of the poem is upon the *variety* of Gregory's talents; and although the lines about Gregory the painter are among the best in the poem, the repeated refrain summing up his achievements

Soldier, scholar, horseman, he

does not even include the artist. Certainly there is nothing whatever in the poem to match the explicit suggestion in the obituary that war was an escape from the loneliness of art.

At one point Kermode seems close to recognizing that this is the case: 'I speak as though Gregory were treated in this poem as an artist-contemplative and as nothing else; and this is almost true' (p. 38). It is not even 'almost true'; this acknowledgement that it is not entirely true seems at least to prepare the way for a statement of justification – but none follows. In the course of acknowledging that 'the richness and variety of [Gregory's] powers are there, of course', the discussion passes to the subject of verse form, and the matter is left unresolved. If Yeats is using Gregory to serve his mythology, Kermode is using the poem to serve the purposes of his history. □

(C.K. Stead, *Pound, Yeats, Eliot and the Modernist Movement*, 1986)[74]

While Kermode used this poem to place Yeats at the centre of the modern romantic tradition, Stead uses it to show why Yeats does not belong anywhere near the centre of modernism alongside Pound and Eliot. For Stead, this elegy is a perfect example of a poem that Yeats fails, rather spectacularly, to modernise, trying far too hard to fit the expressions of everyday speech into a traditional lyric form. Yeats simply plans too much and thinks too much, turning what could be an authentic, even if somewhat untidy, cry from the heart into what Stead calls a 'cold poem'. And it was precisely this need to tidy things up, to come to some conclusion about the subjects of his poems before he actually wrote them, that prevented Yeats from taking that further step, from being merely modern to becoming an open-form modernist.

Although Stead wanted to correct his own earlier error of seeing the later Yeats as a modernist, he agreed with Ellmann that Pound had made him at least a modern poet. In a book published in 1988 that closely examines those three winters that Yeats and Pound spent together at Stone Cottage, James Longenbach argues that it was not Pound who dragged Yeats, kicking and screaming, into modernism, but just the opposite. It was not Pound who influenced an old Yeats, but Yeats who influenced a young Pound. As Longenbach notes, he is not the first critic to question Pound's role in shaping Yeats' poetry; Thomas Parkinson (1920–92) had done so in an essay published in *Comparative Literature* as far back as 1954, which Stead dismissed in an endnote as unconvincing since it relies on 'insufficient evidence' to make its case.[75] In that short essay, Parkinson says Yeats may have been looking for something new when he met Pound, but the last thing he wanted was to become an imagist or a modernist:

■ 'How the hell many points of agreement,' Ezra Pound asks a correspondent, 'do you suppose there were between Joyce, W. Lewis, Eliot and yrs. truly in 1917; or between [the French sculptor Henri] Gaudier [1891–1915] and Lewis in 1913; or between me and Yeats, etc.?'[76] The question was rhetorical and it is perhaps impolite to answer it; but it has been answered with apparent conviction by several critics recently, and answered too simply, especially with respect to Pound and Yeats. Thus John Berryman [1914–72] says of the change in Yeats' style that he has '... always supposed Pound the motor';[77] and, though Hugh Kenner [1923–2003] and F.R. Leavis are more restrained in their conclusions, Leavis finds that Pound '... influenced ... Yeats beneficently at a crucial moment ...'[78] and Kenner that Pound '... effected some transfusion of ironic discipline into Yeats ... .'[79] A.N. Jeffares and Vivienne Koch also argue that Pound's influence on Yeats was profound, and it is fast becoming a platitude that Pound was one major – if not *the* major – force in creating Yeats' later style. Like all such platitudes it will not bear close inspection, but on critical examination alters to an hypothesis that bears little resemblance to the original flat statement. There is little evidence pointing to Pound's influence on Yeats; there is not much more indicating that Yeats was very important to Pound; and there is a great deal to support the view that the two men present the unusual instance of master and disciple outgrowing one another in areas eccentric to the original points of agreement. Yet they remained bound to one another by affection and the tension of fruitful disagreement.

The tension is exhibited in a letter from Pound to Sarah Perkins Cope (1934) in which he betrays his uneasiness in dealing with Yeats' later poetry: 'Are you still young enough to read Ole Uncl. William Yeats? Or at least to tell me how it strikes the young and tender of your generation?'[80] Pound, with his admirable and almost compulsive desire to keep up with and remain capable of instructing 'les jeunes' [the young], is here betraying a certain uneasiness before a poetry that, while not to his taste, had an apparent and puzzling vital attainment to recommend it. Nor is it any mere habit of thinking antithetically that compelled Yeats to write, in *A Packet for Ezra Pound* [1929], that Pound was a man '... whose art is the opposite of mine, whose criticism commends what I most condemn, a man with whom I should quarrel more than with anyone else if we were not united by affection ... .'[81] When Pound was at work on the *Cantos* and Yeats at work on *A Vision* and his later poems, the two men regarded one another with respect tinged by suspicion.

This ultimate disagreement indicates that perhaps the relations between the pair in the period 1908–17 were not so simple and unilateral as Kenner and others now assume. For if Pound taught Yeats how to write major poetry there is something a little unsettling in his judgment of Yeats – after the publication of *The Wild Swans at Coole* [1917]. With this first of Yeats' later books available to him, Pound wrote to William Carlos Williams that Yeats had 'faded.' Apparently he was a little annoyed with his pupil, as he was in the 1930s when he returned to Yeats the lyrics from *The King of the Great Clock Tower* [1934] with the single comment 'putrid.' His lack of sympathy for Yeats' later poems and Yeats' dubious appreciation of the *Cantos* tend to undermine the view that Pound could radically alter the poetry of a man some twenty years older than himself, a man distinguished, Irish, and stubborn. □   (Thomas Parkinson, 'Yeats and Pound', 1954)[82]

Parkinson goes on to argue that Pound was still using archaic diction and inverted syntax years after Yeats had given them up, that Pound was unable to persuade Yeats to take an interest in any poetry later than Browning and Morris and that Yeats was writing non-naturalistic plays for the Abbey Theatre long before Pound introduced him to Japanese Noh drama at Stone Cottage. While Longenbach would agree that Pound did not have a great effect on Yeats' thinking about poetry, he would disagree with Parkinson about the effect Yeats had on Pound. When they left for Sussex for their first winter at Stone Cottage, there was very little that Pound could teach Yeats, especially since Pound was still learning to write his own poems by reading the poems Yeats had written when he was about Pound's age:

■ Although Pound is often thought of as the poet who dragged the reluctant Yeats into the twentieth century, the actual turns of influence reveal

Yeats as the dominant force. Pound himself felt that Yeats's transformation was due to Synge's influence more than his own:

> There is little use discussing the early Yeats, everyone has heard all that can be said on the subject. The new Yeats is still under discussion. Adorers of the Celtic Twilight are disturbed by his gain of hardness. Some of the later work is not so good as the Wind Among the Reeds, some of it better, or at least possessed of new qualities. Synge had appeared. There is a new strength in the later Yeats on which he & Synge may have agreed between them. Poems like 'The Magi' & 'The Scholars,' and 'No Second Troy' have in them a variety that the earlier work had not.[83]

Pound wrote these sentences in 1915 for an aborted book called *This Generation*; had he published them, our sense of his role in Yeats's artistic development might have been quite different. Over the last fifty years, Pound's supposed influence on the Yeats of *Responsibilities* has become part of the mythology of literary modernism, primarily because of the well-known story of Pound's minor revisions of poems Yeats offered to *Poetry* magazine late in 1912. While the young Pound may have been proud of his brazened 'corrections' of the older poet, Yeats thought of the corrections as nothing more than that – 'misprints' he called them in a letter to Lady Gregory, 'Ezra's fault.'[84] A transformation of style is not founded on misprints. Yet Yeats did come to accept Pound's suggestions, and at the same time he wrote to Lady Gregory praising his young critic: 'He is full of the middle ages and helps me to get back to the definite and the concrete away from modern abstractions. To talk over a poem with him is like getting you to put a sentence into dialect. All becomes clear and natural.'[85] In a speech Yeats gave at a *Poetry* magazine banquet the following year he repeated this praise, claiming that he 'had a young man go over all my work with me to eliminate the abstract.'[86] If Yeats thought Pound had taught him this lesson, Pound himself felt he had first learned about the clarity of poetic diction from Yeats; he wrote in *This Generation* that some of the poems in *The Wind Among the Reeds* 'run with the simplicity of a good prose sentence, and that, I think, shows a very fine art.'[87]

Yeats did not need Pound's criticism to transform his style, yet one senses that his praise of Pound's critical eye is not disingenuous. The extravagance of his statements to Lady Gregory and at the *Poetry* magazine banquet grew from his desire to reciprocate the praise Pound had been heaping on him for several years. The words William Horton wrote to Yeats in 1916 are probably true: 'What is astonishing is that you do not see what Ezra is to you.'[88] To Yeats, Pound was most valuable as a great admirer during a time when Yeats himself was enormously insecure about the quality of his work. Pound helped to fill the gap left by Synge, the man who first taught Yeats to 'express the individual.' It is not difficult to see why Yeats would have found the opening sentences of Pound's 'Status Rerum' (January 1913) flattering: 'I find Mr. Yeats the only poet worthy of serious study. Mr. Yeats' work is already a recognized classic and is part of the required reading in the Sorbonne. There is no need of proclaiming him to the American public.'[89] Pound's typescript for this essay reveals that this lavish praise for Yeats was originally far more personal. When he sent the essay to Harriet Monroe for publication in *Poetry*, the first sentence read, 'I find Mr. Yeats the only poet worthy of *my* serious study.' □   (James Longenbach, *Stone Cottage*, 1988)[90]

As Ellmann also suggested, one of the things that brought Yeats and Pound closer together just before their winters at Stone Cottage was the arrival of the Bengali poet Rabindranath Tagore in London. They took turns boasting that Tagore was the greatest poetic discovery of the age, with Pound even comparing his arrival with the rediscovery of Greek culture in the Renaissance – or even what it must have been like for Boccaccio (1313–75) to read Theocritus (third century BC) for the first time. But the curious thing about this discovery, says Longenbach, is that Yeats and Pound did not want to share Tagore with others, jealously protecting him from the public and printing only limited editions of his poetry. They were, in effect, creating a secret society that consisted of Yeats, Pound and whomever else they chose to include – and they did not choose to include many. Pound had always envied Yeats his membership in the Rhymers' Club, which Longenbach describes as a sort of 'poetic aristocracy, meeting in private, ignoring the demands of a vastly inferior public'.[91] In the months before they first left for Stone Cottage, Pound had begun to imagine an even more exclusive club, which he called somewhat jokingly the Order of the Brothers Minor, a separate society that would allow select poets space to write without having to worry about paying the rent and buying the groceries. Pound could probably not believe his luck, then, when Yeats offered to provide just that for the two of them at Stone Cottage for the winter. London and Dublin were incredibly busy places for both poets, keeping them apart rather than bringing them together to realise Pound's dream of this new order:

■ Yet that dream was more complicated than Pound would have had some of his contemporaries believe. Despite the fact that Pound reiterated his feelings of unity with Yeats several times between 1911 and 1913, both poets were still involved in many other activities during that time. The ambitious and energetic Pound had more to benefit from this sense of unity and probably felt it rather more strongly than Yeats. Without Pound, the older poet was spending a good amount of time and energy running the Abbey Theatre and fighting to keep Hugh Lane's collection of Impressionist paintings in Dublin. He pursued his experiments in psychic research with a new intensity. In the spring of 1912 he met Elizabeth Radcliffe, a medium whom he would consult intermittently throughout 1912 and intensively between May and August 1913. Early in 1913, when Pound visited Eva Fowler at Daisy Meadow along with Yeats and Olivia Shakespear, he reported that Yeats 'insisted on talking ghosts.'[92] Yeats continued talking: later that year he completed an account of Elizabeth Radcliffe's automatic writing ('Preliminary Examination of the Script of E.R.'), and on All Hallow's Eve he gave a lecture in Dublin titled 'Ghosts and Dreams,' in which he described his research and concluded that the 'great controversy was closed':[93] for Yeats there was no longer any question that the soul survived the body and that supernatural phenomena could be explained by the theories of spiritualism. His account of those theories in 'Preliminary Examination' would be extended in 'Swedenborg, Mediums, and the Desolate Places' (1914), *Per Amica Silentia Lunae* (1918), and finally in 'The Gates of Pluto,' the last chapter of the 1925 version of *A Vision*.

While Yeats was holding court for ghosts at Daisy Meadow, Pound was instructing younger poets to 'go in fear of abstractions.'[94] Despite his use of the Tagore 'boom' to emphasize his exclusive relationship with Yeats, Pound was involved with a circle of younger artists (Aldington, H.D., Gaudier-Brzeska, [Jacob] Epstein [1880–1959], Lewis) who had little interest in anyone of Yeats's generation. Pound felt the tensions of this double life. The Imagist manifestos seem designed to counteract the dreamy symbolism of both Yeats's and (more to the point) Pound's early verse. But in writing the manifestos, Pound was formulating a literary movement for 'les jeunes.' Even though Yeats had come to the same conclusions about poetic diction a decade earlier, he could have no part in the movement.

From the start, though, Pound maintained a private conception of Imagism, distinct from the publicized goals of 'A Few Don'ts by an Imagiste'; and for his own purposes, Pound considered Yeats a seminal part of the movement. In 'Imagisme,' first drafted by Pound and then rewritten by F.S. Flint, Flint reported that 'they' (meaning Pound) 'held also a certain "Doctrine of the Image," which they had not committed to writing; they said that it did not concern the public, and would provoke useless discussion.'[95] Twenty-five years later Flint would remark that 'we had a doctrine of the image, which none of us knew anything about.'[96] Only a very select few knew the secret. Pound did commit the doctrine to writing and then unveiled it in 'Ikon,' a prose poem published in the December 1913 issue of the *Cerebralist*. 'Ikon' is preceded in the *Cerebralist* by a long article that was probably written by Richard Aldington. Many of Pound's readers have suspected that some kind of visionary impulse lurks behind the clipped precision of Imagist poetics, and while Aldington's essay rehearses the litany of Imagist 'Don'ts,' 'Ikon' makes the visionary impulse of Pound's own work clear:

> It is in art the highest business to create the beautiful image; to create order and profusion of images that we may furnish the life of our minds with a noble surrounding.

And if – as some say, the soul survives the body; if our consciousness is not an intermittent melody of strings that relapse between whiles into silence, then more than ever should we put forth the images of beauty, that going out into tenantless spaces we have with us all that is needful – an abundance of sounds and patterns to entertain us in that long dreaming; to strew our path to Valhalla; to give rich gifts by the way.[97]

This prose-poem is Pound's most revealing statement about the nature of Imagist poetics. And the Yeatsian quality of both the language and the sentiment of 'Ikon' is striking. In his notes to *The Wind Among the Reeds* Yeats had written that 'The image – a cross, a man preaching in the wilderness, a dancing Salome, a lily in a girl's hand, a flame leaping, a globe with wings, a pale sunset over still waters – is an eternal act; but our understandings are temporal and understand but a little at a time.'[98] 'Ikon,' which describes how the Image is a necessary accompaniment to life after death, almost seems to be a response to Yeats's excursions into the spirit world with Elizabeth Radcliffe: while Yeats decided that the 'great controversy was closed' – that the soul does indeed survive the body – Pound described how art can 'entertain us in that long dreaming' and 'strew our path to Valhalla' with the eternal Image.

The first winter at Stone Cottage strengthened Pound's belief that Yeats held a seminal position in his secret 'Doctrine of the Image.' When he reviewed Yeats's *Responsibilities* in May 1914, he asked, 'Is Mr. Yeats an Imagiste?' and answered 'No, Mr. Yeats is a symbolist, but he has written *des Images* as have many good poets before him.'[99] While Yeats (like Pound himself) did not always conform to the Imagist 'Don'ts' that Aldington belabored in the *Cerebralist*, he did subscribe to the secret 'Doctrine of the Image.' It is not coincidental that the lines from Yeats's 'The Magi' which Pound quotes as 'a passage of *imagisme*' present a visionary experience:

Now as at all times I can see in the mind's eye,
In their stiff, painted clothes, the pale unsatisfied ones
Appear and disappear in the blue depth of the sky
With all their ancient faces like rain-beaten stones,
And all their helms of silver hovering side by side.

Pound goes on in his review of *Responsibilities* to hint that the poet who best achieved the visionary goals of Imagism described in 'Ikon' was Yeats himself. First Pound repeats the opening phrases of 'Ikon': 'It is perhaps the highest function of art that it should fill the mind with a noble profusion of sounds and images, that it should furnish the life of the mind with such accompaniment and surrounding.' Then he adds, in homage to the man whom he still considered 'the best poet in England,' that 'Mr. Yeats' work has done this in the past and still continues to do so.'

Only the initiated members of the Brothers Minor would understand that Pound was presenting Yeats as the ultimate poet of the secret

'Doctrine of the Image.' By the time 'Ikon' appeared in the *Cerebralist*, Pound and Yeats were hiding by the waste moor in Sussex, writing letters and poems, reading Swedenborg and Noh plays. The Yeatsian cadences of Pound's 'Ikon' lead us to the door of Stone Cottage. A few days after they settled in, Pound wrote to William Carlos Williams that he was 'getting our little gang after five years of waiting.'[100] Pound was referring to 'les jeunes' but the irony of the letter is that Pound wrote it while alone with the older master, having left his contemporaries behind. The first meeting of the Brothers Minor, a club even more exclusive than the Rhymers', had convened. □

(James Longenbach, *Stone Cottage*, 1988)[101]

While Stead had insisted that Yeats did not belong in the company of modernists like Pound and Eliot, Longenbach argues that modern poetry as we now know it depended on Yeats not only spending long winters huddled together with Pound but also providing Pound with its esoteric poetics. According to Longenbach, the only ones who really knew what was going on with modern poetry at that time were Pound and Yeats – and they were not in the mood to tell anyone about it. In his revision of modern literary history, Longenbach suggests it was not so much that Pound helped the old Yeats write *Responsibilities* as it was that Yeats helped the young Pound write *Lustra* (1916). Despite what Pound seemed to have said to those outside this little circle in that review published in *Poetry* magazine in May 1914, when Pound thought of modernism, he thought of Yeats.

CHAPTER FOUR

Yeats and Nationalism

In the 1930s, the world suddenly seemed to be more interested in politics than it had been before – and so did its poets. There was the Salt March of Mahatma Gandhi (1869–1948) in India (1930), the Long March of Mao Tse-tung (1893–1976) in China (1934–5) and the Jarrow Hunger Marches in England (1933–4). Japan invaded Manchuria (1931), Italy conquered Abyssinia (1935) and Germany annexed Austria (1938) and took control of Czechoslovakia (1939). The Spanish Civil War (1936–9) came to a bloody end and what would quickly become the Second World War had a bloody start. But while the younger generation of poets, like Auden, MacNeice and Stephen Spender (1909–95), responded to these worrying events by turning to the left, the older generations often turned to the right. Pound wrote a book comparing the Italian dictator Benito Mussolini to the American president Thomas Jefferson (1743–1826) and Yeats wrote a handful of marching songs for Ireland's Blueshirts. The thirties was also one of Yeats' most productive decades, during which he wrote more than a hundred poems, including volumes such as *The Winding Stair and Other Poems* (1933), *New Poems* (1938) and *Last Poems* (1939). Those productive years were, of course, his last and, following his death in the south of France on 28 January 1939, poets and critics began to re-evaluate a long literary career that had begun in the romantic days of Irish nationalism and ended in the troubling times of international fascism.

Given the concerns of those times, it is little wonder that the first commentators on that career could not help but mention Yeats' politics alongside his poetry. Fascism definitely did not mean in 1939 what it means today, but the fact that Yeats had taken a particular interest in Italian politics and its potential implications for the Irish Free State in the last decade or so of his life could not simply be ignored. When J.M. Hone was asked to contribute a piece on Yeats to a commemorative issue of the *London Mercury* in March 1939, he was clearly aware that the recently deceased's taste in politics might do some damage to his reputation as Ireland's greatest modern poet. Hone had agreed to write Yeats' biography, of course, within weeks of his death and he knew that part of his job would be to define those politics as best he could. He admits that some have called the older Yeats a 'reactionary' but, stepping back and looking at his life as a whole, Hone argues that he should be seen as an Irish nationalist, even if that nationalism went from allegedly belonging to the Irish Republican Brotherhood towards the beginning of his career to supporting anyone who would oppose Sinn Fein and the IRA towards its end:

■ The artist was always implicit in Yeats, whatever the subject of his utterance: Ireland, the philosophy of politics, religion, morals, even economics. He had been brought up by his father, a distinguished and interesting painter, to think of the arts as superior to all other forms of human activity, and early reading of Blake, and the associations which as a young man in London, he formed with the poets of the 'nineties and with William Morris did not tend to shake him in that belief. I have never quite understood, nor did he ever fully explain, what brought him into the Irish movement, dominated in his youth as now, by men who were more interested in elections than in literature, and who supposed that their ideas could be verified at the polls.

The elder Yeats's conversation, as I remember, was sprinkled with derogatory remarks about the English, usually very witty. In nineteenth-century Ireland, a sort of platonic hatred of England appeared frequently among the purest Anglo-Irish (as it does in America among the descendants of the *Mayflower*) who yet might never touch popular politics or mix with their Catholic countrymen. Neither this inheritance, nor a natural love of Ireland, common enough among Irish Protestants, is sufficient to account for the active nationalism of Yeats.

An impressive old man, an ex-Fenian and booklover, John O'Leary, introduced him to Irish patriotic poetry, Davis, Mangan, Ferguson, and instilled into him the belief that Irish writers must seek Irish theme and Irish feeling; and if, as is said, he became a member of the Irish Republican Brotherhood, we may suspect that it was because he wished to please Miss Maud Gonne, 'that new wonder,' as he described her in a youthful contribution to the Boston *Pilot*, 'a beautiful woman who makes speeches.' Mr Horace Reynolds, who recently edited Yeats's work in the *Pilot*, says that nationalism for Yeats was precious, not so much because it served Ireland as because it served art. It may be so, and the 'importance of a subject' was a part of his first literary creed. But he must always have felt a deep impulse towards organization and leadership. In spite of his estheticism, he was never indifferent to external events and contemporary history; he became quite early a great orator, and in the last forty years there was never a period in which his countrymen did not regard him as a public figure.

At the start his Nationalist politics were of the orthodox sort, and he was ready to denounce Cromwell, the Danes, 'West Britons,' Anglo-Irish and landlords with the rest. This did not last long. When I first knew him he was immersed in the management of the Abbey Theatre, and at quarrel with all the little semi-literary and semi-political clubs and societies out of which the Sinn Fein movement grew. The issue, which came to a head when Synge's *Playboy of the Western World* [1907] was produced, went deep, for, although Yeats still held that there could be 'no fine literature without nationality,' he could not admit – nor indeed had he ever admitted – that the criterion by which Irish work should be judged was its effectiveness as melodramatization of the sorrows of Ireland or its power to shoulder an idealistic conception of Irish character and provide useful political thoughts. The 'ignominy of public manners,' shown in Synge's treatment, and still more in that of Hugh Lane, together perhaps with an impression made by [the German philosopher Friedrich] Nietzsche [1844–1900], resulted in Yeats becoming very hostile to democracy in the political and every other sense. He wrote lines meant to be offensive to the lower middle class of Sinn Fein, and called upon those who should have been the inheritors of the aristocratic Whig tradition of Grattan to take the lead in their country's aesthetic progress, and 'leave Paudeens to their pitch and toss' ['To a Wealthy Man who promised a second Subscription to the Dublin Municipal Gallery if it were proved the People wanted Pictures'], or their 'greasy till' ['September 1913']. But the minor poets' rising of 1916 moved him deeply, and he commemorated the sacrifice of Pearse, [Thomas] MacDonagh [1878–1916] and [Joseph Mary] Plunkett [1887–1916] in poetry of passionate intensity. His verses on this occasion were no doubt remembered in his favour; when the Free State was established he was offered a place among the thirty senators to be nominated for their special qualifications, or because they represented groups or parties not adequately represented in the lower house.

Unlike his fellow mystic, A.E., who told Mr Cosgrave's messenger that he 'must consult the Gods' before giving a reply, Yeats accepted the senatorship with alacrity. [Mr Cosgrave was William Thomas Cosgrave (1880–1965), first President (1922–32) of the Irish Free State.] His speeches, it is almost unnecessary to say, were the most distinguished and eloquent utterances of that body; the most notable and the most carefully prepared was his attack on theocratic principles in connection with the law abolishing divorce in the Free State. There was no slightest chance of the defeat of the measure, and, therefore, much as he resented the attempt to force the Catholic view of marriage upon the Protestant minority, he had no reason to be politic, and in one passage of his speech he gave free rein to the spirit of mischief. A month before we had met in Rome, and he seemed so preoccupied with the speech he was about to make that I was not surprised when, on our going with him to call on the charming and very intelligent daughter of Prince Scipio Borghese, he opened the conversation by saying: 'May I ask you to give your views on divorce?' I had told him that there was no divorce in Italy.

She replied to the effect that easy divorce in America seemed to be founded on a Puritan sentimentality which was unlikely to commend itself to her compatriots as a means of mitigating marriage. The look of gratification on Yeats's face showed that he had got the answer he wanted, which, with evidence from Balzac, and also from G.K. Chesterton [1874–1936], would show that the Catholic view of marriage was based on the family and on the family only. He would be able on the authority of 'an Italian of an illustrious Catholic house from which have come cardinals and, I believe, one Pope,' to tell his Catholic fellow senators that American public opinion in regard to illicit relations between the sexes was considered extremely harsh in Italy and was explained by the ease of divorce, which made such relations seem inexcusable.

It was the same speech in which he said vehemently:

> I am proud to consider myself a typical man of that minority. We are the people of Burke; we are the people of Grattan; we are the people of Swift, the people of Parnell. We have created the most of the modern literature of this country. We have created the best of its political intelligence.

While in the senate Yeats acted chiefly with what was known as the Southern Unionist Group, chosen by Mr Cosgrave from the peerage and from important business and professional interests. 'Berkeley,' he wrote to me, 'is of the utmost importance to the Ireland that is coming into existence. I want Protestant Ireland to base some part of its culture upon Swift, Burke and Berkeley.' He wished to insinuate into the ex-Ascendancy Senators a nationalism conceived imaginatively as their heritage from the magnanimity of Swift, Burke and Grattan, 'who gave though free to refuse.' The senators of the group often sought his advice on practical matters and one of them said: 'Yeats would have made an admirable banker,' and another, 'A great lawyer was lost in the poet.' Among the new men of the time, Kevin O'Higgins [1892–1927] commanded his admiration –;

A great man in his pride
Confronting murderous men.
['Death']

because O'Higgins seemed to come nearest of all the moderns to the realistic and authoritarian tradition of Irish leadership, cherished by old Parnellites like himself. O'Higgins was the freest mind in Mr Cosgrave's cabinet, and through his good offices Yeats secured some valuable modifications in the Literary Censorship Bill. □

(J.M. Hone, 'Yeats as Political Philosopher', 1939)[1]

Hone goes on to relate Yeats' political thought not only to Burke and Swift but also to the German philosophers G.W.F. Hegel (1770–1831)

and Karl Marx (1819–83), the Italian thinker Giambattista Vico
(1668–1744) and the French essayist Joseph de Maistre (1753–1821):

■ It is difficult to give a name to a poet's politics. If the Whig is for the
exceptional man and the Tory for the common or natural man (so long as
he is kept in his place), Yeats was a Whig. But up to the end he continued
to employ the resources of his imagination to transfigure Irish nationality,
and whether he read Swift, Burke or Hegel – his favourite political
philosophers – he sought in them for some idea of national life, or of the
State, which he could identify with his romantic belief in Ireland. I remember
his delight in finding in the Anglo-Irish writers of the eighteenth century
'a common hatred of abstraction,' which he characterized (in spite of
De Valera's successes) as peculiarly Irish; and in his play, *The Words upon
the Window Pane* [1930], he made Swift foresee the triumph of the
abstract reason in the French Revolution and the rise of 'mathematical
democracy.' He had found in the fourth *Drapier Letter* [1724] the creation
of the political nationality of Ireland, and in the *Discourse of the Contests
and Dissensions of Athens and Rome* [1701], where Swift defines the balance between the One, the Few and the Many, a theory of the State as
the incarnation of reason and liberty, not unlike Hegel's and Vico's,
because by the *vox populi* [voice of the people] or 'universal bent and current,' Swift is not thinking of majorities, or of what the modern man
means by liberty, but of the unity of being of a people, its right to express
itself as it would through such men as had won or inherited general con-
sent. Yeats even read Marx as preaching a return to a primeval State, so
that a new civilization might arise with its One, its Few and its Many.

The later Yeats was called a reactionary; but he would have replied that
only in Anglo-Saxon nations, impelled by moral enthusiasm, does progress
seem a perpetual straight line. To him, as for de Maistre, contempt for
Locke and for the pragmatic and atomistic tendency of English thought is
the beginning of knowledge. The speculations of his old age in the domains
of politics and of the philosophy of history had the same source in a passion for spiritual unity as his early revolt against 'an international art, picking its symbols and stories where it chose' and as the mystical beliefs
which inspired his 'fairy' poetry. Whether in all this he expressed the
instincts of the Irish mind is indeed another question. Our scholars and our
inductive reasoners unite with our Philistines in saying that he did not.

The certain thing is that Yeats, unlike most of his contemporaries,
never became disillusioned or cynical, much as he raged at some of the
recent aberrations of Irish nationalism, such as the destruction of our
Georgian monuments and the pedantry of Catholic Gaelicism. When the
Nobel prize came to him, he wrote to me that he chiefly took pride in the
award because of the recognition thus given to the Irish literary movement: 'I am content,' he said. □

(J.M. Hone, 'Yeats as Political Philosopher', 1939)[2]

As this letter suggests, Yeats and Hone had got to know each other quite well in the twenties and thirties and, more often than not, their correspondence and conversation turned to the sad state of Irish politics. They discussed much more than divorce when they met in Rome in January 1925, including the possible organisation of a new anti-democratic party in Ireland loosely based on Mussolini's political experiment in Italy. O'Higgins had also shown an interest in Mussolini, taking a tough stance as minister for External Affairs in Cosgrave's government towards unreconstructed republicans. Yeats was deeply disturbed when he heard that O'Higgins had been shot and killed on his way to Mass in July 1927, with rumours going round that Maud Gonne's son, Seán MacBride, had pulled the trigger. However, Hone still insists that, even if his politics went from his father's dislike of everything English to his own eventual dislike of dissident republicans like MacBride and his mother, Yeats was always an Irish nationalist.[3]

Not everyone agreed in 1939. Some were not bothered by the politics and kept reading the poems anyhow, some were so bothered by the politics that they could read the poems no longer, while others kept reading the poems but were still bothered by the politics. One of these was the poet W.H. Auden, who was asked to contribute something on Yeats for the Spring 1939 edition of the *Partisan Review*. Auden had been influenced by the older writer's poetry ever since the late twenties and Yeats admired some of the younger writer's poetry and drama in the thirties, but each seemed to be of two minds about the other. As a result, Auden divided his tribute into two, beginning with the arguments against Yeats as a great poet and ending with the arguments for. One of the more personal arguments for the prosecution accuses Yeats of being an awful editor, with Auden no doubt baffled and slightly offended by Yeats' decision to include only four of his lesser known poems in *The Oxford Book of Modern Verse*: 'It's no use raising a Shout', 'This lunar beauty', 'Before this loved one' and 'The Silly Fool'. MacNeice also had four poems chosen for the anthology, while Spender had just two. When it comes to politics, the prosecution dismisses nationalism as far too easy an explanation for Yeats' various causes and, although the f-word is not actually used, it is certainly implied:

■ THE PUBLIC PROSECUTOR:
  Gentlemen of the Jury. Let us be quite clear in our minds as to the nature of this case. We are here to judge, not a man, but his work. Upon the character of the deceased, therefore, his affectations of dress and manner, his inordinate personal vanity, traits which caused a fellow countryman and former friend to refer to him as 'the greatest literary fop in history', I do not intend to dwell. I must only remind you that there is usually a close connection between the personal character of a poet and his work, and that the deceased was no exception.

Again I must draw your attention to the exact nature of the charge. That the deceased had talent is not for a moment in dispute; so much is freely admitted by the prosecution. What the defence are asking you to believe, however, is that he was a *great* poet, the greatest of this century writing in English. That is their case, and it is that which the prosecution feels bound most emphatically to deny.

A great poet. To deserve such an epithet, a poet is commonly required to convince us of these things: firstly a gift of a very high order for memorable language, secondly a profound understanding of the age in which he lived, and thirdly a working knowledge of and sympathetic attitude towards the most progressive thought of his time.

Did the deceased possess these? I am afraid, gentlemen, that the answer is, no.

On the first point I shall be brief. My learned friend, the counsel for the defence, will, I have no doubt, do his best to convince you that I am wrong. And he has a case, gentlemen. O yes, a very fine case. I shall only ask you to apply to the work of the deceased a very simple test. How many of his lines can you remember?

Further, it is not unreasonable to suppose that a poet who has a gift for language will recognise that gift in others. I have here a copy of an anthology edited by the deceased entitled *The Oxford Book of Modern Verse*. I challenge anyone in this court to deny that it is the most deplorable volume ever issued under the imprint of that highly respected firm which has done so much for the cause of poetry in this country, the Clarendon Press.

But in any case you and I are educated modern men. Our fathers imagined that poetry existed in some private garden of its own, totally unrelated to the workaday world, and to be judged by pure aesthetic standards alone. We know that now to be an illusion. Let me pass, then, to my second point. Did the deceased understand his age?

What did he admire? What did he condemn? Well, he extolled the virtues of the peasant. Excellent. But should that peasant learn to read and write, should he save enough money to buy a shop, attempt by honest trading to raise himself above the level of the beasts, and O, what a sorry change is there. Now he is the enemy, the hateful huxter whose blood, according to the unseemly boast of the deceased, never flowed through *his* loins. Had the poet chosen to live in a mud cabin in Galway among swine and superstition, we might think him mistaken, but we should admire his integrity. But did he do this? O dear no. For there was another world which seemed to him not only equally admirable, but a deal more agreeable to live in, the world of noble houses, of large drawing rooms inhabited by the rich and the decorative, most of them of the female sex. We do not have to think very hard or very long, before we shall see a connection between these facts. The deceased had the feudal mentality. He was prepared to admire the poor just as long as they remained poor and deferential, accepting without protest the burden of maintaining a little Athenian band of literary landowners, who without their toil could not have existed for five minutes.

For the great struggle of our time to create a juster social order, he felt nothing but the hatred which is born of fear. It is true that he played a certain part in the movement for Irish Independence, but I hardly think my learned friend will draw your attention to that. Of all the modes of self-evasion open to the well-to-do, Nationalism is the easiest and most dishonest. It allows to the unjust all the luxury of righteous indignation against injustice. Still, it has often inspired men and women to acts of heroism and self-sacrifice. For the sake of a free Ireland the poet Pearse and the countess [Constance] Markiewicz [1868–1927] gave their all. But if the deceased did give himself to this movement, he did so with singular moderation. After the rebellion of Easter Sunday 1916, he wrote a poem on the subject which has been called a masterpiece. It is. To succeed at such a time in writing a poem which could offend neither the Irish Republican nor the British Army was indeed a masterly achievement.

And so we come to our third and last point. The most superficial glance at the last fifty years is enough to tell us that the social struggle towards greater equality has been accompanied by a growing intellectual acceptance of the scientific method and the steady conquest of irrational superstition. What was the attitude of the deceased towards this? Gentlemen, words fail me. What are we to say of a man whose earliest writings attempted to revive a belief in fairies and whose favourite themes were legends of barbaric heroes with unpronounceable names, work which has been aptly and wittily described as Chaff about Bran?

But you may say, he was young; youth is always romantic; its silliness is part of its charm. Perhaps it is. Let us forgive the youth, then, and consider the mature man, from whom we have a right to expect wisdom and common sense. Gentlemen, it is hard to be charitable when we find that the deceased, far from outgrowing his folly, has plunged even deeper. In 1900 he believed in fairies; that was bad enough; but in 1930 we are confronted with the pitiful, the deplorable spectacle of a grown man occupied with the mumbo-jumbo of magic and the nonsense of India. Whether he seriously believed such stuff to be true, or merely thought it pretty, or imagined it would impress the public, is immaterial. The plain fact remains that he made it the centre of his work. Gentlemen, I need say no more. In the last poem he wrote, the deceased rejected social justice and reason, and prayed for war. Am I mistaken in imagining that somewhat similar sentiments are expressed by a certain foreign political movement which every lover of literature and liberty acknowledges to be the enemy of mankind?

THE COUNSEL FOR THE DEFENCE:
Gentlemen of the Jury. I am sure you have listened with as much enjoyment as I to the eloquent address of my learned friend. I say enjoyment because the spectacle of anything well-done, whether it be a feat of

engineering, a poem, or even an outburst of impassioned oratory, must always give pleasure.

We have been treated to an analysis of the character of the deceased which, for all I know, may be as true as it is destructive. Whether it proves anything about the value of his poetry is another matter. If I may be allowed to quote my learned friend: 'We are here to judge, not a man, but his work.' We have been told that the deceased was conceited, that he was a snob, that he was a physical coward, that his taste in contemporary poetry was uncertain, that he could not understand physics and chemistry. If this is not an invitation to judge the man I do not know what it is. Does it not bear an extraordinary resemblance to the belief of an earlier age that a great artist must be chaste? Take away the frills, and the argument of the prosecution is reduced to this: 'A great poet must give the right answers to the problems which perplex his generation. The deceased gave the wrong answers. Therefore the deceased was not a great poet.' Poetry in such a view is the filling up of a social quiz; to pass with honours the poet must score not less than 75%. With all due respect to my learned friend, this is nonsense. We are tempted so to judge contemporary poets because we really do have problems which we really do want solved, so that we are inclined to expect everyone, politicians, scientists, poets, clergymen, to give us the answer, and to blame them indiscriminately when they do not. But who reads the poetry of the past in this way? In an age of rising nationalism, Dante looked back with envy to the Roman Empire. Was this socially progressive? Will only a Catholic admit that Dryden's 'The Hind and the Panther' [1687] is a good poem? [This poem by John Dryden (1631–1700) was published two years after his conversion to Catholicism.] Do we condemn Blake because he rejected Newton's theory of light, or rank Wordsworth lower than Baker, because the latter had a deeper appreciation of the steam engine?

Can such a view explain why

> Mock Emmet, Mock Parnell
> All the renown that fell
>
> ['Three Marching Songs']

is good; and bad, such a line as

> Somehow I think that you are rather like a tree.

In pointing out that this is absurd, I am not trying to suggest that art exists independently of society. The relation between the two is just as intimate and important as the prosecution asserts.

Every individual is from time to time excited emotionally and intellectually by his social and material environment. In certain individuals this excitement produces verbal structures which we call poems; if such a verbal structure creates an excitement in the reader, we call it a good poem. Poetic talent, in fact, is the power to make personal excitement socially available. Poets, i.e. persons with poetic talent, stop writing good poetry when they stop reacting to the world they live in. The nature of that reaction, whether it be positive or negative, morally admirable or morally disgraceful, matters very little; what is essential is that the reaction should genuinely exist. The later Wordsworth is not inferior to the earlier because the poet had altered his political opinions, but because he had ceased to feel and think so strongly, a change which happens, alas, to most of us as we grow older. Now, when we turn to the deceased, we are confronted by the amazing spectacle of a man of great poetic talent, whose capacity for excitement not only remained with him to the end, but actually increased. In two hundred years when our children have made a different and, I hope, better social order, and when our science has developed out of all recognition, who but a historian will care a button whether the deceased was right about the Irish Question or wrong about the transmigration of souls? But because the excitement out of which his poems arose was genuine, they will still, unless I am very much mistaken, be capable of exciting others, different though their circumstances and beliefs may be from his.

However since we are not living two hundred years hence, let us play the schoolteacher a moment, and examine the poetry of the deceased with reference to the history of our time.

The most obvious social fact of the last forty years is the failure of liberal capitalist democracy, based on the premises that every individual is born free and equal, each an absolute entity independent of all others; and that a formal political equality, the right to vote, the right to a fair trial, the right of free speech, is enough to guarantee his freedom of action in his relations with his fellow men. The results are only too familiar to us all. By denying the social nature of personality, and by ignoring the social power of money, it has created the most impersonal, the most mechanical and the most unequal civilisation the world has ever seen, a civilisation in which the only emotion common to all classes is a feeling of individual isolation from everyone else, a civilisation torn apart by the opposing emotions born of economic injustice, the just envy of the poor and the selfish terror of the rich.

If these latter emotions meant little to the deceased, it was partly because Ireland compared with the rest of western Europe was economically backward, and the class struggle was less conscious there. My learned friend has sneered at Irish Nationalism, but he knows as well as I that Nationalism is a necessary stage towards Socialism. He has sneered at the deceased for not taking arms, as if shooting were the only honourable and useful form of social action. Has the Abbey Theatre done nothing for Ireland?

But to return to the poems. From first to last they express a sustained protest against the social atomisation caused by industrialism, and both in their ideas and their language a constant struggle to overcome it. The fairies and heroes of the early work were an attempt to find through folk tradition a binding force for society; and the doctrine of Anima Mundi found in the later poems is the same thing in a more developed form, which has left purely local peculiarities behind, in favour of something that the deceased hoped was universal; in other words, he was looking for a world religion. A purely religious solution may be unworkable, but the search for it is, at least, the result of a true perception of a social evil. Again, the virtues that the deceased praised in the peasantry and aristocracy, and the vices he blamed in the commercial classes, were real virtues and vices. To create a united and just society where the former are fostered and the latter cured is the task of the politician, not the poet.

For art is a product of history, not a cause. Unlike some other products, technical inventions for example, it does not re-enter history as an effective agent, so that the question whether art should or should not be propaganda is unreal. The case for the prosecution rests on the fallacious belief that art ever makes anything happen, whereas the honest truth, gentlemen, is that, if not a poem had been written, not a picture painted, nor a bar of music composed, the history of man would be materially unchanged.

But there is one field in which the poet is a man of action, the field of language, and it is precisely in this that the greatness of the deceased is most obviously shown. However false or undemocratic his ideas, his diction shows a continuous evolution towards what one might call the true democratic style. The social virtues of a real democracy are brotherhood and intelligence, and the parallel linguistic virtues are strength and clarity, virtues which appear ever more clearly through successive volumes by the deceased.

The diction of *The Winding Stair* is the diction of a just man, and it is for this reason that just men will always recognise the author as a master. □

(W.H. Auden, 'The Public v. the Late Mr. William Butler Yeats', 1939)[4]

Auden may have been of two minds about Yeats but, in the months following the poet's death, he clearly thought him a great poet and, even though they may have argued over the cure, Auden certainly agreed with Yeats that the modern industrial world was far from well. More importantly, this mock trial of the dead poet helped the living one rethink his own poetics, questioning whether his own poems about the civil war in Spain, for example, had had any effect whatsoever on its outcome. As he said in his famous elegy to Yeats written at roughly the same time as the tribute above:

■ You were silly like us; your gift survived it all:
The parish of rich women, physical decay,
Yourself. Mad Ireland hurt you into poetry.
Now Ireland has her madness and her weather still,
For poetry makes nothing happen: it survives
In the valley of its making where executives
Would never want to tamper, flows on south

From ranches of isolation and the busy griefs,
Raw towns that we believe and die in; it survives,
A way of happening, a mouth. □
('In Memory of W.B. Yeats')

It was after writing his tribute and his elegy to Yeats that Auden went back to a poem like 'Spain 1937' and edited out its support for some of the brutal killing that had taken place during the three years of civil war there; he would eventually disown the poem altogether. It was not that his re-evaluation of Yeats made Auden completely rethink his own poetics, but it certainly gave him the opportunity to refine that rethinking and publish it.

Louis MacNeice no doubt welcomed this public about-face. While his old mates from Oxford and fellow thirties poets, Auden and Spender, had had little objection to using poetry as a platform for political causes, MacNeice was never as comfortable with that as they were. As MacNeice had said in 1938, 'The world no doubt needs propaganda, but propaganda ... is not the poet's job. He is not the loudspeaker of society, but something much more like its still, small voice.' While he definitely disagreed with Auden's prosecution that Yeats could not be a great poet because his politics were not progressive enough, he could not agree with the defence either that poetry makes nothing happen. In a study published in 1941 that is still one of the best introductions to Yeats' poetry around, MacNeice said that Yeats and the thirties poets may have been ambivalent about one another and occasionally denounced one another's politics, but the latter actually had more in common with Yeats than they ever had with Eliot. While all the poets saw falling towers in the thirties, says MacNeice, Eliot was the only one who did not see something else slowly rising from their ruins:

■ In England about 1930 a school of poets appeared who mark more or less of a reaction against the influence of Eliot. Curiously, in spite of their violently 'modern' content, they were not so much in reaction against Yeats, who for his part found them, on occasions, sympathetic, and discovered in them a 'concentrated passion' which, according to him, distinguished their poetry from Eliot's. This distinction is fallacious but they can be grouped with Yeats rather than with Eliot on the following grounds. Eliot [in his essay 'After Strange Gods' (1934)] had maintained that the poet must adapt himself to his world; if his world is difficult and complex, his poetry must be difficult and complex (a theory exemplified by The Waste Land). Poets like Auden and Spender abandoned this feminine conception of poetry and returned to the old, arrogant principle – which was Yeats's too – that it is the poet's job to make sense of the world, to simplify it, to put shape on it. The fact that these younger poets proposed to stylize their world in accordance with communist doctrine or psycho-analytical theory (both things repugnant to Yeats) is comparatively irrelevant. Whatever their system was, they stood with Yeats for system against chaos, for a positive art against a passive impressionism. Where Eliot had seen misery, frustration, and ruins, they saw heroic struggle – or, sometimes, heroic defeat – and they saw ruins rebuilding. The two earlier English poets who chiefly influenced my generation were Donne [1573–1631] and Blake; it is significant that, whereas we shared Donne with Eliot, we shared Blake with Yeats; our aim was to use our brains, as Donne and Eliot had done, but to follow Blake in not abjuring life or the world of 'created things.' Eliot has deplored the 'diabolic influence' in modern literature; we may remember that Blake wrote of Milton: 'he was a true Poet and of the Devil's party without knowing it.'

Yeats found much of this new poetry exasperatingly obscure and ostentatiously experimental. He distrusted *deliberate* originality and had written in *Per Amica Silentia Lunae* (1917): 'It is not permitted to a man, who takes up pen or chisel, to seek originality, for passion is his only business, and he cannot but mould or sing after a new fashion because no disaster is like another.' But, if the younger poets sometimes seemed wilfully original, he recognized also that they had their own disasters, that they could not be expected to write to his own recipe. He must have considered their content too heterogeneous and must have disliked Auden's guide-book curiosity; if Auden had written poems about the Rosses he would never have left out the Metal Man who stands in the harbour. On the other hand he welcomed their vigour of thought, being tired no doubt of the spineless elegance of some of his own imitators. He approved also their return, though 'with a new freedom,' to the traditional metres and to the personal lyric. And he liked their zest, a quality which, except in his own poetry, had been notably lacking in English verse for some time.

I will not push these comparisons any further. It is fashionable in some circles in England to-day to dismiss Yeats as a mere reactionary, a man who wrote elegantly in an outmoded manner and preached a gospel which was not only obsolete but vicious. This very superficial view has been well combated in an article by Auden entitled The Public v. the late Mr W.B. Yeats (published in *The Partisan Review*), which takes the form of a speech for the prosecution and a speech for the defence. The defence argue – quite rightly – that a work of art cannot be assessed merely by its political reference. Auden, however, as was natural in a poet who had abruptly abandoned the conception of art as handmaid of politics for the conception of art as autotelic [art as an end in itself], overstates his case; he says that the case for the prosecution rests on the fallacy that art ever makes anything happen. The case for the prosecution does rest on a fallacy but it is not this. The fallacy lies in thinking that it is the *function* of art to make things happen and that the effect of art upon actions is something either direct or calculable. It is an historical fact that art *can* make things happen and Auden in his reaction from a rigid Marxism seems in this article to have been straying towards the Ivory Tower. Yeats did not write primarily in order to influence men's actions but he knew that art can alter a man's outlook and so indirectly affect his actions. He also recognized that art can, sometimes intentionally, more often perhaps unintentionally, precipitate violence. He was not sentimentalizing when he wrote, thinking of *Cathleen ni Houlihan* [1902]:

> Did that play of mine send out
> Certain men the English shot?
>   ['Man and the Echo'] □
>   (Louis MacNeice, *The Poetry of W.B. Yeats*, 1941)[5]

MacNeice admits that Yeats may have been, as Auden suggested in his elegy, a bit silly at times, that his poems sometimes expressed theories that could not be supported by the facts themselves and that he stubbornly refused to budge when confronted with evidence to the contrary, but that did not mean that Yeats was a dishonest poet. Rather, it is an indication of his poetic integrity:

■ Poets of my generation, who distrust *a priori* methods, tend to found – or think they found – their own beliefs and their own moral principles on evidence. These beliefs and principles are, in their opinion, of the utmost importance to their poetry. So they are, but not necessarily because they are the 'right' beliefs. Poetry gains body from beliefs, and the more suited the belief is to the poet, the healthier his poetry; one poet can thrive on pantheism and another on Christianity; [A.E.] Housman [1859–1936] *as a poet* flourished on beliefs the opposite of Browning's. It is not the absolute, or objective, validity of a belief that vindicates the poetry; it is a gross over-simplification to maintain that a right belief makes a poem good and a wrong belief makes a poem bad. First, beliefs are not so easily sorted out into merely right and merely wrong; secondly, by the time a belief is embodied in a poem, it has suffered a biochemical change, has become blended inextricably with mood, picture, and drama. We can, however, say that at certain times in certain places there are certain beliefs affecting us so widely and deeply that they are for us the right ones. This being so, we can argue that some of Yeats's beliefs were wrong and can go on to infer that better, or greater, or more 'significant' poetry than Yeats's could be made, given better ingredients. This inference, too, is possibly correct (though we must remember that a belief, in the narrow sense, is only one ingredient out of many), but we should be mistaken if we inferred that *Yeats* could have written better poetry if he had had the 'right' ingredients; he probably could not have assimilated them. Yeats, like Gerard Manley Hopkins [1844–89], was a special case. Those critics are fools who lament that, if Hopkins had not been a Jesuit, he would have written much better poetry. If Yeats had been different from what he was, if he had had different beliefs, or even been capable of different beliefs, he might not have written at all. The spiritual lesson that my generation (a generation with a vastly different outlook) can learn from Yeats is to write according to our lights. His lights are not ours. *Go thou and do otherwise.* □

(Louis MacNeice, *The Poetry of W.B. Yeats*, 1941)[6]

Even though MacNeice argues that Yeats would not have been a better poet if he had had better politics and that he should be considered, like Hopkins, a 'special case', this does not mean that MacNeice ever approved of Yeats' politics. Nor did he simply ignore them, as some critics have done. He can look at a poem like 'The Second Coming' and see how some readers, like Spender, think they can detect an image of the rise of fascism there – and a worrying relish in that rise. MacNeice is willing to admit that this probably suggests that 'Yeats had a budding fascist inside himself'[7] but, once again, he sees a similarity there between Yeats and the thirties poets as well as a difference. If the left shared anything with the right, says MacNeice, it was a firm belief at that time that the coming of violence as depicted in 'The Second Coming' was inevitable.

While Auden was half willing to make a connection between Yeats' politics and 'a certain foreign political movement' and MacNeice was at least willing to concede that the Irish poet had 'a budding fascist inside himself', George Orwell was the first major writer not to pull his punches and simply state that Yeats was a fascist. In what was a curiously belated review of V.K. Narayana Menon's *The Development of William Butler Yeats* (1933), first published in *Horizon* in January 1943, Orwell wonders whether a criticism can be contrived that tells a poet's politics from the style of his poems alone. He is convinced that such connections between political tendencies and poetical textures definitely exist, arguing that everyone knows that 'a Socialist would not write like Chesterton or a Tory imperialist like Bernard Shaw'.[8] The same goes for Yeats, whose 'wayward, even tortured style of writing' must have something to do with 'his rather sinister vision of life'. He acknowledges that the way-wardness of Yeats' writing is often dismissed as some sort of harmless Irishness, but Orwell believes that its 'quaintness' is really the sign of someone who desperately hates the modern world and everything it stands for, including democracy, equality and progress:

■ Mr. Menon's book is incidentally a short biography of Yeats, but he is above all interested in Yeats's philosophical 'system', which in his opinion supplies the subject-matter of more of Yeats's poems than is generally recognized. This system is set forth fragmentarily in various places, and at full length in *A Vision*, a privately printed book which I have never read but which Mr. Menon quotes from extensively. Yeats gave conflicting accounts of its origin, and Mr. Menon hints pretty broadly that the 'documents' on which it was ostensibly founded were imaginary. Yeats's philosophical system, says Mr. Menon, 'was at the back of his intellectual life almost from the beginning. His poetry is full of it. Without it his later poetry becomes almost completely unintelligible.' As soon as we begin to read about the so-called system we are in the middle of a hocus-pocus of Great Wheels, gyres, cycles of the moon, reincarnation, disembodied spirits, astrology and what-not. Yeats hedges as to the literalness with which he believed in all this, but he certainly dabbled in spiritualism and astrology, and in earlier life had made experiments in alchemy. Although almost buried under explanations, very difficult to understand, about the phases of the moon, the central idea of his philosophical system seems to be our old friend, the cyclical universe, in which everything happens over and over again. One has not, perhaps, the right to laugh at Yeats for his mystical beliefs – for I believe it could be shown that *some* degree of belief in magic is almost universal – but neither ought one to write such things off as mere unimportant eccentricities. It is Mr. Menon's perception of this that gives his book its deepest interest. 'In the first flush of admiration and enthusiasm,' he says, 'most people dismissed the fantastical philosophy as the price we have to pay for a great and curious intellect. One did not quite realise where he was heading. And those who did, like Pound and perhaps Eliot, approved the stand that he finally took. The first reaction to this did not come, as one might have expected, from the politically minded young English poets. They were puzzled because a less rigid or artificial system than that of *A Vision* might not have produced the great poetry of Yeats's last days.' It might not, and yet Yeats's philosophy has some very sinister implications, as Mr. Menon points out.

Translated into political terms, Yeats's tendency is Fascist. Throughout most of his life, and long before Fascism was ever heard of, he had had the outlook of those who reach Fascism by the aristocratic route. He is a great hater of democracy, of the modern world, science, machinery, the concept of progress – above all, of the idea of human equality. Much of the imagery of his work is feudal, and it is clear that he was not altogether free from ordinary snobbishness. Later these tendencies took clearer shape and led him to 'the exultant acceptance of authoritarianism as the only solution. Even violence and tyranny are not necessarily evil because the people, knowing not evil and good, would become perfectly acquiescent to tyranny ... . Everything must come from the top. Nothing can come from the masses.' Not much interested in politics, and no doubt disgusted by his brief incursions into public life, Yeats nevertheless makes political pronouncements. He is too big a man to share the illusions of Liberalism, and as early as 1920 he foretells in a justly famous passage ('The Second Coming') the kind of world that we have actually moved into. But he appears to welcome the coming age, which is to be 'hierarchical, masculine, harsh, surgical', and is influenced both by Ezra Pound and by various Italian Fascist writers. He describes the new civilization which he hopes and believes will arrive: 'an aristocratic civilization in its most completed form, every detail of life hierarchical, every great man's door crowded at dawn by petitioners, great wealth everywhere in a few men's hands, all dependent upon a few, up to the Emperor himself, who is a God dependent on a greater God, and everywhere, in Court, in the family, an inequality made law'. The innocence of this statement is as interesting as its snobbishness. To begin with, in a single phrase, 'great wealth in a few men's hands', Yeats lays bare the central reality of Fascism, which the whole of its propaganda is designed to cover up. The merely political Fascist claims always to be fighting for justice: Yeats, the poet, sees at a glance that Fascism means injustice, and acclaims it for that very reason. But at the same time he fails to see that the new authoritarian civilization, if it arrives, will not be aristocratic, or what he means by aristocratic. It will not be ruled by noblemen with Van Dyck [1599–1641] faces, but by anonymous millionaires, shiny-bottomed bureaucrats and murdering gangsters. Others who have made the same mistake have afterwards changed their views, and one ought not to assume that Yeats, if he had lived longer, would necessarily have followed his friend Pound, even in sympathy. But the tendency of the passage I have quoted above is obvious, and its complete throwing overboard of whatever good the past two thousand years have achieved is a disquieting symptom.

How do Yeats's political ideas link up with his leaning towards occultism? It is not clear at first glance why hatred of democracy and a tendency to believe in crystal-gazing should go together. Mr. Menon only discusses this rather shortly, but it is possible to make two guesses. To begin with, the theory that civilization moves in recurring cycles is one way out for people who hate the concept of human equality. If it is true that 'all this', or something like it, 'has happened before', then science and the modern world are debunked at one stroke and progress becomes for ever impossible. It does not matter if the lower orders are getting above themselves, for, after all, we shall soon be returning to an age of tyranny. Yeats is by no means alone in this outlook. If the universe is moving round on a wheel, the future must be foreseeable, perhaps even in some detail. It is merely a question of discovering the laws of its motion, as the early astronomers discovered the solar year. Believe that, and it becomes difficult not to believe in astrology or some similar system. A year before the war, examining a copy of *Gringoire*, the French Fascist weekly, much read by my officers, I found in it no less than thirty-eight advertisements of clairvoyants. Secondly, the very concept of occultism carries with it the idea that knowledge must be a secret thing, limited to a small circle of initiates. But the same idea is integral to Fascism. Those who dread the prospect of universal suffrage, popular education, freedom of thought, emancipation of women, will start off with a predilection towards secret cults. There is another link between Fascism and magic in the profound hostility of both to the Christian ethical code.

No doubt Yeats wavered in his beliefs and held at different times many different opinions, some enlightened, some not. Mr. Menon repeats for him Eliot's claim that he had the longest period of development of any poet who has ever lived. But there is one thing that seems constant, at least in all of his work that I can remember, and that is his hatred of modern Western civilization and desire to return to the Bronze Age, or perhaps to the Middle Ages. Like all such thinkers, he tends to write in praise of ignorance. The Fool in his remarkable play, *The Hour-Glass* [1903], is a Chestertonian figure, 'God's fool' the 'natural born innocent', who is always wiser than the wise man. The philosopher in the play dies on the knowledge that all his lifetime of thought has been wasted (I am quoting from memory):

> The stream of the world has changed its course,
> And with the stream my thoughts have run
> Into some cloudy, thunderous spring
> That is its mountain-source;
> Ay, to a frenzy of the mind,
> That all that we have done's undone
> Our speculation but as the wind.

Beautiful words, but by implication profoundly obscurantist and reactionary; for if it is really true that a village idiot, as such, is wiser than a philosopher, then it would be better if the alphabet had never been invented. Of course, all praise of the past is partly sentimental, because we do not live in the past. The poor do not praise poverty. Before you can despise the machine, the machine must set you free from brute labour. But that is not to say that Yeats's yearning for a more primitive and more hierarchical age was not sincere. How much of all this is traceable to mere snobbishness, product of Yeats's own position as an impoverished offshoot of the aristocracy, is a different question. And the connection between his obscurantist opinions and his tendency towards 'quaintness' of language remains to be worked out; Mr. Menon hardly touches upon it.

This is a very short book, and I would greatly like to see Mr. Menon go ahead and write another book on Yeats, starting where this one leaves off. 'If the greatest poet of our times is exultantly ringing in an era of Fascism, it seems a somewhat disturbing symptom', he says on the last page, and leaves it at that. It *is* a disturbing symptom, because it is not an isolated one. By and large the best writers of our time have been reactionary in tendency, and though Fascism does not offer any real return to the past, those who yearn for the past will accept Fascism sooner than its probable alternatives. But there are other lines of approach, as we have seen during the past two or three years. The relationship between

Fascism and the literary intelligentsia badly needs investigating, and Yeats might well be the starting-point. He is best studied by someone like Mr. Menon, who can approach a poet primarily as a poet, but who knows that a writer's political and religious beliefs are not excrescences to be laughed away, but something that will leave their mark even on the smallest detail of his work. □

(George Orwell, 'W.B. Yeats', 1943)[9]

For Orwell, then, every little archaism or inverted phrase was not to be dismissed as some fanciful bit of Sligo or Galway dialect but yet another sign of Yeats' slinking fascism. However, Orwell was not the only writer in the forties and fifties to call for a new kind of criticism that would reread Yeats and the other modernist poets in the context of postwar politics. The American poet and critic Yvor Winters (1900–68) also called Yeats a fascist, agreeing with Spender that a poem like 'The Second Coming' not only predicts the end of the civilised world as we know it but also approves of its passing. Winters rather vehemently disagreed, though, with all those other critics who argued that it was possible to enjoy this poem without necessarily enjoying the ideas it expressed:

■ We have been told many times that we do not have to take the ideas of W.B. Yeats seriously in order to appreciate his poetry; but if this is true, Yeats is the first poet of whom it has ever been true. We need to understand the ideas of Donne and Shakespeare in order to appreciate their works, and we have to take their ideas seriously in one sense or another, and it is impossible to take their ideas seriously much of the time. A great deal of scholarly work has been done on their ideas, and some of this work has contributed to our appreciation of what they wrote. A great deal of scholarly work has been done on Yeats in recent years; unfortunately, the better one understands him, the harder it is to take him seriously. □

(Yvor Winters, 'The Poetry of W.B. Yeats', 1960)[10]

As this comment at the end of the fifties makes clear, these accusations of fascism had not stopped most scholars from studying Yeats' poetry and those voices in this debate who insisted that any consideration of his greatness as a poet could not go without a consideration of his politics were still relatively few in number. But those few voices were important voices and they were becoming bolder, occasionally targeting those Yeats scholars who did not take his politics as seriously as they took his poetry as misguided apologists.

This somewhat minor debate on whether Yeats was a nationalist, a fascist or something else altogether suddenly became impossible to ignore in 1965 when Conor Cruise O'Brien decided to dedicate his contribution to a collection of essays celebrating the centenary of Yeats' birth to the question. O'Brien was a major figure in both Irish politics and literature, having served in a number of prominent posts for the United Nations and having just accepted the Albert Schweitzer Chair of Humanities at New York University. He came from an influential nationalist family in Dublin but claims he had always been able to read Yeats' poetry without worrying too much about its politics. However, he began to wonder whether Yeats was the political fool his defenders had often suggested he was (and Yeats had sometimes pretended to be) or actually a very clever opportunist, taking full advantage of such public events as the death of Parnell to draw attention to himself as both a poet and a politician. According to O'Brien, Yeats had learned from O'Leary that a poet in Ireland would always need either the Church or the Fenians on his side and, since Yeats would never have the support of the Catholic fathers, he had better get the Fenians'. This is precisely what Yeats did, says O'Brien, defining himself as a nationalist for most of his public life. But everything began to change in 1932 when the party that had won the civil war and ruled Ireland ever since was defeated in a general election by the party that had lost the war. To Yeats, this victory for de Valera and the former forces of the IRA signalled the start of mob rule in Dublin. In opposition to this, a paramilitary movement made up of disgruntled members of the defeated Cosgrave government began to form around General Eoin O'Duffy (1892–1944), calling themselves the Blueshirts (after the Blackshirts in Italy and the Brownshirts in Germany). Yeats wrote a handful of marching songs for this paramilitary organisation but, when de Valera banned a planned march by the Blueshirts through the streets of Dublin in August 1933, the movement suddenly seemed to collapse and so did Yeats' hopes for a new anti-democratic government in Ireland:

■ It is customary to say that, at this point, Yeats had become 'disillusioned with Fascism'. One may accept this judgment, but must also remark that the principal illusion which had been dissipated was the illusion that Fascism in Ireland stood a good chance of winning. In the spring and summer of 1933, the Fascism of the Irish Blueshirts looked to many people like a possible winner and in this phase Yeats was with the Blueshirts. By the autumn and winter of 1933–34, the Government's energetic measures – described by Yeats as 'panic measures' – made it clear that de Valera was no von Papen. [Franz von Papen (1879–1969) was briefly Chancellor of Germany in 1932, but soon yielded to Adolf Hitler (1889–1945) and became his Vice Chancellor until the Night of the Long Knives in June 1934.] O'Duffy, failing to devise anything effective in reply, revealed that he was no Hitler. The blue began to fade, and Yeats's interest in it faded proportionately.[11]

Commenting on a mildly anti-Blueshirt anecdote in a letter of Yeats, Professor Jeffares says: 'This ironic attitude to the Blueshirts reveals the true Yeats, detached and merely playing with his thoughts, except for the intervals when he wanted to achieve complete directness and accuracy'.

The date of the anecdote in question is February 1934, by which date the Blueshirts were beginning to look a little silly. The thoughts Yeats had 'played with' in the days when they had looked possibly formidable were less 'detached'. I cannot see on what grounds we are to regard the Yeats who began to sneer at the Blueshirts when they proved a flop, as being more 'real' than the Yeats who was excited about them when he thought they might win. It was the same Yeats, strongly drawn to Fascism, but no lover of hopeless causes.

In April 1934 ... he was still advocating 'force, marching men' to break the reign of the mob, but professing, somewhat disingenuously, that 'no such party' as would undertake this work had yet appeared. By August 1934 – when the party for which he had in fact written the songs was on the verge of public disintegration – he has found that that party 'neither could nor would' do what he proposed for it. This, it will be noted, does *not* amount to a disavowal of the programme of 'force, marching men' to 'break the reign of the mob'. The irony and detachment of the poem 'Church and State' belong to the period after the final break-up of the Blueshirt movement.

Comment on the question of Yeats's attitude to Fascism has been bedevilled by the assumption that a great poet must be, even in politics, 'a nice guy'. If this be assumed then it follows that, as Yeats obviously was a great poet, he cannot *really* have favoured Fascism, which is obviously not a nice cause. Thus the critic or biographer is led to postulate a 'true Yeats', so that Yeats's recorded words and actions of Fascist character must have been perpetrated by some bogus person with the same name and outward appearance.[12]

If one drops the assumption, about poets having always to be nice in politics, then the puzzle disappears, and we see, I believe, that Yeats the man was as near to being a Fascist as his situation and the conditions of his own country permitted. His unstinted admiration had gone to Kevin O'Higgins, the most ruthless 'strong man' of his time in Ireland, and he linked his admiration explicitly to his rejoicing at the rise of Fascism in Europe – and this at the very beginning, within a few weeks of the March on Rome. Ten years later, after Hitler had moved to the centre of the political stage in Europe, Yeats was trying to create a movement in Ireland which would be overtly Fascist in language, costume, behaviour and intent. He turned his back on this movement when it began to fail, not before. Would the irony and detachment of this phase of disillusion have lasted if a more effective Fascist leader and movement had later emerged? One may doubt it. Many in Germany who were 'disillusioned' by the failure of the Kapp *putsch* and the beer-cellar *putsch* were speedily 'reillusioned' when Hitler succeeded – and 'disillusioned' again when he lost the war.

Post-war writers, touching with embarrassment on Yeats's pro-Fascist opinions, have tended to treat these as a curious aberration of an idealistic but ill-informed poet. In fact such opinions were quite usual in the Irish Protestant middle-class to which Yeats belonged (as well as in other middle-classes), in the 'twenties and 'thirties. The *Irish Times*, spokesman of that class, aroused no protest from its readers when it hailed Hitler (4 March 1933) as 'Europe's standard bearer against Muscovite terrorism' and its references to Mussolini were as consistently admiring as those to Soviet Russia were consistently damning. But the limiting factor on the pro-Fascist tendencies of the *Irish Times* and of the Irish Protestant middle-class generally was the pull of loyalty to Britain – a factor which did not apply – or applied only with great ambivalence – in the case of Yeats. Mr. T.R. Henn is quite right when he says that Yeats was 'not alone in believing at that moment of history, that the discipline of Fascist theory might impose order upon a disintegrating world'. I cannot follow Mr. Henn, however, to his conclusion that 'nothing could be further from Yeats's mind than [Fascism's] violent and suppressive practice'.[13] 'Force, marching men' and 'the victory [in civil war] of the skilful, riding their machines as did the feudal knights their armoured horses' (*On the Boiler*), surely belong to the domain of violent and suppressive practice.

Just as one school is led to claim that the pro-Fascist Yeats was not the 'true' Yeats, so another tries to believe that the Fascism to which Yeats was drawn was not a 'true' Fascism.

Several critics have assured us that he was drawn not really to Fascism, but to some idealized aristocracy of eighteenth-century stamp. 'In all fairness', writes Dr. Vivian Mercier, 'we should allow that his views were closer to Hamilton's or even to Jefferson's than they were to Mussolini's.'[14] As far as political theory is concerned this is probably correct – although the name of Swift would seem more relevant than that of Hamilton or of Jefferson. [Alexander Hamilton (1755–1804) was one of America's so-called founding fathers, arguing against Jefferson for a much stronger federal government, even supporting the abolishment of the states and a president-for-life.] But it ignores one important reality: that Yeats was interested in contemporary politics and that he was a contemporary, not of Swift's or Jefferson's, but of Mussolini's.[15]

He would certainly have preferred something more strictly aristocratic than Fascism, but since he was living in the twentieth century he was attracted to Fascism as the best available form of anti-democratic theory and practice. Mr. Frank O'Connor [1903–66], who knew him well in his last years and – politics apart – greatly admired and liked him, has told us plainly that 'he was a fascist and authoritarian, seeing in world crises only the break-up of the "damned liberalism" he hated'.[16]

George Orwell, though critical, and up to a point percipient, about Yeats's tendencies, thought that Yeats misunderstood what an authoritarian society would be like. Such a society, Orwell pointed out, 'will not be ruled by noblemen with Van Dyck faces, but by anonymous millionaires, shiny-bottomed bureaucrats and murderous gangsters'. This implies a degree of innocence in Yeats which cannot reasonably be postulated. O'Higgins and O'Duffy were not 'Duke Ercole and Guidobaldo' ['To a Wealthy Man who promised a second Subscription to the Dublin Municipal Gallery if it were proved the People wanted Pictures'], and Yeats had considerable experience of practical politics, both in the 'nineties and in the early 'twenties. 'In the last forty years,' wrote J.M. Hone in the year of Yeats's death, 'there was never a period in which his countrymen did not regard him as a public figure.'[17] When he thought of rule by an *élite*, it was a possible *élite*, resembling in many ways the nominated members of the Senate in which he had sat.[18] Its membership – bankers, organizers, ex-officers – would correspond roughly to what Orwell, in more emotive language, describes. Nor should it be assumed – as Orwell with his 'murderous gangsters' seems to imply – that the sensitive nature of the poet would necessarily be revolted by the methods of rule of an authoritarian state.[19] Yeats – unlike, say, his brother, or Lady Gregory – was not, in politics, a very squeamish person. Seventy-seven executions did not repel him; on the contrary, they made him admire O'Higgins all the more. At least one of his associates of the early 'thirties might have been described as a 'murderous gangster'. And when, in 1936, Ethel Mannin [1900–84] appealed to him for a gesture which would have helped the German writer [Carl von] Ossietzki [1887–1938], then in a Nazi concentration camp, Yeats refused. 'Do not', he said, 'try to make a politician of me ... .'[20]

It is true that neither Yeats nor anyone else during Yeats's lifetime knew what horrors Fascism would be capable of. But the many who, like Yeats, were drawn to Fascism at this time knew, and seemed to have little difficulty in accepting, or at least making allowances for, much of what had already been done and continued to be done. 'The Prussian police', wrote the *Irish Times* in an editorial of February 1933, 'have been authorized by Herr Hitler's Minister to shoot Communists – a term which in Germany has a wide political connotation – on sight.' The same editorial which contained this information ended with the words: 'Naturally the earlier phases of this renascence are crude, but Germany is finding her feet after a long period of political ineptitude'.[21]

Yeats read the newspapers; he also read, as Hone records, several books on Fascist Italy and Nazi Germany.[22] If, then, he was attracted to the dominant movements in these countries, and if he supported a movement in his own country whose resemblances to these Continental movements he liked to stress, it cannot be contended that he did so in ignorance of such 'crude' practices as the *Irish Times* described.[23]

Some writers – notably Professor Donald Torchiana in his well-documented study *W.B. Yeats, Jonathan Swift and Liberty*[24] – have insisted that, in spite of Yeats's authoritarian and Fascist leanings, he was essentially a friend of liberty. 'Both Swift and Yeats', Torchiana concludes, 'served human liberty.' The senses in which this is true for Yeats are important but clearly limited. He defended the liberty of the artist, consistently. In politics, true to his duality, he defended the liberty of Ireland against English domination, and the liberty of his own caste – and sometimes, by extension, of others – against clerical domination. Often these liberties overlapped, and the cause of artist and aristocrat became the same; often his resistance to 'clerical' authoritarianism (his position on the Lock-out, on divorce, on censorship) makes him appear a liberal. But his objection to clerical authoritarianism is not the liberal's objection to *all* authoritarianism. On the contrary he favours 'a despotism of the educated classes' and in the search for this, is drawn towards Fascism. It is true that Fascism was not in reality a despotism of the educated classes, but it was a form of despotism which the educated classes in the 'twenties and 'thirties showed a disposition to settle for – a disposition proportionate to the apparent threat, in their country, of Communism or 'anarchy'. In assessing Yeats's pro-Fascist opinions, there is no need to regard these as so extraordinary that he must either not have been himself, or not have known what he was about. □

(Conor Cruise O'Brien, 'Passion and Cunning', 1965)[25]

While O'Brien argues that the true Yeats was definitely a fascist in the early thirties, he also says it is true that Yeats went through manic phases when he suddenly became obsessed with politics and depressive phases when he could have hardly cared less. The manic phases almost always coincided with decisive moments in Irish history when the country was divided over its immediate future, including the death of Parnell in the early nineties, the civil war in the early twenties and the flirtation with fascism in the early thirties. O'Brien believes that, if the Blueshirts had been more of a success, Yeats still would have lost interest in politics once again, since the fascists would have needed the support of the Catholic Church in order to succeed in Ireland and the Protestant Yeats would never have supported that. In fact, Yeats changed his mind about de Valera and his government once he realised that the new president of the Executive Council had no intention whatsoever of moving Ireland from a democracy to a communist state. Yeats' son, Michael, even became a senator after the war as a member of de Valera's party.

Following the publication of O'Brien's extended essay, this question became the loudest debate in Yeats studies for the next few years. Numerous critics responded to O'Brien's charge, including David Bradshaw, Rivers Carew, Joseph Chadwick, Elizabeth Cullingford, Denis Donoghue (born 1928), William Empson (1906–84), David Fitzpatrick, Grattan Freyer (1915–83), Joseph Hassett (born 1943), Samuel Hynes, William Johnsen, John Kelly, Bernard Krimm, Michael

North (born 1951), Edward Said (1935–2003), Paul Scott Stanfield (born 1954), Geoffrey Thurley and Terence de Vere White (1912–94). But one of the most polemical early responses to O'Brien was Patrick Cosgrave's essay 'Yeats, Fascism and Conor O'Brien', published in *London Magazine* in July 1967. Cosgrave (born 1941) argues that O'Brien may know a lot about politics and literature, but his understanding of Irish history leaves a little to be desired, often burying anything that might contradict his case in a brief footnote. For Cosgrave, Yeats was always an Irish nationalist and whatever political interests he had over his long and complicated literary career can best be explained in the context of that nationalism, not fascism:

■ Yeats's post-independence political hopes were focused on the Cosgrave Government's powerful Minister for Justice, Kevin O'Higgins. When O'Higgins was assassinated by a dissident Republican, Yeats's last political hero had gone. This is the period when Yeats first showed himself interested in the doctrines of Fascism, then first appearing in Europe. It is likewise in this period that Professor O'Brien finds the bulk of his material for the final, triumphant statement of his argument.

It is a part of the O'Brien case that O'Higgins was a Fascist, standing for 'what was most ruthless and implacable in the party of property'. As is by this stage in his essay usual, Mr de Vere White's contradictory evidence (from his definitive biography of O'Higgins) is relegated to a dismissive footnote. Mr White gives evidence from O'Higgins's papers and speeches to the effect that his views, particularly for such a crisis-torn period were, if anything, exceptionally democratic, and evidence of O'Higgins's anxiety for the humanitarian treatment of political prisoners and rigid fairness in the appointment of non-party members to the judicial bench (a rarity in Ireland now) supports his case. All this Professor O'Brien puts in a footnote, while his own aspersions on O'Higgins are unsupported by any evidence, let alone evidence of comparable quality.

As evidence of Yeats's Fascism, Professor O'Brien quotes a letter from the poet to Ethel Mannin in which he said he would rejoice in a victory for Franco in Spain because this would weaken the British Empire. But Professor O'Brien ignores the important emphasis, 'But this is mere instinct. A thing I would never act on. Then I have a horror of modern politics ... .' For further support Professor O'Brien cites Yeats's 1938 work *On the Boiler* – an expression of all his bitterness about the failure of Ireland to live up to his dreams – as a celebration of 'force and marching men' and a prophecy of Fascist victory in a coming war. He regards this work as 'a sort of political testament'.

Professor O'Brien answers the argument that Yeats's seeming attraction towards Fascism was a naïve thing representing no real political preference, by recounting the events of 1932. In that year the Cosgrave

Government fell and there ascended to power the civil war rebels under De Valera. In the panic and fear succeeding this event, many of the Cosgrave party formed themselves into a Fascist style opposition group called the Blueshirts, led by a former chief of police, Eoin O'Duffy. Yeats summoned O'Duffy to him to discuss writing an anti-democratic hymn for the Blueshirts. Thus, Professor O'Brien comments, if Yeats was attracted intellectually to the doctrines of Fascism and supported a Fascist movement in his own country, then he did so in full knowledge of all the 'crude practices' that Fascist government entailed. Two years after this event Yeats disengaged from the Blueshirts but this, says Professor O'Brien, should be attributed to his cunning realization that Fascism had no chance of success in Ireland, while his subsequent opposition to the Catholic Front (successor to the Blueshirts) should be put down to the clericalist element in this successor movement to the Blueshirts.

First, let us take Yeats's initial attraction to the Blueshirts. It is curious that Professor O'Brien should ascribe to *On the Boiler* the status of a political testament while completely ignoring Yeats's real poetic, historical, philosophical and political legacy contained in *A Vision*. Yeats, when he first met O'Duffy, was re-writing the section of that work dealing with the future. It was in terms of historically determinist prophecy that he saw the Blueshirt leader as, he wrote, 'a plastic man'. The term 'plastic' is here a technical one: it meant that Yeats, by the process of historical determinism that characterizes *A Vision*, had predicted for himself, as Professor Donoghue shows, that the Blueshirts were the next phase in the progress of the world towards the 'violent annunciation' presaged in *A Vision*. Likewise, 'The second coming', a poem which Professor O'Brien sees as prophesying Fascism:

> And what rough beast, its hour come round at last,
> Slouches towards Bethlehem to be born?

is a complex and far from unequivocal poem:

> The ceremony of innocence is drowned;
> The best lack all conviction, while the worst
> Are full of passionate intensity.

'Anyone is free,' as Professor Donoghue says, 'to decide that the theory of *A Vision* is nonsense ... . But it is not cool, crafty, calculating nonsense.' Nor is it related to the advocation of the practice of Fascism. Of that practice by O'Duffy Yeats wrote in 1933, 'Doubtless I shall hate it (though not so much as I hate Irish democracy) ... .' And of all the references to O'Duffy in Yeats's letters, not one is notable for any mark of enthusiasm. Even Professor O'Brien admits that Yeats's (wildly inaccurate) description of De Valera as a Fascist is difficult to reconcile with pro-Fascism and opposition to De Valera. (The translation of the title of De Valera's party, Fianna Fail, as 'Soldiers of Destiny' and the dark clothes favoured by its leaders gave rise to similar impressions outside Ireland in 1933.) All this in fact indicates the bedrock of historical determinism (an emotionally neutral attitude of mind) lying beneath Yeats's political views at this time. The disappointment of his Utopian dreams for Ireland made him bitterly disillusioned with the forms of Irish democracy, but his attitude to what he saw as the coming force was far from unambiguously favourable. □

(Patrick Cosgrave, 'Yeats, Fascism and Conor O'Brien', 1967)[26]

This ambiguous attitude towards the future of both Ireland and Europe, argues Cosgrave, is even more pronounced in Yeats' poetry than it is in his prose, particularly in poems such as 'The Second Coming' and 'Under Ben Bulben'. Cosgrave suggests that when everything Yeats wrote is taken into consideration – as well as the proper historical research on figures like O'Leary, O'Higgins and O'Duffy – it becomes clear that Yeats had only two significant political concerns throughout his life: the first was Irish nationalism and the second was his desire for a government in Dublin that would function as a patron of the arts, not only for individual poets and other artists but for national theatres and museums. Much of his despair and desperation in the thirties, says Cosgrave, can be explained by the failure of the Irish Free State to do just that. O'Brien may feel that Yeats' fascism has been overlooked by scholars for fear of what they may find, but it is O'Brien who has overlooked the historical facts themselves.

It was not until the early 1980s that book-length studies on the subject of Yeats and politics began to appear and, as Grattan Freyer noted in one of those books, *W.B. Yeats and the Anti-Democratic Tradition* (1981), almost all the essential essays on this subject up to that point had been hostile. The real hostility began, of course, with Orwell, whose unshakeable belief in democratic society slowly progressing towards full egalitarianism was bound to clash with Yeats' belief that, with another spin of the gyres, a benevolent aristocracy would rule once more. This whimsical Irish poet was almost certain to rub that most practical of English novelists the wrong way. In fact, Freyer argues that rubbing readers the wrong way was the whole point of Yeats' last writings on politics, particularly those pieces published after his death as *On the Boiler*. While O'Brien had called Yeats a political opportunist, Freyer suggests that these writings were a wholly personal harangue, with Yeats fully aware of just how unpopular they would prove. Yeats knew that even close friends would be upset by what he wrote in them and, in the spirit of a mad old man, relished the thought. The original plan was to publish these ramblings twice a year in the form of a periodical, taking its title from Yeats' childhood memory of a crazy ship's carpenter who had the habit of using an old boiler as his soapbox down by the

Sligo docks. Although the poems Yeats wrote following the death of Parnell and the Easter Rising might have been a touch more opportunist than these last writings were, Freyer still does not think that the tag fits, nor does he accept O'Brien's argument that the goal of either Yeats or the Blueshirts was a fascist dictatorship in Ireland:

■ O'Brien's essay was a broadside attack on two fronts. The first charge is that the poet was a political opportunist. In O'Brien's view, Yeats was not, as he wished to suggest in a much-quoted poem, 'A foolish passionate man' ['A Prayer for Old Age'], but 'something much more interesting: a cunning passionate man'. The second charge is that, in his political involvements, Yeats was explicitly pro-fascist. We must examine each of these concepts in turn.

O'Brien cites in evidence on the first count the short poem *Mourn – And Then Onward!*, which Yeats wrote on the day of Parnell's death and ... took round immediately to the offices of the old Parnellite paper, *United Ireland*, in which it appeared on 10 October 1891 among the first of several poetic tributes to the lost leader. Yeats was twenty-six at the time, and he wrote with some complacency to his sister in London that the poem had been a success. In fact, as he soon realised, since he never reprinted it, it was an incredibly tawdry effort. Yeats was not a disciple of Parnell at that time. Almost certainly, he shared his father's view that Parnell was inferior to Butt. [The barrister, politician and novelist Isaac Butt (1813–79) founded both the Home Government Association and the Home Rule League. Parnell replaced him as MP for Limerick and leader of the nationalist parliamentary party.] But Yeats and Parnell had a common enemy: the priest's mob. Yeats noted with elation the anti-clericalism of many of the banners carried at the funeral and of tributes at the graveside.

It seems a little hard to interpret this episode, as O'Brien does, as a bid by Yeats 'by bringing poetry into the political vacuum left by Parnell's death, to become as a poet something like what Parnell had been in politics: a virtual dictator in Ireland: a power, and sometimes an arbiter in England'. Yeats was already pushing his way as an intellectual leader, but his subsequent encouragement of the very different talents of Synge and then Joyce suggests that the role he envisaged was that of first among equals, rather than dictator.

When O'Brien moves on to the 1916 period, the charge of opportunism appears nearer substantiation. Yeats wrote the vigorous vindication of *Easter 1916* under the emotional impact of the Rising. He printed twenty-five copies later that year for private circulation only, and he chose not to include it in either the Cuala Press collection, *The Wild Swans at Coole*, in 1917 or in the general Macmillan edition of 1919. It was released to the general public only in 1920, when it appeared simultaneously in the London *New Statesman* and the New York *Dial*. It does seem possible that Yeats delayed publication out of a prudent wish not to alienate English friends. Publication even in 1920, however, when the outcome of the Black and Tan war in Ireland was still uncertain, was a defiant indication of which side his sympathies lay. After his first anguish and anger at the fate of the 1916 leaders, he fell into a curious indolence, almost indifference, with regard to politics. Both Lady Gregory and Maud Gonne remarked on this, the latter with some scorn. It seems that personal preoccupations – his renewed courtship first of Maud, then of Iseult – account for this. We must remember, however, that in 1917 Yeats was working on the uncompromisingly nationalist play, *The Dreaming of the Bones*, which he did offer, unsuccessfully, for immediate publication.

The second part of O'Brien's essay, based on Yeats's letters and Senate speeches, parallels the account given in earlier chapters [of Freyer's book] of the poet's involvement in the politics of the Irish Free State. Where the viewpoint differs is in suggesting that first O'Higgins, and then O'Duffy and the Blueshirt movement, aimed at full fascist-style dictatorship. O'Brien's view of O'Higgins as 'the most ruthless "strong man" of his time in Ireland' was the commonplace of republican propaganda during the 1920s and 1930s. There is no support for it in the carefully documented life of O'Higgins by Terence de Vere White, published in 1948, nor in the *Official Report* of O'Higgins's speeches in Dail Eireann. O'Higgins, like other members of the first Cosgrave government, felt driven to desperate actions by desperate times. In private he deplored them. There is a certain irony in the fact that just a decade after the publication of this essay, O'Brien found himself a member of another Cosgrave's government [headed by William Thomas Cosgrave's son, Liam Cosgrave (born 1920), who was Taoiseach 1973–77] which, in far less threatening times, felt it again necessary to revoke many of the safeguards of civil liberties and to resolve not to yield to the blackmail of the hunger-striker.

There is no evidence to suggest the Blueshirt movement was a concerted bid for a fascist dictatorship. It has already been pointed out that the origin of the movement was to protect freedom of speech, which was being thwarted by the then IRA. If the Free State politicians who supported the Blueshirts had wished to overthrow parliamentary government in Ireland, they would surely have staged their *coup d'état* when they were defeated at the polls a few years earlier. They then held control of the army, and had O'Duffy as head of the police. Yeats certainly wished for authoritarian government, but he dreamed of the eighteenth-century elitism. He became disillusioned with practical politics when he realised the only likely replacement of parliamentarianism in Ireland would be by a clerical autocracy. O'Brien claimed he would rapidly have become 'reillusioned' if an effective fascist leader had emerged. We must leave that an open question. □

(Grattan Freyer, *W.B. Yeats and the Anti-Democratic Tradition*, 1981)[27]

What is clear is that Yeats became disillusioned with fascist politics faster than some others did, perhaps partly because of his experience with the Blueshirts in Ireland, and that many writers and politicians who supported Mussolini before the war swiftly switched sides once the bombing began. Neville Chamberlain (1869–1940), Winston Churchill (1874–1965) and Lloyd George all switched sides when they began to see Mussolini as a threat to the traditional balance of power in Europe and even Wyndham Lewis recanted his earlier writings in praise of Hitler from the safety of Canada. Only Ezra Pound hung on until the bitter end, paying for that continued support by being put into a cage at the conclusion of the war and accused of treason by the American government. However, Freyer suggests that Yeats would probably have been as disillusioned with fascism during the war as he was in the years just before it:

■ We must hazard a guess that it is unlikely that the outbreak of the Second World War would have occasioned any modification of Yeats's views. He had remained indifferent to the general hysteria which greeted the outbreak of the 1914 war. His letters to Ethel Mannin show him watching with equal impartiality the lead-up to that of 1939. The poem he worked on and completed a week before he died, *The Black Tower*, was probably his most enigmatic ever. We have the word of Mrs Yeats, reported by G.B. Saul, that the subject is 'political propaganda'. We have her testimony also that Yeats was preoccupied towards the end of his life with the dilemma of Christian belief. It seems probable the line

   Those banners come to bribe or threaten

refers equally to the advances of fascism in Europe, to Ethel Mannin's anti-fascist arguments, and to Christian apologetics. In any case, the standpoint of the poem is that all such blandishments are rigorously defied. *On the Boiler* makes clear that Yeats would have endorsed firmly de Valera's action in declaring Irish neutrality and preparing to defend Ireland against all comers. Yeats had advocated the building of armed forces ready 'to throw back from our shores the disciplined uneducated masses of the commercial nations', and in general he welcomed the approach of war as offering occasion, as the Irish troubles of twenty years back had, for able, courageous men to move to the fore.

   In any case we have seen that his practical interest in fascism had already waned. He could hardly have foreseen that Mussolini's final period would prove as buffoonish as that of General O'Duffy, and his end more sordid, but it had been less Mussolini's person than the political organisation and cultural aspects of the regime which attracted him. He never visited Nazi Germany. His library contained some works on the German youth movement, and he found aspects of German race philosophy interesting, notably a law passed by the Nazis to allow landed estates which had passed to the hands of 'non-Aryans' to be returned to their earlier owners.

But there is no trace of anti-semitism anywhere in Yeats's writings, a noteworthy omission when one remembers that two of his closest friends in later years, Oliver St John Gogarty and Ezra Pound, were outspokenly anti-semitic. He did believe in racial characteristics. Celts in general, he felt, were more imaginative and artistic than their pragmatically-minded neighbours. Further, he believed the small section of the Irish race to which he himself belonged, that of the former Protestant ascendancy, had virtues of pride and independent judgment out of all proportion to their numbers. As Conor Cruise O'Brien pointed out, his attitude here was akin to that of a caste-loyalty. But he did not despise Catholic Irishmen as such. From early youth he had admired the simple country-men of Sligo and Galway, believing their way of life enshrined a wisdom which the more affluent classes had stifled. Subsequently, he hated the rising Catholic middle-class democracy which he witnessed rejecting the Lane pictures and pillorying Synge. But he believed history would repair these shortcomings and provide Catholic names in the mould of Kevin O'Higgins to fill out the great tradition. □

(Grattan Freyer, *W.B. Yeats and the Anti-Democratic Tradition*, 1981)[28]

And it is precisely that great Irish tradition that Freyer believes was Yeats' concern from the beginning of his literary career to its end, suggesting once again that, when it comes to politics, he was essentially a national-ist, not a fascist. He may have welcomed violence, but only as part of the inevitable historical cycle that would bring about the benevolent rule of the best educated few for the benefit of the many, not fascist dictatorship. In order to imagine this new Irish society, argues Freyer, Yeats looked to England for some of those things he wanted it to ignore just as he looked to eighteenth-century Ireland and to pre-war Italy for some of those things he wanted it to imitate. Freyer says that other Irishmen and women may have imagined other Irelands, but Yeats' Ireland was far from the sort of fascist society that led to the gas ovens.

Published the same year as Freyer's book, Elizabeth Cullingford's *Yeats, Ireland and Fascism* was also largely a response to O'Brien's nagging essay, though she argued that not only was Yeats a nationalist rather than a fascist, but he was a left-wing not a right-wing nationalist. Yeats was a student of the school of O'Leary and that school taught a respect for tradition not racial pride, the sort of nationalism that Giuseppe Mazzini (1805–72) wanted for Italy and not the sort of nationalism that Hitler wanted for Germany. Yeats' lessons on nationalism had also been significantly influenced by the socialism of William Morris, which Cullingford suggests helps to explain such later public stances as his sup-port for the workers during the Dublin lock out, stances that have sometimes baffled those critics who insist on seeing Yeats as a budding fascist. Even those Anglo-Irish with whom Yeats chose to identify himself were almost always of a left-wing nationalist or republican persuasion, with both Lady Gregory and Yeats supporting the redistribution of land in the west of Ireland. But his sympathies for the politics of the left only went so far and, when the disgruntled losers of the civil war took control of the government in 1932 under de Valera, Yeats was afraid those old revolutionaries would side with revolutionaries elsewhere in Europe, bringing communism (and probably anarchy) to Ireland. Yeats may have disliked democracy, but he disliked communism even more and, in the thirties, fascism was the official opposition to bolshevism. However, Cullingford argues that Yeats' brief fascination with fascism can be better understood in an Irish than a European context:

■ Irish fascism, indeed, was always far more Irish than fascist. The Blueshirts began as the Army Comrades Association, a friendly society for ex-members of the Free State Army founded in February 1932. The ACA feared that De Valera would not prove well disposed to an army which had loyally supported Cosgrave, and were further worried by IRA threats against the 'betrayers of the Republic'. Armed with the slogan, 'No free speech for traitors', the IRA took to breaking up Cumann na nGaedheal [Party of the Irish] meetings. In August 1932 T.F. O'Higgins, leader of the ACA, announced the formation of a volunteer force to protect the freedom of speech. He also took the opportunity of stating that the ACA was opposed to communism: a dig at the IRA, who were popularly suspected of Marxist tendencies. *An Phoblacht* [*Republican News*], the left-wing newspaper, instantly responded by calling the ACA 'fascist'. Thus, although the ACA continually proclaimed their independence from party politics, the polarization was clear: the IRA was Republican and supposedly communist, while the ACA was Treatyite and supposedly fascist. Despite the fact that the ACA did develop outward similarities with continental fascism – shirts, salutes, drill – the Irish label had more validity than the international one.

The ACA volunteer force grew rapidly: by autumn 1932 it claimed 30,000 members. It provided bodyguards on request for political meetings; technically for any party, actually for Cumann na nGaedheal and the new Centre Party. Although they masqueraded as the guardians of law and order, their presence was naturally provocative, and violent clashes between the ACA and IRA or Fianna Fáil supporters grew increasingly frequent towards the end of 1932. Resumption of civil strife seemed a real possibility.

Yeats, who was away in America from October 1932 to January 1933, missed the period of the ACA's spectacular expansion and the worst of the violent clashes. At first he attached little importance to the ACA, whom he saw simply as a group of bodyguards, without significant ideological direction. Not until July 1933 did he take any active interest in them. His attention was focused upon the threat of communism in Ireland.

Most historians agree that this threat was never very real, although 'communist' was a favourite term of abuse in the Dublin of the thirties. Yeats never suspected either De Valera or Fianna Fáil of such tendencies, but the IRA and fringe groups such as Saor Eire [Free Ireland] did provide some justification of his fears. To Yeats's unconcealed delight the leader of Saor Eire, Peadar O'Donnell [1893–1987], came in secret to offer him a play for the Abbey. Yeats wrote: 'He is the head of the most extreme of all Irish organizations and of course my bitter opponent politically ... . But I have told you enough of the Irish political underworld, the strange gallery I and mine play our part before.'[29] Yeats's thirst for drama and involvement kept him in touch with the Irish political underworld: what he found there convinced him that there was indeed some danger of the extension of communist influence.

The sensation of crisis was intensified by a serious new development: the increasing alienation from the Government of its erstwhile supporters, the IRA. De Valera showed himself determined to keep their illegal activities in check, and they were soon openly hostile to Fianna Fáil. Conservative onlookers therefore feared an IRA-based and communist-oriented coup. Added to this was the chaos caused by the economic war with England. Yeats respected both De Valera's intransigence towards the British and his refusal to compromise with the IRA. He wrote: 'This country is exciting. I am told that De Valera has said in private that within three years he will be torn in pieces. It reminds me of a saying by O'Higgins to his wife, "Nobody can expect to live who has done what I have."'[30] However, if De Valera were to be 'torn in pieces' by the IRA, communism might gain a foothold in Ireland. In March 1933 an hysterical wave of anti-communist feeling swept Dublin. Early in April Yeats wrote: 'At the moment I am trying in association with [an] ex-cabinet minister, an eminent lawyer, and a philosopher, to work out a social theory which can be used against Communism in Ireland – what looks like emerging is Fascism modified by religion.'[31] Tantalizingly, Yeats fails to mention the specific modifications he desires: a fascism truly modified by religion would not be fascism at all. However, since Yeats took the essentials of fascism to be order, hierarchy, discipline, devotion to culture, and the rule of the most educated, the addition of religion would have produced the Toryism of an Eliot rather than the Catholic dictatorship of a [Francisco] Franco [1892–1975].

Among the participants in these discussions was an ACA organizer, Yeats's old friend Captain Dermot MacManus, who in June 1933 drew his attention to the Blueshirts as a force which might dedicate itself to hierarchical principles and unity of culture, and which was already opposed to communism. The Blueshirts were making their own way towards fascism without any assistance from Yeats, but he liked to think that he had provided the fascist impetus himself:

> Capt. Macmanus ... his head full of vague Fascism, got probably from me, decided that Gen[eral] O'Duffy should be made leader of a body

of young men formed to keep meetings from being broken up. He put into O'Duffy's head – he describes him as a 'simple peasant' – Fascist ideas and started him off to organise that body of young men.[32]

But Yeats was not as near to the centre of things as he supposed. Although a personal friend of T.F. O'Higgins, MacManus was not particularly prominent in the Blueshirts, and himself disclaims all responsibility for the choice of O'Duffy. Yeats was friendly with both Desmond Fitzgerald [1888–1947] and Ernest Blythe [1889–1975], ex-ministers of the Cosgrave Government now active in the Blueshirts, but he was close to sources of information rather than power.

The intensity of Yeats's excitement about the Blueshirts, which was matched only by its brevity, stemmed partly from the general hysteria in Dublin in the months of June, July and August 1933. In February 1934, when the fever had entirely cooled, Yeats apologized for his temporary aberration:

> In politics I have one passion and one thought, rancour against all who, except under the most dire necessity, disturb public order, a conviction that public order cannot long persist without the rule of educated and able men ... . Some months ago that passion laid hold upon me with the violence which unfits the poet for all politics but his own. While the mood lasted, it seemed that our growing disorder, the fanaticism that inflamed it like some old bullet imbedded in the flesh, was about to turn our noble history into an ignoble farce.[33]

De Valera's feud with the IRA seemed to Yeats the major cause of unrest. That 'old bullet imbedded in the flesh', legacy of the Civil War, was about to invalidate all the heroic sacrifices made previously in the name of Irish freedom. Not realizing that the Blueshirts themselves were also essentially a legacy of the Civil War, nor that their activities had considerably increased the growing disorder, Yeats turned to them as a force above party politics which might help to subdue old antagonisms and promote unity:

> When nations are empty up there at the top,
> When order has weakened or faction is strong,
> Time for us all to pick out a good tune,
> Take to the roads and go marching along.
>
> ['Three Songs to the Same Tune']

Yeats later realized that to be 'rioters in the cause of peace'[34] is a contradiction in terms, and that marching feet produce not order but more marching feet. At the time, however, he gave his excitement full rein. There is a tone of flamboyant bravado about his letters during these three months that indicates that the mood was too extravagant to last long.

On 13 July, a week before O'Duffy took over the leadership of the Blueshirts, Yeats wrote:

> Politics are growing heroic. De Valera has forced political thought to face the most fundamental issues. A Fascist opposition is forming behind the scenes to be ready should some tragic situation develop. I find myself constantly urging the despotic rule of the educated classes as the only end to our troubles.[35]

The 'Fascist opposition', Yeats thought, was to act only if the IRA brought off their coup. 'If the I.R.A. attempts to seize power (& MacManus believes they will but I do not) or if the economic war brings chaos, then democratic politics will be discredited in this country & a substitute will have to be found.'[36] Yeats's advocacy of his substitute, the despotic rule of the educated classes, must be seen in the context of civil disorder, fears about communism and the IRA, and economic breakdown. Yeats himself was not planning a coup, but wondering how to salvage an already chaotic situation. Like his early advocacy of 'authority' in the aftermath of the Civil War, his enthusiasm for 'despotism' was a response to Irish violence.

The Blueshirts were not, in any case, likely to promote the rule of the educated classes, nor indeed, any of Yeats's cherished ideals. Although Yeats knew this well enough, MacManus persuaded him that the party had potential. It is difficult to envisage the rank and file Blueshirts, mostly uneducated thugs, as the servants of unity of culture, but Diarmuid Brennan recalls that Yeats

> insisted there could be no boundary to the advance of a nation once its intellectual forces were properly harnessed.
>
> But how, I wondered, could a dream of cultural fusion be achieved other than by governmental power.
>
> 'By militants', he said; and he said it so passionately a look of youngness transformed his face. 'By marching men'.[37]

At no time were the Blueshirts animated by 'a dream of cultural fusion', but Yeats was too excited to notice such details, though even at the height of his enthusiasm there is evident a touch of ironic self-mockery. On 13 July, some days before his first meeting with O'Duffy, he wrote:

> It is amusing to live in a country where men will always act. Where nobody is satisfied with thought. There is so little in our stocking that we are ready at any moment to turn it inside out, and how can we not feel emulous when we see Hitler juggling with his sausage of stocking. Our chosen colour is blue, and blue shirts are marching about all over the country ... . The chance of being shot is raising everybody's spirits enormously.[38]

Yeats had created for himself a fantasy world of action, drama, and self-aggrandizement, centred on the idea of the Blueshirts. For the first and only time he identified himself with them, speaking of 'our' chosen colour. But apart from MacManus and the two ex-ministers he had never met a grass-roots Blueshirt. His encounter with General O'Duffy on 24 July did something to dispel his illusions.

MacManus brought O'Duffy to see Yeats so that he could 'talk my anti-democratic philosophy. I was ready, for I had just re-written for the seventh time the part of *A Vision* that deals with the future.'[39] Yeats had cast O'Duffy, as he had already cast Mussolini, as an antithetical hero. Mussolini survived in Yeats's imagination because he had never seen the reality, but contact with a home-made Mussolini sowed the first seeds of doubt. Yeats treated O'Duffy to a disquisition on his *Vision*-based philosophy:

> Talk went in the usual line: the organized party directed from above. Each district dominated through its ablest men. My own principle is that every government is a tyranny that is not a government by the educated classes and that the state must be hierarchical throughout ... . I urged the getting of a recent 3 volume description of the Italian system (Fitzgerald talks of it) & putting some Italian scholars to make a condensation of it. I urged also that unless a revolutionary crisis arose they must make no intervention. They should prepare themselves by study to act without hesitation should the crisis arise. Then, & then only, their full program. I talked the 'historical dialectic,' spoke of it as proving itself by events as the curvature of space was proved (after mathematicians had worked it out) by observation during an eclipse. O'Duffy probably brought here that I might talk of it.[40]

MacManus, who says that he had indeed envisaged Yeats as the philosopher of the movement, admits that the project was hopeless. After this meeting both men were hysterical with laughter. O'Duffy understood not a word of Yeats's rhetoric, and Yeats called O'Duffy an uneducated lunatic. The encounter revealed to him that fascism, though desirable in comparison with democracy, might not be so aristocratic and cultured after all: 'Italy, Poland, Germany, then perhaps Ireland. Doubtless I shall hate it (though not so much as I hate Irish democracy) but it is September and we must not behave like the gay young sparks of May or June.'[41] Not until he met a real Irish fascist did he begin to think that he might hate fascism. Hannah Arendt [1906–75] writes: 'There is an abyss between the men of brilliant and facile conceptions and the men of brutal deeds ... which no intellectual explanation is able to bridge.'[42] Yeats faced O'Duffy across that abyss. □

(Elizabeth Cullingford, *Yeats, Ireland and Fascism*, 1981)[43]

While O'Brien argued that the Blueshirts began to fall apart when de Valera banned their march through Dublin in August 1933, Cullingford suggests that they simply responded by becoming more overtly political. Yeats had hoped they were above the party politics that had plagued

Ireland ever since the civil war, but he was soon disabused of this notion when O'Duffy became leader of the newly formed Fine Gael party in September, a merger between Cumann na nGaedheal and the Centre Party that made it clear, even to Yeats, just whose side they were on. When Yeats first published the three marching songs he wrote for the movement as 'Three Songs to the Same Tune' in the *Spectator* in February 1934, he attached a long note disassociating himself from the Blueshirts. O'Brien saw this disassociation as Yeats' attempt to abandon a sinking ship, but Cullingford cites political historians who argue that the Blueshirts had become more popular in Ireland by this time not less, winning the support of the farmers and fighting openly with the IRA. In any case, Cullingford seems more than a bit surprised that such a minor flirtation with fascism has become the single political fact of Yeats' life that everyone seems to know, especially since it did not last longer than the summer of 1933 and existed for the most part in the mind of the poet himself.

Long responses to O'Brien's essay were still being published in the late 1980s. In his book *Yeats and Politics in the 1930s* (1988), Paul Scott Stanfield agrees with Cullingford that Yeats did not turn his back on the Blueshirts because he saw them as a bunch of losers with no hope of success in Ireland, as O'Brien had suggested, but because of their absorption into a popular political party. While Cullingford argued that it was this descent into the old battles of party politics that had disillusioned Yeats in the autumn of 1933, Stanfield believes it was the democratisation of the movement itself that upset him. In fact, it was the democratisation of nationalism that had disillusioned Yeats with Irish politics in the first place, as he always wanted that movement to be led by an educated elite not public mandate. When it was decided under de Valera's government that senators should be elected rather than appointed for their specialist knowledge and abilities, as Yeats had been, it seemed that this democratisation was all but complete. It was not that Yeats was not fascist enough or violent enough to be a proper Blueshirt, says Stanfield, but that the Blueshirts were not anti-democratic enough for Yeats:

■ Conor Cruise O'Brien has argued that Yeats withdrew from the Blueshirts because, by February 1934, they 'were beginning to look a little silly' and had 'proved a flop'. Yeats, being 'no lover of hopeless causes', severed his ties to the moribund organisation.[44] However persuasive one finds O'Brien's perceptive and informed essay, which twenty years after its writing remains the best single effort on the subject of Yeats's politics, one has to pull up at this. The man who wooed Maud Gonne, tried to revive the poetic drama, battled the Irish Catholic Church over divorce, sang the greatness of the vanishing Protestant Ascendancy, wrote 'The Two Titans' at the beginning and 'The Black Tower' at the end of his career, no lover of hopeless causes? Yeats loved hopeless causes to distraction. If the Blueshirts had represented what he wished them to represent, he would have been prouder of his association with them with every setback they suffered. It was in September 1933, when the Blueshirts had arrived as near as they ever would to ordinary political success, and long before they had been embarrassed by name changes, legal squabbles, electoral defeats and O'Duffy's erratic leadership, that Yeats became capable of irony about them.

Many have followed T.R. Henn in arguing that while Yeats, like others of his time, may have thought that 'the discipline of fascist theory might impose order upon a disintegrating world', certainly 'nothing could be farther from Yeats's mind than its violent and suppressive practice'.[45] Yeats's attitude towards political violence was not so simple as this. Certainly, in 'Nineteen Hundred and Nineteen', in 'The Stare's Nest at my Window' and in 'Reprisals' he drew its terrors as well as anyone ever has. However, violence did not make him queasy, he did not believe mankind would ever be able to do without it, and he believed governments could legitimately employ it. He took pains to free himself of every kind of cant about violence, and so often appeared to speak of it with unnecessary relish. We can say he was merely being outrageous when, during the Civil War, he was asked by an English statesman whether he supported Cosgrave and answered, 'Oh, I support the gunmen – on both sides.'[46] We can say he was merely dealing in metaphysics when he startled an interviewer by picking up Sato's sword, swinging it over his head, and crying, 'Conflict! More conflict!'[47] We can say he was merely speaking from a poetic persona when he wrote 'a good strong cause and blows are delight' ['Three Marching Songs'] or the third section of 'Under Ben Bulben'.[48] We can even say he was merely fantasising when he predicted a civil war in the near future between the 'educated classes' and the 'uneducatable masses', with 'the victory of the skilful, riding their machines as did the feudal knights their armoured horses'.[49] At other times, however, he addressed the problem more plainly and more seriously.

> If human violence is not embodied in our institutions the young will not give them their affection, nor the young and old their loyalty. A government is legitimate because some instinct has compelled us to give it the right to take life in defence of its laws and its shores.[50]

So Yeats argued in 1938, and so he had argued in 1930:

> Much of the emotional energy in our civil war came from the indignant denial of the right of the State, as at present established, to take life in its own defence, whether by arms or by process of law, and that right is still denounced by a powerful minority. Only when all permit the State to demand the voluntary or involuntary sacrifice of its citizens' lives will

Ireland possess that moral unity to which England, according to Coleridge, owes so large a part of its greatness.[51]

Yeats went so far as to base the legitimacy of the Free State not on (as Free State spokesmen preferred to maintain) its having won a democratic election, but on its having passed 'the only effective test: it has been permitted to take life'.[52] That Yeats defended in principle and practice the Free State's incarceration and execution of its political enemies by no means implies that he would have looked tolerantly upon what took place in Germany and Russia. It does show, though, that we are presumptuous in thinking he must have shared our dislike for the Blueshirts' tactics.

In the 1930s, we ought to remember, people occupied with politics took force and violence for granted, whether their allegiance was to right, left or centre. The liberal E.M. Forster disliked violence intensely, but by 1939 felt compelled to admit that 'all society rests upon force', that force was 'the ultimate reality on this earth', that violence was the 'major partner' in the 'muddled establishment' of human violence and human creativity.[53] When the young Stephen Spender, on first meeting T.S. Eliot, asked for an opinion on 'the future of Western civilisation', Eliot 'indicated ... there was no future "except" – I remember the phrase because I did not quite understand it – "internecine conflict". I asked him what exactly he meant by this, and he said: "People killing one another in the streets."'[54] In the catalogue of duties dictated by the needs of the hour in 'Spain 1937', Auden included 'the deliberate increase in the chances of death' and 'the conscious acceptance of guilt in the necessary murder' along with 'the expending of powers / On the flat ephemeral pamphlet and the boring meeting'.[55] George Orwell objected to what he considered the intellectual's pose in the matter-of-factness of these lines, saying, 'It could only be written by a person to whom murder is at most a *word*.'[56] Orwell himself, though, in a review of Arthur Koestler's [1905–83] *Spanish Testament* [1937], had written, 'The only apparent alternatives are to smash dwelling houses to powder, blow out human entrails and burn holes in children with lumps of thermite, or to be enslaved by people who are more ready to do these things than you are yourself; as yet no one has suggested a practicable way out.'[57] George Watson [born 1927], in his *Politics and Literature in Modern Britain* [1977], has gathered example upon example of intelligent leftist Englishmen out-doing each other in steely-eyed pragmatism as they explain the necessity of the Stalinist purges.[58] Yeats was only one of many to conclude that politics could not be divorced from violence, and though he did not encourage the violent tendencies of the Blueshirts, if we are to judge from the advice he gave O'Duffy, it is not likely that those tendencies repelled him. At the time he became interested in the group, it had made what reputation it possessed by cracking heads and was given to boasting of its 'strong hands and stout sticks'.[59] In a letter to

Olivia Shakespear Yeats mentions that 'The chance of being shot is raising everybody's spirits enormously.'[60] After he had abandoned his hopes for the Blueshirts, still hoping that some party might yet transform Ireland, he wrote:

> If any Government or party undertake this work it will need force, marching men (the logic of fanaticism, whether in a woman or a mob is drawn from a premise protected by ignorance and therefore irrefutable); it will promise not this or that measure but a discipline, a way of life ... .[61]

Once again Yeats expresses his preference of the strength derived from obeying a self-created, self-imposed code to the strength derived from obeying the dictates of a 'mechanically' produced argument. Besides that, he says as plainly as possible that the one kind of strength will not triumph over the other without using force. It was not, then, the cracking of heads that did the most to dissuade Yeats from his belief that the Blueshirts were the party of his hopes.

It has been much more pertinently suggested that Yeats ended by detecting a democratic bias in the Blueshirts, by seeing in those who would impose order on the mob the worst traits of the mob – the theme of the short poem 'Church and State'. In 1947, Grattan Freyer wrote that Yeats eventually saw in both Italian and German fascism 'indications of a faith in numbers, an uncritical emphasis on quantity irrespective of quality, even cruder than that which he despised under democracy'.[62] In the 1960s Donald Torchiana made much the same point, with especial reference to the Blueshirts, when he described the differences between Yeats's ideal of a modern Grattan's Parliament and 'the grubby, thick-witted pomposities of over 100,000 marching farmers, firebrands, backwater attorneys, auctioneers, and disgruntled merchants, who looked to an uninspiring megalomaniac for their leadership'.[63] In 1981, Grattan Freyer added that Yeats 'dreamed of the eighteenth-century elitism' and fell away from the Blueshirts when he saw they represented only 'clerical autocracy'.[64] As the way I have approached the topic shows, I too believe this was the case. To say Yeats looked for eighteenth-century virtues in the Blueshirts, however, is to portray him as somewhat more naïve than he was. Moreover, it leaves the door open for such mistaken conclusions as those of George Watson, who has written that 'fascism was too vulgar a phenomenon to attract Yeats consistently and for long. Snobbery, that supreme discriminator, always held him back where the fervour of political conviction might have pressed him onwards into final commitment.'[65] Yeats did not begin by thinking fascism a modern version of aristocracy and end by thinking it mob rule. Rather, he began by thinking it the stage succeeding communism in the breaking-up of democracy, and ended by thinking it the last, hysterical constriction of democracy, a finale rather than a prelude. □

(Paul Scott Stanfield, *Yeats and Politics in the 1930s*, 1988)[66]

Drawing upon some unpublished prose by Yeats written in the spring and summer of 1933, Stanfield notes that the poet was already coming to the conclusion that Irish fascism would never be anything like Italian fascism, since O'Duffy's power was not coming from within himself but from without. This conclusion was confirmed, of course, when O'Duffy accepted the leadership of the Fine Gael party, making himself subject not only to the whims of the Irish people but, much more worrying for Yeats, to the whims of the Catholic Church. For Yeats, proper government would resemble the old appointed senate more than it would the new elected senate, with senators making their decisions to please their own personal standards and not the public standards of those who merely put them and perhaps kept them there.

In an essay first published as a pamphlet by the Field Day Theatre Company the same year as Stanfield's book, Edward Said also notes that Yeats' attitude towards political violence was far from squeamish. But Said sees this violence as an inevitable part of the anti-imperialist process, not an excuse for fascism. Taking a postcolonial view of his poetry, Said says that Yeats was clearly an Irish revivalist and a European modernist, but he also belongs to the global tradition of 'the great nationalist artists of decolonization and revolutionary nationalism' that includes Aimé Césaire (born 1913), Mahmud Darwish (born 1941), Faiz Ahmad Faiz (1914–78), Pablo Neruda (1904–73), Leopold Sedar Senghor (1906–2001), Rabindranath Tagore and César Vallejo (1892–1938). Although Said concedes that many may not consider Yeats to be a card-carrying member of this particular club, he argues that Yeats' nationalism also served an anti-imperialist purpose, beginning where all postcolonial cultures do with an attempt to redefine Ireland against the imposing imperial power but eventually moving towards a postnationalist way of thinking that involves neither Ireland as it has been nor Irishness. For Said, this is the moment of liberation, when something absolutely unexpected is glimpsed that defies both the old colonial definitions and the new postcolonial redefinitions. These moments are almost always violent and their consequences far from certain, which is why Said suggests some readers of Yeats' poetry think that Yeats is on their side against the revolution, while others think that he is on theirs, welcoming the violence as the birth of at least something different from what was there before:

■ In the first volume of his memoirs Neruda speaks of a writer's congress in Madrid held in 1937 in defense of the Republic. 'Priceless replies' to the invitations 'poured in from all over. One was from Yeats, Ireland's national poet; another, from Selma Lagerlöf [1858–1940], the notable Swedish writer. They were both too old to travel to a beleaguered city like Madrid, which was steadily being pounded by bombs, but they rallied to the defense of the Spanish Republic' (*Memoirs*, 130). This passage comes as a surprise to someone who like myself had once been influenced by Conor Cruise O'Brien's famous account of Yeats's politics, an essay whose claims are, it seems to me, hopelessly inadequate when contrasted with the information and analysis put forward by Elizabeth Cullingford's *Yeats, Ireland and Fascism* (which also refers to the Neruda recollection). Just as Neruda saw no difficulty in thinking of himself as a poet who dealt both with internal colonialism in Chile and with external imperialism throughout Latin America, we should think of Yeats, I believe, as an Irish poet with more than strictly local Irish meaning and applications. Neruda takes him as a national poet who represents the Irish nation in its war against tyranny, and, according to Neruda, Yeats responded positively to that unmistakably antifascist call, despite his frequently cited dispositions toward European fascism.

There is a justly famous poem, 'El pueblo,' by Neruda in the 1962 collection *Plenos Poderos* (a collection translated by Alistair Reid, whose version I have used, as *Fully Empowered*). The resemblance between Neruda's poem and Yeats's 'The Fisherman' is striking, because in both poems the central figure is an anonymous man of the people, who in his strength and loneliness is also a mute expression *of* the people; and it is this quality that inspires the poet in his work. Yeats: 'It is long since I began / To call up to the eyes / This wise and simple man. / All day I'd look in the face / What I had hoped 'twould be / To write for my own race / And the reality.' Neruda:

> I knew that man, and when I could
> when I still had eyes in my head,
> when I still had a voice in my throat,
> I sought him among the tombs and I said to him,
> pressing his arm that still was not dust:
> 'Everything will pass, you will still be living.
> You set fire to life.
> You made what is yours.'
> So let no one be perturbed when
> I seem to be alone and am not alone;
> I am not without company and I speak for all.
> Someone is hearing me without knowing it,
> But those I sing of, those who know,
> go on being born and will overflow the world.[67]

The poetic calling develops out of a pact made between people and poet; hence the power of such invocations to an actual poem as those provided by the popular but silent figures both men seem to require. But the chain does not stop there, since Neruda goes on (in 'Deber del Poeta') to claim that 'through me, freedom and the sea / will call in answer to the shrouded heart,' and Yeats in 'The Tower' speaks of sending imagination forth 'and call[ing] images and memories / From ruin or from ancient trees.' Yet because such protocols of exhortation and expansiveness are announced from under the shadow of domination, we would not be wrong to connect them with the new, and perhaps even underground narrative of liberation depicted so memorably in [Frantz] Fanon's [1925–61] *Wretched of the Earth* [1961]. For whereas the divisions and separations of the colonial order freeze the population's captivity into a sullen torpor, 'new outlets ... engender aims for the violence of colonized peoples.'[68] Fanon specifies such things as declarations of human rights, clamors for free speech, trades-union demands; later, as the violent confrontation escalates, there is an entirely new history that unfolds subterraneously, as a revolutionary class of militants, drawn from the ranks of the urban poor, the outcasts, criminals, and *déclassés* [people who have fallen in social status], takes to the countryside, there slowly to form cells of armed activists, who return to the city for the final stages of the insurgency.

The extraordinary power of Fanon's writing is that it is presented as a surreptitious counternarrative to the aboveground force of the colonial regime, which in the teleology of Fanon's narrative is certain to be defeated. The difference between Fanon and Yeats is, I think, that Fanon's theoretical and perhaps even metaphysical narrative of anti-imperialist decolonization is cadenced and stressed from beginning to end with the accents and inflections of liberation. Fanon's is a discourse of that anticipated triumph, liberation, which marks the second moment of decolonization. Yeats, on the other hand, is a poet whose early work sounds the nationalist note and stands finally at the very threshold it cannot actually ever cross. Yet it is not wrong to interpret Yeats as in his poetry setting a trajectory in common with other poets of decolonization, like Neruda and Darwish, which he could not complete, even though perhaps they could go further than he did. This at least gives him credit for adumbrating the liberationist and utopian revolutionism in his poetry that had been belied, and to some extent canceled out, by his late reactionary politics.

It is interesting that Yeats has often been cited in recent years as someone whose poetry warned of nationalist excesses. He is quoted without attribution, for example, in Gary Sick's book (*All Fall Down* [1985]) on the Carter administration's handling of the Iranian hostage crisis in 1979–81; and I can distinctly recall that the *New York Times* correspondent in Beirut in 1975–76, James Markham, quotes the same passages from 'The Second Coming' in a piece he did about the onset of the Lebanese civil war in 1977. 'Things fall apart; the centre cannot hold' is one phrase. The other is 'The best lack all conviction, while the worst / Are full of passionate intensity.' Sick and Markham both write as Americans frightened of the revolutionary tide sweeping through a Third World once contained by Western power. Their use of Yeats is minatory: remain orderly, or you're doomed to a frenzy you cannot control. As to how, in an inflamed colonial situation, the colonized are supposed to remain orderly and civilized – given that the colonial order has long since profited the oppressor and has long since been discredited in the eyes of the colonized – neither Sick nor Markham tells us. They simply assume that Yeats, in any event, is on our side, *against* the revolution. It's as if both men could never have thought to take the current disorder back to the colonial intervention itself, which is what Chinua Achebe [born 1930] does in 1958, in his great novel *Things Fall Apart*.

The point, I believe, is that Yeats is at his most powerful precisely as he imagines and renders that very moment itself. His greatest decoloniz-ing works quite literally conceive of the birth of violence, or the violent birth of change, as in 'Leda and the Swan,' instants at which there is a blinding flash of simultaneity presented to his colonial eyes – the girl's rape, and alongside that, the question 'did she put on his knowledge with his power / Before the indifferent beak could let her drop?' Yeats situates himself at that juncture where the violence of change is unarguable, but where the results of the violence beseech necessary, if not always suffi-cient, reason. More precisely, Yeats's greatest theme in the poetry that culminates in *The Tower* is, so far as decolonization is concerned, how to reconcile the inevitable violence of the colonial conflict with the every-day politics of an on-going national struggle, and also how to square the power of each of the various parties in the colonial conflict, with the dis-course of reason, of persuasion, of organization, with the requirements of poetry. Yeats's prophetic perception that at some point violence cannot be enough and that the strategies of politics and reason must come into play is, to my knowledge, the first important announcement in the con-text of decolonization of the need to balance violent force with an exi-gent political and organizational process. Fanon's assertion, almost half a century later than Yeats, that the liberation cannot be accomplished simply by seizing power (though he says, 'Even the wisest man grows tense with some sort of violence' ['Under Ben Bulben']), underlines the importance of Yeats's insight. That neither Yeats nor Fanon offers a pre-scription for undertaking the transition from direct force to a period *after* decolonization when a new political order achieves moral hegemony, is part of the difficulty we live with today in Ireland, Asia, Africa, the Caribbean, Latin America, and the Middle East. □

(Edward W. Said, 'Yeats and Decolonization', 1990)[69]

For Said, Yeats took poetry in Ireland well beyond the nationalism of Davis, Mangan and Ferguson but he still stopped short of taking it to the moment of full postimperialist liberation, stuck on that threshold where he could only pose and repose the question of what was to follow all the violence. Yeats may have been a bit ahead of his time, but he still some-times thought like a colonialist where, according to Fanon, the subject sees himself as a child protected by his colonial mother not from the vio-lent outside world but from himself, whose own nature is violent and even suicidal. Said suggests that Yeats' obsession with cycles, pernes and gyres was a similar sort of protection, helping him to cope with the inevitable violence and political uncertainty of all colonial situations. Yeats may have failed to imagine a fully liberated Ireland but, for poets around the world in similar situations, he showed what a nationalist poet could do and what a postnationalist poet might be.

CONCLUSION

So where do we place Yeats, then?

In the middle of the 1960s, four of the most prominent poets writing in Ireland, England and America met for a public discussion of what had happened to poetry since the death of Yeats. Stephen Spender had probably been invited to speak for the politically engaged poets of the 1930s, although he had converted from a dedicated member of the Communist Party to an outspoken anti-communist long ago. W.D. Snodgrass (born 1926) was probably there to represent the so-called confessional poets, since critics could not resist comparing his book *Heart's Needle* (1959) to the recent publications of Robert Lowell (1917–77), Anne Sexton (1928–74) and Sylvia Plath (1932–63), even though Lowell himself perhaps more appropriately described him as 'the American Philip Larkin'. Thomas Kinsella had probably been asked to come and talk on behalf of the younger generation of Irish poets writing at that time, as well as someone who had helped revive the Cuala Press in Dublin and who was now in America working on new translations of old Irish texts like the *Táin Bó Cuailnge*. Besides being asked to join in the debate because of his reputation as an old literary rascal who could be counted on to disagree with everyone else on the panel, Patrick Kavanagh was no doubt there to speak from his own personal experience as an Irish poet writing in the massive shadow of Yeats.

Spender began the discussion by placing Yeats amongst the modernists, arguing that he belonged to that generation of poets who very deliberately decided to write great poems:

■ Someone said this afternoon that Mr. Padraic Colum [1881–1972] was the last of the dinosaurs. Of course what he meant by that was Mr. Colum belonged to the generation of the very great poets early in this century, W.B. Yeats and then later on T.S. Eliot and I would include James Joyce. We feel that since then poets are not so concentrated on trying to produce great works. There's such a thing as deliberately setting out to write great poetry. At the beginning of this century writers deliberately set out to write great works and I think one reason why they did this was that they thought they were living at a time in which their civilization was perhaps coming to an end and they were occupied in making the last great statements about this civilization.[1] □

Those statements were made in a 'language of the dead', one that allowed them to invoke the great poets of the past as well as speak for the doomed present, wringing with nostalgia. Poets since Yeats, argues Spender, have not been nearly as ambitious as the modernist poets, nor nearly as nostalgic. Instead of deliberately deciding to write great poems, they have deliberately decided not to, with a poet like Auden perfectly content to write poems about such insignificant subjects as the bathroom of his house in Austria. They may seem like minor poets in comparison to great dinosaurs like Yeats, Pound and Eliot, but you cannot be nostalgic forever.

Yeats was not an early modernist, according to Snodgrass, but the last of the symbolist poets. And it was his strict adherence to symbolist poetics that allowed him to write his great poetry of maturity and middle age, whereas almost all poets since Yeats have produced a few good early books, and the occasional good book late in life, but nothing of note in between. Even modernist poets, argues Snodgrass, had a tendency to come to certain conclusions in their middle ages, to adopt a system of belief that helped them make sense of the world around them, even though they sometimes acknowledged the difference between that system and the world itself:

> ■ Yeats's idea system, on the other hand, silly as it may look at first, does tend to correspond to the outside world. In a very odd way he became so very much like his world, like his civilization, like the ancient edifice identified with the faith that was destroying him that he has only to describe his own feelings and he describes that culture. He says, 'Why should not old men be mad?' He was, after all, a wild, old, wicked man identified with a wild, old, wicked civilization in its decay and corruption and he had something to say for it. He needs only to report his feelings – 'the best lack all conviction while the worst are full of passionate intensity' ['The Second Coming'] – and he reports the case with his culture. As he gets older he gets closer and closer to the physical, to difference, to the sharp-edged reality, where most of our poets are trying to hold themselves away from that. Besides, Yeats had a taste for confusion. It seems to me that's essential in an artist almost more than anything else. He had an ear for intolerable music. He had a tolerance for all the insane awfulness of this world as almost no one else has had since. Although he was the last of the symbolists and although he engaged as they all did in a search for stasis, for a state of being, an ecstasy which would be literally a standing out of this world, it never could satisfy him as it could some of them.[2] □

Yeats may have had his own silly system but, never forgetting the essential connection between symbolism and occultism, he never tried to impose reason upon it, always suspicious of even temporary stays against confusion. You cannot tidy up Yeats' system of belief any better than you can tidy up Shakespeare's messy plots, says Snodgrass, and any attempt to do so is to bowdlerise both of them. As middle age approached, Pound, Eliot, Stevens, Williams, Robert Frost (1874–1963) and E.E. Cummings (1894–1962) all opted for a belief in something that brought order to a disorderly world, but not Yeats.

Unconvinced by either Spender or Snodgrass, Kinsella suggests that Yeats was not an early modernist or a late symbolist, but the last romantic poet. Clearly familiar with Kermode's argument that the romantic poet must suffer for his images in isolation from the rest of modern society, Kinsella argues that the future that Yeats anticipated in 'The Second Coming' has become all too true and the result is that everyone is now isolated, not just the poets:

■ Among the first of the properties to go in the destruction of the old order was the great poetic stance of romantic isolation, represented so beautifully by Yeats himself. He is the nearest to us of the great images of poetic isolation, an isolation by reference to a more or less homogeneous society of which he is not really a part. He is almost certainly the last … . After the deluge, the poet is still, naturally, isolated; but so now is every man. The repeated cruel checks to reasonable hope which the world has suffered have destroyed the cohesion of the modern social organism. The organism continues to function but the most sensitive individuals have been shaken loose into disorder, conscious of a numbness and dullness in themselves, a pain of dislocation and loss which may be the simplest meaning, the general human truth, that underlay the Romantic intuition … . Everywhere in modern writing the stress is on personal versions of the world, in which basic things are worked out repeatedly as if for the first time, and there are no fixed stars. The detailed exploration of private miseries is an expedition into the interior to find what may guide us in the future. It is out of ourselves and our wills that the chaos came, and out of ourselves that some order will have to be constructed.[3] □

If the idea of the romantic poet isolated from the rest of modern society no longer describes the situation of the poet in our postwar world, argues Kinsella, the idea of the romantic image itself may have to change. Whereas Kermode had suggested that the romantic image was intensely personal, earned by the poet in exchange for his or her exile, Kinsella wonders whether the romantic image should be something shared by everyone in his or her mutual isolation, not Yeats' rough beast slouching towards Bethlehem but our shared vision of the atomic clouds above Hiroshima and Nagasaki.

Living up to his reputation as a cantankerous old Irish poet, Kavanagh was having none of this. Not only was he bored to tears by all these arguments, but Kavanagh could not have cared less whether Yeats belonged to the modernists, the symbolists or the romantics. His only concern was to insist, as he had for years now, that Yeats was not Irish, but an English poet belonging very much to the English tradition. Quickly dismissing all the contemporary poets that had been praised by the other members of the panel, Kavanagh asserted that the only writers doing anything interesting at the present moment were the Beats, as well as, somewhat curiously, George Barker (1913–91), an English poet sometimes described as the last of the Bohemians and the youngest poet Yeats had included in the *Oxford Book of Modern Verse* back in 1936. At that point, the intended exchange of views turned into an exchange of insults, aimed either at the poets each of the panel members had put forth as potential worthy successors to Yeats or at the panel members themselves, with scattered applause from the audience. Before the discussion became an exchange of blows, the four poets decided to abandon the debate, with Kinsella proposing they all go off for a dance instead. Discussions of Yeats and his poetry are usually more polite than this, but not always. And the discussion about where we should place Yeats and to whom he properly belongs seems no more settled now than it was when these four poets met in the middle of the 1960s, with views as wide apart as ever. Although the publication of this book suggests that readers of Yeats' poetry need a guide through the occasionally overwhelming amount of criticism it has produced, this is surely a healthy sign and a clear indication that his poems will continue to be read and discussed for a long time to come.

NOTES

A Note on the Text: Whenever an excerpt from one of Yeats' poems is identified by its title, the title is taken from *The Collected Works of W.B. Yeats, Volume 1: The Poems*, 2nd edn, ed. Richard J. Finneran (New York: Scribner, 1997).

INTRODUCTION

1 These letters are cited in Richard J. Finneran, *Editing Yeats's Poems: A Reconsideration* (London: Macmillan – now Palgrave Macmillan, 1990), pp. 153–4.

2 W.B. Yeats, *The Collected Works of W.B. Yeats, Volume 3: Autobiographies*, ed. William H. O'Donnell and Douglas N. Archibald (New York: Scribner, 1999), pp. 56–8.

3 Finneran, *Editing Yeats's Poems*, p. 174.

4 Curtis Bradford, 'The Order of Yeats's *Last Poems*', *Modern Language Notes*, 76.6 (1961), 515–16.

5 Cited in Phillip L. Marcus, 'Yeats's *Last Poems*: A Reconsideration', *Yeats Annual*, 5 (1987), 4–5.

6 Bradford, 'Yeats's *Last Poems* Again' in Liam Miller (ed.), *Dolmen Press Yeats Centenary Papers*, 8 (Dublin: Dolmen, 1966), p. 261.

7 Seamus Heaney, Review of W.B. Yeats, *The Poems: A New Edition*, ed. Richard J. Finneran, and Richard J. Finneran, *Editing Yeats's Poems*, *Yeats: An Annual of Critical and Textual Studies*, 3 (1985), 263.

CHAPTER ONE

1 Cited in Richard Ellmann, *Yeats: The Man and the Masks* (London: Faber, 1961), pp. 5–6. Originally published in 1948.

2 W.B. Yeats, *Essays and Introductions* (New York: Macmillan, 1961), pp. 509–10.

3 Yeats, *The Collected Works of W.B. Yeats, Volume 3: Autobiographies*, ed. William H. O'Donnell and Douglas N. Archibald (New York: Scribner, 1999), pp. 104–5.

4 Ellmann, *Yeats*, pp. 1–2.

5 Ibid., p. 4.

6 R.F. Foster, *W.B. Yeats, A Life, Volume 1: The Apprentice Mage, 1865–1914* (Oxford: Oxford University Press, 1997), pp. xxvi–vii.

7 Foster, *W.B. Yeats, A Life, Volume 2: The Arch-Poet, 1915–1939* (Oxford: Oxford University Press, 2003), p. xx.

8 Some other very readable biographies of Yeats have also been produced as part of a series, including Augustine Martin's *W.B. Yeats*, published for the Gill's Irish Lives series in 1983, and Alasdair D.F. Macrae's *W.B. Yeats: A Literary Life*, published for the Macmillan Literary Lives series in 1995.

9 Terence Brown, *The Life of W.B. Yeats: A Critical Biography* (Dublin: Gill & Macmillan, 1999), p. 379.

10 Brenda Maddox, *George's Ghosts: A New Life of W.B. Yeats* (London: Picador, 1999), p. xix.

11 Helen Vendler, 'Lives', *Yeats Annual*, 9 (1992), 327.

CHAPTER TWO

1 W.B. Yeats, *Autobiographies*, ed. William H. O'Donnell and Douglas N. Archibald (New York: Scribner, 1999), p. 47.

2 [Ryan's note:] An Irish literary weekly, started early in the eighties, by the proprietor of the *Freeman's Journal*. James Murphy, the novelist, was its first editor. It did much to encourage young Irish writers, and for a long time was really racy of the soil.

3 [Ryan's note:] Fairies, pronounced *Shee*.

4 W.P. Ryan, *The Irish Literary Revival: Its History, Pioneers and Possibilities* (London: W.P. Ryan, 1894), pp. 132–6.

5 Ibid., p. 180.

6 Ernest A. Boyd, *Ireland's Literary Renaissance* (Dublin: Maunsel, 1916), pp. 122–3.

7 Ibid., pp. 126–8.

8 This poem is now better known by its revised title, 'To Ireland in the Coming Times'.

9 Boyd, *Literary Renaissance*, pp. 132–5.

10 Patrick Kavanagh, *Collected Prose* (London: MacGibbon and Kee, 1967), p. 13.

11 Ibid., pp. 254–6. This essay was originally published in *Kilkenny Magazine* in Spring 1962.

12 [Henn's note:] See Lady Gregory, *Journals*; in particular the chapters called 'The Terror' and 'The Civil War'.

13 [Henn's note:] As in *Visions and Beliefs*. She had popularized it, though Standish O'Grady and Douglas Hyde were the pioneers.

14 [Henn's note:] See *Autobiographies*, pp. 258, 261. George Moore gives a good account of this in his boyhood: adding the interesting opinion that the best and purest English was spoken by gamekeepers.

15 T.R. Henn, *The Lonely Tower: Studies in the Poetry of W.B. Yeats* (London: Methuen, 1965), pp. 3–7.

16 [Henn's note:] See the account of this ceremony in Honor Tracy's *The Straight and Narrow Path*.

17 Henn, *The Lonely Tower*, pp. 7–9.

18 [Torchiana's note:] 'Ireland, 1921–1931,' *Spectator*, 30 January 1932, p. 137.

19 [Torchiana's note:] Ibid., pp. 137–8.

20 [Torchiana's note:] Hugh A. Law, 'The Anglo-Irish,' *Irish Statesman*, 17 August 1929, p. 467. See also 'The Anglo-Irish Tradition,' *Irish Statesman*, 15 December 1928, pp. 289–90. Yeats had been from his youth familiar enough with the histories of eighteenth-century Ireland by Froude and Lecky. See *Letters to the New Island*, ed. Horace Reynolds (Cambridge, Mass., 1934), p. 90, and 'The Thirty Best Irish Books,' *United Ireland*, 16 March 1895.

21 [Torchiana's note:] Swift, *Works*, ed. Sheridan (London, 1784), XIV, 195.

22 [Torchiana's note:] David H. Greene and Edward M. Stephens, *J.M. Synge 1871–1909* (New York, 1959), p. 1.

23 [Torchiana's note:] *Autobiographies*, pp. 33–4.

24 [Torchiana's note:] Oliver St. John Gogarty, *Mourning Becomes Mrs. Spendlove* (New York, 1948), pp. 211–24.

25 [Torchiana's note:] David H. Greene, 'Synge and the Irish,' *Colby Library Bulletin*, Series IV (February 1957), p. 159.

26 [Torchiana's note:] See, for instance, *Brendan Behan's Ireland* (New York, 1962), p. 18.

27 [Torchiana's note:] Denis Ireland, 'Fog in the Irish Sea,' *Threshold*, V (Autumn–Winter 1961–62), 65–7.

28 [Torchiana's note:] Yeats probably knew well John Eglinton's sympathetic attempt to define that genius in the opening pages of *Anglo-Irish Essays* (Dublin, 1917).

29 [Torchiana's note:] *Wheels and Butterflies*, p. 10, n. 1. This cousin was probably Dr. Francis Butler Yeats of Dunliam, Quebec. See his obituary in the *Irish Independent*, 19 February 1923.

30 [Torchiana's note:] J.B. Yeats, *Letters to his son W.B. Yeats and others 1869–1922*, ed. Joseph Hone (London, 1944), p. 23. See also 'The Anglo-Irish Strain,' *Bell*, II (September 1941), 25, and Hone's 'Edmund Burke,' *Envoy*, II (April 1950), 26–7.

31 [Torchiana's note:] *Senate Speeches*, p. 99.

32 Donald T. Torchiana, *W.B. Yeats & Georgian Ireland* (Washington: The Catholic University of America Press, 1966), pp. 85–90.

33 Thomas Kinsella, 'The Irish Writer' in Roger McHugh (ed.), *Davis, Mangan, Ferguson? Tradition & the Irish Writer* (Dublin: Dolmen, 1970), pp. 57–9.

34 Ibid., pp. 61–4.

35 [Thuente's note:] Yeats, 'A General Introduction for My Work', 511.

36 [Thuente's note:] Ferguson, *Congal*, viii; Yeats, 'The Poetry of Sir Samuel Ferguson – I' (1886), *Uncollected Prose* I, 81–7.

37 [Thuente's note:] O'Grady, *History of Ireland* II, 28, 44.

38 [Thuente's note:] Yeats, 'General Introduction', 512–13.

39 [Thuente's note:] Phillip Marcus, *Standish O'Grady*, 18.

40 [Thuente's note:] Yeats, *Letters to Katharine Tynan*, 64, 76.

41 [Thuente's note:] Yeats, 'The Poetry of R.D. Joyce' (1886), *Uncollected Prose* I, 112.

42 [Thuente's note:] Yeats, 'Tales from the Twilight' (1890), *Uncollected Prose* I, 170.

43 Mary Helen Thuente, *W.B. Yeats and Irish Folklore* (Dublin: Gill and Macmillan, 1980), pp. 20–4.

44 [Deane's note:] Myron F. Brightfield, *John Wilson Croker* (London, 1940). See also Croker's *Essays on the Early Period of the French Revolution* (London, 1857), and L.J. Jennings (ed.), *The Correspondence and Diaries of the late Right Honourable John Wilson Croker*, 3 vols (London, 1884).

45 [Deane's note:] *Essays and Introductions* (London, 1961), p. 25.

46 Seamus Deane, *Celtic Revivals: Essays in Modern Irish Literature 1880–1980* (London: Faber, 1985), pp. 28–9.

47 Ibid., p. 31.

48 [Deane's note:] R. Theodore Hoppen, 'Politics in Mid-Nineteenth-Century Ireland', in *Studies in Irish History*, eds. A. Cosgrove and D. McCartney (Dublin, 1979), p. 222.

49 [Deane's note:] See Cathal G. O Hainle, 'Towards the Revival: Some Translations of Irish Poetry 1789–1897', in *Literature and the Changing Ireland*, ed. Peter Connolly (London, 1982), pp. 37–58.

50 [Deane's note:] *Plays and Controversies* (London, 1923), p. 198.

51 [Deane's note:] Samuel Hynes, *Edwardian Obsessions* (London, 1972), pp. 1–12.

52 [Deane's note:] Cyril Connolly, *Previous Convictions* (London, 1967), p. 252.

53 Deane, *Celtic Revivals*, pp. 33–7.

54 [McCormack's note:] *The Catholic Bulletin*, vol. 12, No. 1 (January 1922), p. 5.

55 W.J. McCormack, *From Burke to Beckett: Ascendancy, Tradition and Betrayal in Literary History* (Cork: Cork University Press, 1994), pp. 311–12. This book was first published in 1985 as *Ascendancy and Tradition in Anglo-Irish Literary History from 1789 to 1939*.

56 [McCormack's note:] *The Catholic Bulletin*, vol. 14, No. 1 (January 1924), p. 5.

57 [McCormack's note:] Ibid., pp. 6–7.

58 [McCormack's note:] See 'The Very Newest History of Ireland', vol. 14, No. 1 (January 1924), pp. 48–53, 'Mr. Stephen Gwynn's Historical Propaganda', No. 2 (February 1924), pp. 126–31, 'Shane Leslie Patronises the Irish', vol. 14, No. 3 (March 1924), pp. 211–17.

59 [McCormack's note:] Agnes O'Farrelly was a lecturer in modern Irish at University College, Dublin, whose poem 'The Old House' had appeared in *The Irish Independent* of 29 January 1924; for a contrasting assimilation of her name into literature, see the analysis of *Finnegans Wake* on pp. 279–80 above. For the bashaws, see *The Catholic Bulletin*, vol. 14, No. 3 (March 1924), p. 171.

60 [McCormack's note:] Ibid., vol. 14, No. 3 (March 1924), p. 171.

61 [McCormack's note:] Ibid., vol. 14, No. 7 (July 1924), pp. 556 and 565.

62 [McCormack's note:] Ibid., vol. 14, No. 10 (October 1924), p. 861 etc.

63 [McCormack's note:] Ibid., vol. 14, No. 11 (November 1924), p. 937. Something of the condition in which the academic teaching of literature existed in Ireland at the time may be judged from this editorial. It began by quoting with approval the opinion of W. Fitzjohn Trench, professor of English at Trinity College, on the subject of *Ulysses* ('rakes hell and the sewers for dirt'). It ended by commending a speech at the Annual Conference of the Catholic Truth Society by Robert Donovan: 'some of the very worst writings came from men who from their names and origin, might have been expected to be on the C.T.S. platform.' Robert Donovan held the chair of English literature at University College, and later combined that honour with chairmanship of the Censorship Board in which connection he banned the novels of his former colleague, Austin Clarke. A member of the Trinity English department subsequently served on the Censorship Appeals Board.

64 [McCormack's note:] Ibid., vol. 14, No. 12 (December 1924), pp. 1021–2. In 1925 the *Bulletin* published several further attacks on 'ascendancy outposts in medicine' (January) and maintained its interest in history, 'The Ascendancy Church and Popular Education (1824–1827)' (April).

65 [McCormack's note:] Donald R. Pearse, ed., *The Senate Speeches of W.B. Yeats* (London: Faber, 1961), pp. 89–102, 156–60 (quotation p. 99).

66 McCormack, *Burke to Beckett*, pp. 315–18.

67 Ibid., p. 325.

68 [Kiberd's note:] W.B. Yeats, *Autobiographies*, London 1955, 541.

69 [Kiberd's note:] For an extended discussion of this, see Louis MacNeice, *The Poetry of W.B. Yeats*, London 1967, 102–39.

70 [Kiberd's note:] *Autobiographies*, 27.

71 [Kiberd's note:] Ibid., 130.

72 [Kiberd's note:] *Autobiographies*, 463.

73 Although Kiberd cites p. 778 of *The Variorum Edition of the Poems of W.B. Yeats* as his source for these lines, this is not how they appear there.

74 [Kiberd's note:] J.M. Synge, *Letters to Molly: John M. Synge to Maire O'Neill*, ed. Ann Saddlemyer, Cambridge, Mass. 1971, passim.

75 [Kiberd's note:] Vivian Mercier, *Beckett / Beckett*, London 1977, 46.

76 Declan Kiberd, *Irish Classics* (London: Granta, 2000), pp. 440–4.

77 Ibid., pp. 14–15.

78 [Kiberd's note:] *Autobiographies*, 277.

79 [Kiberd's note:] See Robert Langbaum, *The Mysteries of Identity: A Theme in Modern Literature*, Chicago 1982, 3–24.

80 [Kiberd's note:] W.B. Yeats, *On the Boiler*, Dublin 1939, 22.

81 Kiberd, *Irish Classics*, pp. 458–60.

CHAPTER THREE

1 Ezra Pound, 'Status Rerum', *Poetry*, I (1913), 123–7.

2 [Pound's note:] *Vide* [See] POETRY for March, 1914, p. 223.

3 Pound, 'The Later Yeats' in T.S. Eliot (ed.), *Literary Essays of Ezra Pound* (London: Faber, 1954), pp. 378–81. This essay was originally published in *Poetry* in May 1914.

4 Pound, 'Mr Yeats' New Book', *Poetry*, IX (1916), 150–1.

5 Edmund Wilson, *Axel's Castle: A Study in the Imaginative Literature of 1870–1930* (New York: Scribners, 1931), p. 2.

6 Ibid., pp. 265–7.

7 Ibid., pp. 287–90.

8 F.R. Leavis, *New Bearings in English Poetry: A Study of the Contemporary Situation* (London: Chatto & Windus, 1932), pp. 17–18.

9 [Leavis' note:] p. 430.

10 [Leavis' note:] *Autobiographies*, pp. 141–2.

11 [Leavis' note:] Ibid., p. 101.

12 [Leavis' note:] Ibid., p. 372.

13 [Leavis' note:] *Early Poems and Stories*, p. 466.

14 [Leavis' note:] Ibid., p. 485.

15 [Leavis' note:] Ibid., p. 471.

16 [Leavis' note:] *Autobiographies*, p. 395.

17 [Leavis' note:] Ibid., pp. 142–3.

18 [Leavis' note:] Ibid., p. 101.

19 [Leavis' note:] Ibid., p. 343.

20 [Leavis' note:] Ibid., p. 314.

21 Leavis, *New Bearings*, pp. 26–9.

22 Ibid., pp. 33–4.

23 Ibid., p. 36.

24 Frank Kermode, *Romantic Image* (London: Routledge, 1957), pp. 28–33.

25 [Stead's note:] *Romantic Image*, 1957, p. 5.

26 [Stead's note:] Ibid., p. 47.

27 [Stead's note:] Ibid., p. 11.

28 [Stead's note:] 'Per Amica Silentia Lunae' (1917), *Mythologies*, 1959, p. 331.

29 [Stead's note:] Ibid., p. 334.

30 [Stead's note:] *Selected Prose* (Penguin), 1953, p. 202.

31 [Stead's note:] *The Letters of W.B. Yeats*, p. 591.

32 [Stead's note:] *Letters of J.B. Yeats*, edited by J. Hone, 1944, p. 168.

33 [Stead's note:] *Letters*, p. 583.

34 [Stead's note:] J.B. Yeats wrote again shortly afterwards, reminding his son 'The chief thing to know and never forget is that art is dreamland … .' *Letters of J.B. Yeats*, p. 198.

35 [Stead's note:] *Autobiographies*, pp. 532–3.

36 C.K. Stead, *The New Poetic: Yeats to Eliot* (London: Hutchinson, 1964), pp. 30–5.

37 [Bloom's note:] *The Letters of W.B. Yeats*, ed. Allan Wade (New York, 1955), 447.

38 [Bloom's note:] *Letters*, 446.

39 Harold Bloom, *Yeats* (Oxford: Oxford University Press, 1970), pp. 83–8.

40 Richard Ellmann, *Eminent Domain: Yeats Among Wilde, Joyce, Pound, Eliot and Auden* (New York: Oxford University Press, 1967), p. 3.

41 [Ellmann's note:] Letter from J.B. Yeats to W.B. Yeats, 12 March 1918, in J.B. Yeats, *Letters to His Son W.B. Yeats and Others*, ed. Joseph Hone (New York, 1946), pp. 244–5.

42 [Ellmann's note:] A.R. Jones, *The Life and Opinions of Thomas Ernest Hulme* (London, 1960), pp. 29–31.

43 [Ellmann's note:] T.S. Eliot, 'A Foreign Mind,' [review of Yeats's *The Cutting of an Agate*] *Athenaeum* 4653 (4 July 1919), 552–53.

44 [Ellmann's note:] Lawrence, letter to A.W. McLeod, 17 December 1912, in *The Collected Letters of D.H. Lawrence*, ed. Harry T. Moore (New York, 1962), Vol. I, p. 168.

45 [Ellmann's note:] Lawrence, letter to Gordon Campbell, 19 December 1914, ibid., p. 302.

46 [Ellmann's note:] Pound, 'This Hulme Business,' *Townsman* II.5 (January 1939), 15.

47 [Ellmann's note:] Pound, 'Status Rerum,' *Poetry* I.4 (January 1913), 123–27.

48 [Ellmann's note:] Pound, letter to Harriet Monroe, 13 August 1913, in *The Letters of Ezra Pound*, ed. D.D. Paige (New York, 1950), p. 21.

49 [Ellmann's note:] Pound, letter to René Taupin, May 1928, in *Letters*, p. 218.

50 [Ellmann's note:] 'And now one has got with the camera an *enormous* correlation of particulars. That capacity for making contact is a tremendous challenge to literature.' Pound quoted in *Writers at Work* (Second Series) (New York, 1963), p. 41.

51 [Ellmann's note:] Yeats, 'Introduction' to Rabindranath Tagore, *Gitanjali* (New York, 1916), pp. xiii–xv.

52 [Ellmann's note:] Pound, letter to Harriet Monroe, October 1912, in Harriet Monroe, *A Poet's Life* (New York, 1938), p. 262. Cf. Pound, 'Rabindranath Tagore,' *Fortnightly Review* XCIII (N.S.) .555 (1 March 1913), 571–79.

53 [Ellmann's note:] Pound, 'French Poets,' in *Make It New* (New Haven, 1935), p. 245.

54 [Ellmann's note:] W.B. Yeats and T. Sturge Moore, *Their Correspondence*, pp. 22, 190.

55 [Ellmann's note:] Yeats, letter to Dorothy Wellesley, 21 December 1935, in Yeats, *Letters*, p. 846.

56 [Ellmann's note:] Yeats, letter to Edmund Gosse, 25 November 1912, in ibid., pp. 572–3.

57 [Ellmann's note:] Pound, unpublished letter to Harriet Monroe, 4 November 1912, in the University of Chicago Library.

58 [Ellmann's note:] Pound, letter to Harriet Monroe, 26 October 1912, in the University of Chicago Library. It is slightly misquoted in Monroe, *A Poet's Life*, p. 264.

59 [Ellmann's note:] Pound, 'The Later Yeats,' *Poetry* IX.3 (December 1917), 66.

60 [Ellmann's note:] Pound, unpublished letter to Harriet Monroe, 2 November 1912, in the University of Chicago Library.

61 [Ellmann's note:] Pound, letter to Harriet Monroe, also 2 November 1912, but sent separately from the above letter, in the University of Chicago Library.

62 [Ellmann's note:] Pound, 'French Poets,' *Make It New*, p. 245.

63 [Ellmann's note:] Yeats, letter to Lady Gregory, 1 January 1913, in 'Some New Letters from W.B. Yeats to Lady Gregory,' ed. Donald T. Torchiana and Glenn O'Malley, *Review of English Literature* IV.3 (July 1963), 14.

64 [Ellmann's note:] Yeats, 'A General Introduction for My Work,' in *Essays and Introductions* (London, 1961), p. 525.

65 [Ellmann's note:] Yeats, letter to Lady Gregory, 3 January 1913, quoted in A.N. Jeffares, *W.B. Yeats: Man and Poet* (New Haven, 1949), p. 167.

66 [Ellmann's note:] Pound, letter to Harriet Monroe, in *Letters*, p. 49.

67 [Ellmann's note:] W.H. Auden, *The Dyer's Hand* (New York, 1962), p. 50.

68 [Ellmann's note:] Pound, 'The Later Yeats,' p. 67.

69 [Ellmann's note:] Interview with Mrs. W.B. Yeats, 1946.

70 Ellmann, *Eminent Domain*, pp. 61–7.

71 Stead, *Pound, Yeats, Eliot and the Modernist Movement* (London: Macmillan, 1986), pp. 19–21.

72 [Stead's note:] My own discussion of these matters in *The New Poetic* clearly owes a great deal to Kermode's and to his terminology.

73 [Stead's note:] Kermode, *Romantic Image* (London, 1957) pp. 32–3. All quotations from Yeats's obituary notice are taken from Kermode.

74 Stead, *Pound, Yeats, Eliot*, pp. 75–8.

75 Ibid., p. 364.

76 [Parkinson's note:] *The Letters of Ezra Pound, 1907–1941*, ed. D.D. Paige (New York, 1950), p. xxii.

77 [Parkinson's note:] John Berryman, 'The Poetry of Ezra Pound,' *Partisan Review* (April 1949), p. 379.

78 [Parkinson's note:] F.R. Leavis, 'Ezra Pound: The Promise and the Disaster,' *Partisan Review* (Nov.–Dec. 1951), p. 730.

79 [Parkinson's note:] Hugh Kenner, 'Remember That I Have Remembered,' *Hudson Review*, III (1951), 603.

80 [Parkinson's note:] *Letters*, p. 257.

81 [Parkinson's note:] W.B. Yeats, *A Vision* (New York, 1938), p. 3.

82 Thomas Parkinson, 'Yeats and Pound: The Illusion of Influence', *Comparative Literature*, 6 (1954), 256–7.

83 [Longenbach's note:] Pound, *This Generation* (typescript in the Pound Archive, Beinecke Library, Yale University), pp. 36–7.

84 [Longenbach's note:] Yeats to Lady Gregory, 8 January 1913. For an account of Pound's minor revisions of the poems Yeats published in the December 1912 issue of *Poetry*, see Richard Ellmann, *Eminent Domain: Yeats Among Wilde, Joyce, Pound, Eliot, and Auden* (New York: Oxford University Press, 1967), pp. 64–5, or Ellen Williams, *Harriet Monroe and the Poetry Renaissance* (Urbana: University of Illinois Press, 1977), pp. 62–3. Thomas Parkinson has shown that Yeats had begun the process of 'modernization' long before Pound began to tinker with his verse. See 'Yeats and Pound: The Illusion of Influence,' *Comparative Literature* 6 (1954): *passim*.

85 [Longenbach's note:] Yeats to Lady Gregory, 3 January 1913, in A. Norman Jeffares, *W.B. Yeats: Man and Poet* (London: Routledge & Kegan Paul, 1949), p. 167.

86 [Longenbach's note:] *Uncollected Prose by W.B. Yeats*, Vol. 2, ed. John P. Frayne and Colton Johnson (New York: Columbia University Press, 1976), p. 414.

87 [Longenbach's note:] Pound, *This Generation*, p. 37.

88 [Longenbach's note:] George Mills Harper, *W.B. Yeats and W.T. Horton: The Record of an Occult Friendship* (New York: Macmillan, 1980), p. 129.

89 [Longenbach's note:] Pound, 'Status Rerum,' *Poetry* 1 (January 1913): 123. For Pound's revision of the essay see Williams, *Harriet Monroe*, p. 36.

90 James Longenbach, *Stone Cottage: Pound, Yeats & Modernism* (Oxford: Oxford University Press, 1988), pp. 19–20.

91 Ibid., p. 26.

92 [Longenbach's note:] *Ezra Pound and Dorothy Shakespear: Their Letters 1909–1914*, ed. Omar Pound and A. Walton Litz (New York: New Directions, 1984), p. 180.

93 [Longenbach's note:] 'Ghosts and Dreams, Lecture by Mr. W.B. Yeats,' *Irish Times*, 1 November 1913, p. 7. See Yeats's 'Preliminary Examination of the Script of E.R.,' ed. George Mills Harper and John S. Kelly, in *Yeats and the Occult*, ed. George Mills Harper (Niagara Falls: Maclean-Hunter Press, 1975), pp. 130–71. The editors of the manuscript point out that Pound helped Yeats to identify several Provençal lines that emerged in the automatic writing.

94 [Longenbach's note:] *Literary Essays of Ezra Pound*, ed. T.S. Eliot (New York: New Directions, 1968), p. 5.

95 [Longenbach's note:] F.S. Flint, 'Imagisme,' *Poetry* 1 (March 1913): 199.

96 [Longenbach's note:] F.S. Flint, 'The Appreciation of Poetry', in J.B. Harmer, *Victory in Limbo: Imagism 1908–1917* (London: Secker & Warburg, 1975), p. 168.

97 [Longenbach's note:] *Ezra Pound and Dorothy Shakespear: Their Letters 1909–1914*, ed. Pound and Litz, pp. 227–78.

98 [Longenbach's note:] *The Variorum Edition of the Poems of W.B. Yeats*, ed. Peter Allt and Russell K. Alspach (New York: Macmillan, 1957), p. 807.

99 [Longenbach's note:] *Literary Essays of Ezra Pound*, ed. Eliot, p. 378.

100 [Longenbach's note:] *The Selected Letters of Ezra Pound*, ed. D.D. Paige (New York: New Directions, 1971), p. 27.

101 Longenbach, *Stone Cottage*, pp. 29–33.

CHAPTER FOUR

1 J.M. Hone, 'Yeats as Political Philosopher', *The London Mercury*, 39 (1939), 492–5.

2 Ibid., pp. 495–6.

3 MacBride rose through the ranks of the IRA, becoming its Chief of Staff in the late 1930s. However, he broke with the IRA in the 1940s and served in the Irish government as, oddly enough, the minister for External Affairs. He was co-founder of Amnesty International and was awarded the Nobel Peace Prize in 1974.

4 W.H. Auden, 'The Public v. the Late Mr. William Butler Yeats' in Edward Mendelson (ed.), *The English Auden: Poems, Essays and Dramatic Writings 1927–1939* (London: Faber, 1977), pp. 389–93. This essay was originally published in *Partisan Review* in Spring 1939.

5 Louis MacNeice, *The Poetry of W.B. Yeats* (London: Oxford University Press, 1941), pp. 223–5.

6 Ibid., pp. 231–2.

7 Ibid., p. 132.

8 George Orwell, 'W.B. Yeats' in *Collected Essays* (London: Secker & Warburg, 1961), p. 195. This essay was originally published in *Horizon* in January 1943.

9 Ibid., pp. 197–201.

10 Yvor Winters, 'The Poetry of W.B. Yeats', *Twentieth Century Literature*, 6 (1960), 3.

11 [O'Brien's note:] The sequence of events described by Yeats in his September letter involved, in reality, a climb down by O'Duffy who had announced a mass parade of the Blueshirts (National Guard) for 13 August, the anniversary of [Michael] Collins's death. When the National Guard was proclaimed illegal the parade was called off and 'a quiet ceremony at the Cenotaph' was held instead. O'Duffy immediately became, as Yeats noted, leader of the Opposition United Party but, as a historian sympathetic to the opposition has observed: 'from the very outset the new arrangement was thoroughly unsatisfactory, it quickly became apparent that O'Duffy did not possess the special qualities that equip a man for leadership in public life'. (D. O'Sullivan, *The Irish Free State and the Senate*, p. 406.) O'Duffy resigned his chairmanship of the United Party in September 1934.

12 [O'Brien's note:] (There is a sense of course in which the poet, actually engaged in writing his poetry, is 'the true Yeats', but that is another matter.)

13 [O'Brien's note:] *The Lonely Tower*, p. 467.

14 [O'Brien's note:] 'To pierce the dark mind', *Nation* (10 December 1960). My friend Dr. Mercier, like almost all scholars from Ireland who have written on Yeats, finds his aristocratism, as an Anglo-Irish attitude, more congenial than the aboriginal writer of the present essay can find it.

15 [O'Brien's note:] He had, in any case, the assurance of his friend Ezra Pound (*Jefferson and/or Mussolini*) that the Duce was translating Jeffersonian ideas into twentieth-century terms.

16 [O'Brien's note:] 'The Old Age of a Poet', *The Bell* (February 1941). He also mentions an Abbey dispute over an attempt by Yeats to stage *Coriolanus* for purposes of 'fascist propaganda'. Mr. Sean O'Faoláin, a more cautious observer, who also knew Yeats at this time, speaks of his 'fascist tendencies' ('Yeats and the Younger Generation', *Horizon*, January, 1942).

17 [O'Brien's note:] 'Yeats as a Political Philosopher', *London Mercury* (April, 1939). Hone adds that, among Yeats's fellow Senators, a banker thought the poet would have made 'an admirable banker' and a lawyer thought that 'a great lawyer' was lost in him.

18 [O'Brien's note:] 'In its early days', Yeats wrote of the Senate, 'some old banker or lawyer would dominate the House, leaning upon the back of the chair in front, always speaking with undisturbed self-possession as at some table in a board-room. My imagination sets up against him some typical elected man, emotional as a youthful chimpanzee, hot and vague, always disturbed, always hating something or other.' (*On the Boiler*.) In another mood, however, he wrote about these oligarchs in a more disparaging vein. (*A Packet for Ezra Pound*.)

19 [O'Brien's note:] The late Louis MacNeice in *The Poetry of W.B. Yeats* seems to have been the first to lay much stress on Yeats's relation to Fascism, but could not quite make up his mind what that relation was. He refers to Yeats at one point as 'the man who nearly became a fascist' (p. 174), having spoken of him earlier as having arrived at 'his own elegant brand of fascism' (p. 41).

20 [O'Brien's note:] To Ethel Mannin, April 1936. In fairness to Yeats it must be noted, however, that in order to help Ossietzki he would have had to recommend him to the Nobel Committee for consideration for the Nobel Prize – something which, on artistic grounds, he may well have been unwilling to do. His degree of 'toughness' on political matters, minimized as it has been by some of his admirers, should not be exaggerated

either. In the Senate he supported an amendment to the Government's Public Safety Bill intended to secure independent inspection of prisons (Senate Debates, I. Cols. 1440–1; 1638–9). He also sent 'warm blankets' to Maud Gonne when his government put her in jail (Letters, p. 696). But in all essentials he supported the Government's policy of firmness. 'Even the gentle Yeats', wrote Sean O'Casey, 'voted for the Flogging Bill' (i.e. the Public Safety Bill which introduced flogging as a punishment for arson and armed robbery). Yeats voted for the Second Reading (26 July 1923). This was in the aftermath of the Civil War.

21 [O'Brien's note:] The Irish Times was in no way exceptional in this kind of comment. I cite it only because it was the journal of the class to which Yeats belonged, and he read it.

22 [O'Brien's note:] Hone tells us (W.B. Yeats, p. 467) that Yeats had learned with 'great satisfaction' of a law of the Third Reich 'whereby ancient and impoverished families can recover their hereditary properties'. Professor T. Desmond Williams of University College, Dublin, tells me that 'to benefit from the hereditary law [of September 1933] you had to trace your ancestry back to 1760 and you had to be purely Aryan. There was provision for the return of land that had passed into "impure" hands as a result of mortgages.'

23 [O'Brien's note:] It is true that the Blueshirts did not even try to go to anything like the lengths of their Continental models. It is also true that, unlike the case of their models, the Communists whom the Blueshirts were fighting were, in Ireland, largely imaginary.

24 [O'Brien's note:] Modern Philosophy (August 1963).

25 Conor Cruise O'Brien, 'Passion and Cunning: An Essay on the Politics of W.B. Yeats' in A. Norman Jeffares and K.G.W. Cross (eds), In Excited Reverie: A Centenary Tribute to William Butler Yeats 1865–1939 (London: Macmillan, 1965), pp. 256–63.

26 Patrick Cosgrave, 'Yeats, Fascism and Conor O'Brien', London Magazine, 7.4 (1967), 36–8.

27 Grattan Freyer, W.B. Yeats and the Anti-Democratic Tradition (Dublin: Gill & Macmillan, 1981), pp. 125–8.

28 Ibid., pp. 132–3.

29 [Cullingford's note:] Letters of W.B. Yeats, ed. Alan Wade, London, 1954, p. 793.

30 [Cullingford's note:] Letters, p. 809.

31 [Cullingford's note:] Letters, p. 808.

32 [Cullingford's note:] Letters, p. 815.

33 [Cullingford's note:] Variorum Edition of the Poems of W.B. Yeats, ed. Peter Allt and Russell K. Alspach, New York, 1957, p. 543.

34 [Cullingford's note:] Letters, p. 820.

35 [Cullingford's note:] Letters, pp. 811–12.

36 [Cullingford's note:] Quoted in Donald T. Torchiana, W.B. Yeats and Georgian Ireland, Evanston, 1966, p. 161.

37 [Cullingford's note:] 'As Yeats Was Going down Grafton Street', Listener, 6 Feb. 1964, p. 237.

38 [Cullingford's note:] Letters, p. 812.

39 [Cullingford's note:] Ibid.

40 [Cullingford's note:] Quoted in Torchiana, Yeats and Georgian Ireland, p. 161.

41 [Cullingford's note:] Letters, p. 813.

42 [Cullingford's note:] Origins of Totalitarianism, rev. edn, London, 1967, p. 183.

43 Elizabeth Cullingford, Yeats, Ireland and Fascism (London: Macmillan, 1981), pp. 200–5.

44 [Stanfield's note:] Conor Cruise O'Brien, 'Passion and Cunning: an Essay on the Politics of W.B. Yeats', in A. Norman Jeffares and K.G.W. Cross (eds), In Excited Reverie: A Centenary Tribute to Williams Butler Yeats 1865–1939 (New York: St Martin's Press, 1965), p. 257.

45 [Stanfield's note:] T.R. Henn, The Lonely Tower (London: Methuen, 1950; 2nd edn, 1965), p. 344. See also D.E.S. Maxwell, 'Swift's Dark Grove: Yeats and the Anglo-Irish Tradition', in D.E.S. Maxwell and S.B. Bushrui (eds), Centenary Essays on the Art of W.B. Yeats (Nigeria: University of Ibadan Press, 1965), p. 20; Mary Carden, 'The Few and the Many: an Examination of W.B. Yeats's Politics', Studies, LVIII (1969), 61;

Elizabeth Cullingford, *Yeats, Ireland and Fascism* (New York and London: New York University Press, 1981), p. 212.

46 [Stanfield's note:] Grattan Freyer, *W.B. Yeats and the Anti-Democratic Tradition* (Dublin: Gill & Macmillan, 1981), p. 78.

47 [Stanfield's note:] Joseph Hone, *W.B. Yeats: 1865–1939* (London: Macmillan, 1942), p. 459. I have taken liberties with Hone's punctuation. His version reads: 'Conflict, more conflict'.

48 [Stanfield's note:] *The Variorum Edition of the Poems of W.B. Yeats*, eds Peter Allt and Russell K. Alspach (London: Macmillan, 1957; New York: Macmillan, 1957), pp. 545, 616, 638.

49 [Stanfield's note:] *Explorations* (London: Macmillan, 1962; New York: Macmillan, 1962), p. 425.

50 [Stanfield's note:] Ibid., p. 441.

51 [Stanfield's note:] Ibid., pp. 338–9.

52 [Stanfield's note:] *Uncollected Prose by W.B. Yeats*, eds John P. Frayne and Colton Johnson (London: Macmillan, 1976; New York: Columbia University Press, 1976), II, 487.

53 [Stanfield's note:] E.M. Forster, 'What I Believe', in *Two Cheers for Democracy* (London: Edward Arnold, 1951), pp. 80–1.

54 [Stanfield's note:] Stephen Spender, *World Within World* (Berkeley, Calif.: University of California Press, 1966), p. 147.

55 [Stanfield's note:] Edward Mendelson (ed.), *The English Auden* (London: Faber & Faber, 1977), p. 425.

56 [Stanfield's note:] Sonia Orwell and Ian Angus (eds), *The Collected Essays, Journalism and Letters of George Orwell* (London: Secker & Warburg, 1968), II, 516.

57 [Stanfield's note:] Ibid., I, 296.

58 [Stanfield's note:] George Watson, *Politics and Literature in Modern Britain* (Totowa, N.J.: Rowman & Littlefield, 1977), pp. 46–70.

59 [Stanfield's note:] *United Irishman*, 20 May 1933, p. 7.

60 [Stanfield's note:] *The Letters of W.B. Yeats*, ed. Allan Wade (London: Rupert Hart-Davis, 1954; rept. New York: Macmillan 1955; rept. New York: Octagon Books, 1980), p. 812.

61 [Stanfield's note:] *Var. Poems*, p. 837.

62 [Stanfield's note:] Grattan Freyer, 'The Politics of W.B. Yeats', *Politics and Letters*, 1 (1947), 18.

63 [Stanfield's note:] Donald T. Torchiana, *W.B. Yeats and Georgian Ireland* (Evanston, Ill.: Northwestern University Press, 1966), p. 159.

64 [Stanfield's note:] Freyer, *Yeats and the Anti-Democratic Tradition*, pp. 127–8.

65 [Stanfield's note:] Watson, *Politics and Literature in Modern Britain*, p. 78.

66 Paul Scott Stanfield, *Yeats and Politics in the 1930s* (London: Macmillan, 1988), pp. 67–71.

67 [Said's note:] Pablo Neruda, *Fully Empowered*, trans. A. Reid (New York: Farrar, Straus & Giroux, 1975), p. 131.

68 [Said's note:] Frantz Fanon, *The Wretched of the Earth* (New York: Grove Press, 1965), p. 59.

69 Edward W. Said, 'Yeats and Decolonization' in Seamus Deane (ed.), *Nationalism, Colonialism, and Literature* (Minneapolis: University of Minnesota Press, 1990), pp. 87–91.

CONCLUSION

1 Stephen Spender, Patrick Kavanagh, Thomas Kinsella and W.D. Snodgrass, 'Poetry Since Yeats: An Exchange of Views', *Tri-Quarterly*, 4 (1965), 100.

2 Ibid., 103.

3 Ibid., 108.

SELECTED BIBLIOGRAPHY

THE POEMS

Numerous editions of Yeats' selected and collected poems can be bought in bookshops or over the internet. The standard editions of his collected poems are those edited by Richard J. Finneran and A. Norman Jeffares. For a discussion of the controversial differences between these two collections, see the Introduction.

The Collected Works of W.B. Yeats, Volume 1: The Poems, 2nd edn, ed. Richard J. Finneran, (New York: Scribner, 1997).

The Variorum Edition of the Poems of W.B. Yeats, ed. Peter Allt and Russell K. Alspach, (New York: Macmillan, 1957).

Yeats's Poems, 3rd edn, ed. A. Norman Jeffares (London: Macmillan – now Palgrave Macmillan, 1996).

Yeats's Poetry, Drama and Prose: A Norton Critical Edition, ed. James Pethica (New York: Norton, 2000).

SELECTED AND COLLECTED PROSE

Richard J. Finneran and George Mills Harper are the general editors of a new collected edition of the works of W.B. Yeats, with Finneran's collected poems as volume one. Ten volumes have been published so far, with several more still to come. Those works below that are a part of this project have been identified as *CW* and their volume numbers given.

Autobiographies (CW 3), ed. William H. O'Donnell and Douglas Archibald (New York: Scribner, 1999).

The Celtic Twilight and the Secret Rose (CW 11), ed. Warwick Gould, Philip L. Marcus and Michael Sidnell (London: Macmillan – now Palgrave Macmillan, 1992).

Early Articles and Reviews (CW 9), ed. John P. Frayne (London: Macmillan – now Palgrave Macmillan, 1992).

Essays and Introductions (London: Macmillan, 1961).

Interviews and Recollections, ed. E.H. Mikhail (London: Macmillan, 1977).

John Sherman and Dhoya (CW 12), ed. Richard J. Finneran (London: Macmillan – now Palgrave Macmillan, 1991).

Later Articles and Reviews (CW 10), ed. Colton Johnson (New York: Scribner, 2000).

Later Essays (CW 5), ed. William H. O'Donnell and Elizabeth Bergmann Loizeaux (New York: Scribner, 1994).

Letters to the New Island (CW 7), ed. George Bornstein and Hugh Witemeyer (London: Macmillan, 1988).

Memoirs, ed. Denis Donoghue (New York: Macmillan, 1973).

Mythologies (London: Macmillan, 1959).

Prefaces and Introductions (CW 6), ed. William H. O'Donnell (London: Macmillan, 1988).

The Senate Speeches of W.B. Yeats, ed. Donald R. Pearce (Bloomington: Indiana University Press, 1960).

Uncollected Prose by W.B. Yeats, Volume 1, ed. John P. Frayne (London: Macmillan, 1970).

Uncollected Prose by W.B. Yeats, Volume 2, ed. John P. Frayne and Colton Johnson (London: Macmillan, 1975).

A Vision (London: Macmillan, 1962).

SELECTED AND COLLECTED LETTERS

John Kelly is the general editor of a new edition of the collected letters of W.B. Yeats. It is estimated that the edition will eventually contain about a dozen volumes, four of which have been published so far. Until that is complete, readers will still have to rely partly on the Wade edition published in 1954.

The Collected Letters of W.B. Yeats, general ed. John Kelly.

Volume 1: 1865–1895, ed. John Kelly and Eric Domville (Oxford: Clarendon 1986).

Volume 2: 1896–1900, ed. Warwick Gould, John Kelly and Deirdre Toomey (Oxford: Clarendon, 1997).

Volume 3: 1901–1904, ed. John Kelly and Ronald Schuchard (Oxford: Clarendon, 1994).

Volume 4: 1905–1907, ed. John Kelly and Ronald Schuchard (Oxford: Clarendon, 2004).

The Letters of W.B. Yeats, ed. Allan Wade (London: Rupert Hart-Davis, 1954).

The Gonne–Yeats Letters 1893–1938: Always Your Friend, ed. Anna MacBride White and A. Norman Jeffares (London: Hutchinson, 1992).

CD-ROM

The W.B. Yeats Collection, ed. Richard J. Finneran (Cambridge: Chadwyck-Healey, 1998).

INTRODUCTIONS

Archibald, Douglas. *Yeats* (Syracuse: Syracuse University Press, 1983).

Donoghue, Denis. *Yeats* (London: Fontana, 1971).

Ellmann, Richard. *The Identity of Yeats* (London: Macmillan, 1954).

Faulkner, Peter. *Yeats* (Milton Keynes: Open University Press, 1987).

Malins, Edward, and John Purkis. *A Preface to Yeats*. 2nd edn (London: Longman, 1994).

Peterson, Richard. *William Butler Yeats* (Boston: Twayne, 1982).

Rajan, Balachandra. *W.B. Yeats: A Critical Introduction* (London: Hutchinson, 1965).

Smith, Stan. *W.B. Yeats: A Critical Introduction* (London: Macmillan – now Palgrave Macmillan, 1990).

Tuohy, Frank. *Yeats* (London: Macmillan, 1976).

Ure, Peter. *Yeats* (Edinburgh: Oliver and Boyd, 1963).

HANDBOOKS AND GUIDES

Jeffares, A. Norman. *A New Commentary on the Poems of W.B. Yeats* (London: Macmillan, 1984).

O'Donnell, William. *The Poetry of William Butler Yeats: An Introduction* (New York: Ungar, 1986).

Unterecker, John. *A Reader's Guide to William Butler Yeats* (London: Thames and Hudson, 1959).

SCHOLARLY JOURNALS

Yeats: An Annual of Critical and Textual Studies, ed. Richard J. Finneran (Ithaca, NY: Cornell University Press, 1983–5; Ann Arbor: University of Michigan Press, 1986–).

Yeats Annual, ed. Richard J. Finneran (London: Macmillan, 1982–3).

Yeats Annual, ed. Warwick Gould (London: Macmillan, 1985–).

LIVES OF THE POET

Brown, Terence. *The Life of W.B. Yeats: A Critical Biography* (Oxford: Blackwell, 1999).

Ellmann, Richard. *Yeats: The Man and the Masks* (London: Macmillan, 1948).

Foster, R.F. *W.B. Yeats, A Life, Volume 1: The Apprentice Mage, 1865–1914* (Oxford: Oxford University Press, 1997).

——. *W.B. Yeats, A Life, Volume 2: The Arch-Poet, 1915–1939* (Oxford: Oxford University Press, 2003).

Hone, Joseph. *W.B. Yeats, 1865–1939* (London: Macmillan, 1943).

Jeffares, A. Norman. *W.B. Yeats: Man and Poet* (London: Routledge & Kegan Paul, 1949).

——. *W.B. Yeats: A New Biography* (London: Hutchinson, 1988).

Saddlemyer, Ann. *Becoming George: The Life of Mrs W.B. Yeats* (Oxford: Oxford University Press, 2002).

Yeats, W.B. *Autobiographies* (London: Macmillan, 1955).

IRISH CONTEXTS

Brown, Malcolm. *The Politics of Irish Literature: From Thomas Davis to W.B. Yeats* (London: George Allen & Unwin, 1972).

Brown, Terence. *Ireland: A Social and Cultural History 1922–1979* (London: Fontana, 1981).

Deane, Seamus. *A Short History of Irish Literature* (London: Hutchinson, 1986).

Eagleton, Terry. *Crazy John and the Bishop and Other Essays on Irish Culture* (Cork: Cork University Press, 1998).

Ellmann, Richard. *Four Dubliners* (London: Hamish Hamilton, 1987).

Eyler, Audrey S., and Robert F. Garratt (eds). *The Uses of the Past: Essays on Irish Culture* (Newark: University of Delaware Press, 1988).

Fallis, Richard. *The Irish Renaissance: An Introduction to Anglo-Irish Literature* (Syracuse, NY: Syracuse University Press, 1977).

Field Day Theatre Company. *Ireland's Field Day* (London: Hutchinson, 1986).

Foster, R.F. (ed.). *Modern Ireland 1600–1972* (London: Allen Lane, 1988).

Garratt, Robert F. *Modern Irish Poetry: Tradition and Continuity from Yeats to Heaney* (Berkeley: University of California Press, 1986).

Harris, Daniel. *Yeats, Coole Park and Ballylee* (Baltimore: Johns Hopkins University Press, 1974).

Howes, Marjorie. *Yeats's Nations: Gender, Class, and Irishness* (Cambridge: Cambridge University Press, 1996).

Jeffares, A. Norman. *Anglo-Irish Literature* (London: Macmillan, 1982).

Kenner, Hugh. *A Colder Eye: The Modern Irish Writers* (New York: Knopf, 1983).

Kiberd, Declan. *Inventing Ireland* (London: Jonathan Cape, 1995).

Lyons, F.S.L. *Ireland since the Famine* (London: Weidenfeld and Nicolson, 1971).

——. *Culture and Anarchy in Ireland, 1890–1939* (Oxford: Clarendon, 1979).

Marcus, Phillip L. *Yeats and the Beginning of the Irish Renaissance* (Ithaca, NY: Cornell University Press, 1970).

Mercier, Vivian. *Modern Irish Literature: Sources and Founders* (Oxford: Clarendon, 1994).

Pierce, David. *Yeats's Worlds: Ireland, England and the Poetic Imagination* (New Haven, CT: Yale University Press, 1995).

Schirmer, Gregory A. *Out of What Began: A History of Irish Poetry in English* (Ithaca, NY: Cornell University Press, 1998).

Watson, G.J. *Irish Identity and the Literary Revival: Synge, Yeats, Joyce and O'Casey*, 2nd edn (Washington: Catholic University of America Press, 1994).

Welch, Robert. *Irish Poetry from Moore to Yeats* (Gerrards Cross: Colin Smythe, 1980).

——. *Changing States: Transformations in Modern Irish Writing* (London: Routledge, 1993).

Williams, J.E. Caerwyn, and Patrick K. Ford. *The Irish Literary Tradition* (Cardiff: University of Wales Press, 1992).

YEATS AND REVIVALISM

Boyd, Ernest A. *Ireland's Literary Renaissance* (Dublin: Maunsel, 1916).

Deane, Seamus. *Celtic Revivals: Essays in Modern Irish Literature 1880–1980* (London: Faber, 1985).

Henn, T.R. *The Lonely Tower: Studies in the Poetry of W.B. Yeats* (London: Methuen, 1965).

Kavanagh, Patrick. *Collected Pruse* (London: MacGibbon and Kee, 1967).

Kiberd, Declan. *Irish Classics* (London: Granta, 2000).

McCormack, W.J. *From Burke to Beckett: Ascendancy, Tradition and Betrayal in Literary History* (Cork: Cork University Press, 1994).

Ryan, W.P. *The Irish Literary Revival: Its History, Pioneers and Possibilities* (London: W.P. Ryan, 1894).

Kinsella, Thomas. 'The Irish Writer' in Roger McHugh (ed.), *Davis, Mangan, Ferguson?: Tradition & the Irish Writer* (Dublin: Dolmen, 1970).

Thuente, Mary Helen. *W.B. Yeats and Irish Folklore* (Dublin: Gill and Macmillan, 1980).

Torchiana, Donald T. *W.B. Yeats & Georgian Ireland* (Washington: The Catholic University of America Press, 1966).

YEATS AND MODERNISM

Bloom, Harold. *Yeats* (Oxford: Oxford University Press, 1970).

Ellmann, Richard. *Eminent Domain: Yeats Among Wilde, Joyce, Pound, Eliot and Auden* (New York: Oxford University Press, 1967).

Kermode, Frank. *Romantic Image* (London: Routledge, 1957).

Leavis, F.R. *New Bearings in English Poetry: A Study of the Contemporary Situation* (London: Chatto & Windus, 1932).

Longenbach, James. *Stone Cottage: Pound, Yeats & Modernism* (Oxford: Oxford University Press, 1988).

Parkinson, Thomas. 'Yeats and Pound: The Illusion of Influence', *Comparative Literature*, 6 (1954), 256–64.

Pound, Ezra. 'The Later Yeats' in T.S. Eliot (ed.), *Literary Essays of Ezra Pound* (London: Faber, 1954).

Stead, C.K. *The New Poetic: Yeats to Eliot* (London: Hutchinson, 1964).

——. *Pound, Yeats , Eliot and the Modernist Movement* (London: Macmillan, 1986).

Wilson, Edmund. *Axel's Castle: A Study in the Imaginative Literature of 1870–1930* (New York: Scribners, 1931).

YEATS AND NATIONALISM

Auden, W.H 'The Public v. the Late Mr. William Butler Yeats' in Edward Mendelson (ed.), *The English Auden: Poems, Essays and Dramatic Writings 1927–1939* (London: Faber, 1977).

Cosgrave, Patrick. 'Yeats, Fascism and Conor O'Brien', *London Magazine*, 7.4 (1967), 22–41.

Cullingford, Elizabeth. *Yeats, Ireland and Fascism* (London: Macmillan, 1981).

Freyer, Grattan. *W.B. Yeats and the Anti-Democratic Tradition* (Dublin: Gill & Macmillan, 1981).

Hone, J.M. 'Yeats as Political Philosopher', *The London Mercury*, 39 (1939), 492–6.

MacNeice, Louis. *The Poetry of W.B. Yeats* (London: Oxford University Press, 1941).

O'Brien, Conor Cruise. 'Passion and Cunning: An Essay on the Politics of W.B. Yeats' in A. Norman Jeffares and K.G.W. Cross (eds), *In Exited Reverie: A Centenary Tribute to William Butler Yeats 1865–1939* (London: Macmillan, 1965).

Orwell, George. 'W.B. Yeats' in *Collected Essays* (London: Secker & Warburg, 1961).

Said, Edward W. 'Yeats and Decolonization' in Seamus Deane (ed.), *Nationalism, Colonialism and Literature* (Minneapolis: University of Minnesota Press, 1990).

Stanfield, Paul Scott. *Yeats and Politics in the 1930s* (London: Macmillan, 1988).

INDEX

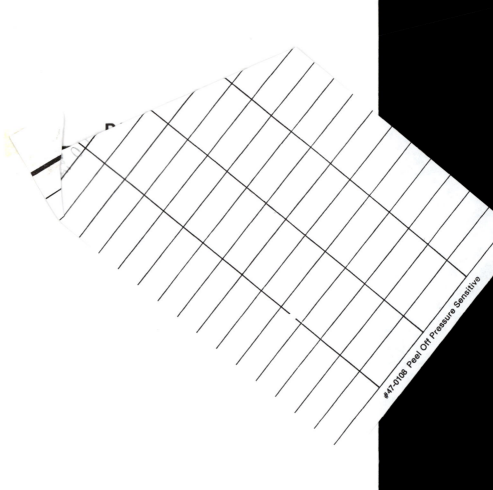

#47-0108 Peel Off Pressure Sensitive